THIS BRIGHT FIELD

THIS BRIGHT FIELD

A TRAVEL BOOK
IN ONE PLACE

WILLIAM TAYLOR

METHUEN

Published by Methuen 2000

1 3 5 7 9 10 8 6 4 2

First published in Great Britain in 2000
by Methuen Publishing Ltd
215 Vauxhall Bridge Road, London SW1V 1EJ

'This Bright Field', from *Collected Poems* by R S Thomas, reproduced by permission of
J M Dent, Publisher. Extract from *The Death and Life of Great American Cities* by Jane
Jacobs reproduced by permission of Jonathan Cape. Extract from *Summoned by Bells* by
John Betjeman reproduced by permission of John Murray (Publishers) Ltd. Extracts
from *The Satanic Verses* (Viking, 1988) and *Imaginary Homelands* (Granta, 1991) by
Salman Rushdie, *Roots Schmoots* by Howard Jacobson (Viking,1993) and *L'Assommoir*
by Emile Zola, translated by L W Tancock (Penguin Classics, 1970) all reproduced by
permission of Penguin Books Ltd. Extract from *Unnecessary Suffering* by Maurice
Glasman reproduced by permission of Verso. Every effort has been made to obtain
permission for use of copyright material; the author and publishers will gladly receive
information allowing them to correct any error in subsequent editions.

Methuen Publishing Limited Reg. No. 3543167

A CIP catalogue record for this book is available from the British Library

ISBN 0 413 74680 1

Typeset in Bembo by MATS, Southend-on-Sea, Essex
Printed and bound in Great Britain by
Creative Print and Design (Wales), Ebbw Vale

Papers used by Methuen Publishing are natural, recyclable products
made from wood grown in sustainable forests. The manufacturing processes
conform to environmental regulations of the country of origin.

For my mother, Jeanie Longbotham,
and in memory of my father,
Francis Hunter Campbell-Taylor
1915-1969

'How shall we sing the Lord's song
in a strange land?' PSALM 137

CONTENTS

THE BRIGHT FIELD

I have seen the sun break through
to illuminate a small field
for a while, and gone my way
and forgotten it. But that was the pearl
of great price, the one field that had
the treasure in it. I realize now
that I must give all that I have
to possess it. Life is not hurrying

on to a receding future, nor hankering after
an imagined past. It is the turning
aside like Moses to the miracle
of the lit bush, to a brightness
that seemed as transitory as your youth
once, but is the eternity that awaits you.

R S Thomas

PROLOGUE

When I went to see the Bishop of Oxford in 1987, the year I sat my final examinations, things were pretty clear in my head. I was going to be a vicar. I'd made my decision and now it was time to get a move on with the career.

Unfortunately the bishop didn't quite see it like that. He let me say my piece and then smiled his disarmingly broad smile and said no, actually he didn't think I was ready. He felt I needed to do some more 'exploring'. He thought perhaps I needed to 'test my vocation' a little. Had I considered getting some 'parish experience'?

I was indignant. Glaring past him out of the bay window into the winter trim of his garden, I became conscious that his bookshelves were completely chock-a-block with his own publications: multiple copies awaiting distribution, no doubt, to potential ordinands such as myself. So *that's* how he spends his days, I thought to myself.

'Do you mean I should go and take sick communion to little old ladies in North Oxford?'

'Maybe it would be better to go somewhere quite different. In the past graduates who were considering holy orders would go and live and work in the East End of London and be based at one of the University Settlements, Toynbee Hall or Oxford House. That's all changed now, of course, but I think the principle is a good one.'

'You think I need to broaden my horizons?'

The bishop tossed his pen irritably on to the table and removed his spectacles. He stood up.

'I think you need to learn a little humility.'

Sod him, I thought as I made my way back along the Banbury Road into the town centre. Maybe I should consider the law.

Shortly before I went to University, my mother had given me her father's ring. An oval sapphire the size of a coffee bean, mounted in diamonds, in a finely chased gold setting, it was fantastically beautiful, in fact rather conspicuously so. It was also slightly too large for my little finger, so before I began to wear it we took it to a jeweller to be shrunk.

The jeweller, who was a little too chirpy for my liking, merrily took down the details and the measurements and, slipping the ring swiftly into a little velvet pouch, said he would give us a tinkle when it was ready. A few days later my mother received a telephone call. It was Deft Fingers himself. Unfortunately and most regrettably, he said, the sapphire had been splintered by the technician performing the specified adjustments as per instruction. However, without prejudice and with discretion, he was apparently prepared to consider a duplicate replacement of the said stone – availability permitting of course – if that was what madam desired. Madam was too upset to desire anything. 'What did he mean?' she asked, putting the receiver down. *Would it ever be the same ring?* I wondered.

My grandfather had been the fourth generation of clergymen who had worn it – it probably started out sometime at the beginning of the nineteenth century – though the line of clerics went back further than that. There is an entry for my great-great-great-grandfather, The Revd William Goodacre, in one of the earliest clerical directories published in 1821. My uncle has a portrait of him looking rather ruddy in his clerical ruff and tailcoat, with a gold ring on his little finger. This William Goodacre spent nearly all of his working life in a single Nottinghamshire benefice, from 1812 to his death in 1859, concerning himself with the motley of parish life. It seems he was unfashionably energetic. In 1825 he sent some doggerel to the Archbishop of York, describing a particularly busy Sunday, which seemed to have involved a fair amount of leaping on and off his horse as well as ascending and descending of pulpits:

'. . . I mounted steed, to Skegby rode,
  Imparted to a female ill
The Holy Eucharist, as before
  She had to me expressed her will.
At this place too I prayed and preached,
  And set the congregation free;
Then mounting steed, to Sutton hied,
  And reached the Church just after three . . .'

The Archbishop responded peremptorily by ordaining him an assistant curate, no doubt to stem the flow of further unwanted verse.

The ring was then passed to his son, a clergyman in Staffordshire, and subsequently to his son, my great-grandfather, a cleric in Oxford, who my grandmother says was also a 'tutor', although quite what or who he taught is unclear. After marrying, he moved to Exeter, where my grandfather was born in 1874. In addition to this one, two of my other three great-grandfathers were men of the cloth, one being a Church of Ireland priest in Dublin, the other a rather fierce-sounding Wee Free minister in the North East Highlands of Scotland. My paternal grandfather (himself a Presbyterian minister) described how, on the sabbath morning the hills around Dornoch would be black with the throng of the faithful making their sober way to his father's kirk. This was serious religion. I have a silver plate that was presented to him in 1865 by his bible class as 'a mark of appreciation' for his 'valuable services and instruction'. By all accounts he was not a man to be trifled with.

The Church of Ireland lot were a sight jollier, or so I imagine them, with their gorgeous lyrical names – my great grandfather, the Revd Ameryld Dancer Purefoy, was of French descent – and a profusion of musical talent which spread through the clerical family like virginia creeper across a wall of granite. Most of my mother's cousins played either the flute or fiddle, a tradition which seems to have gone back several generations. Somewhere there, in the late eighteenth century, there was the learned Matthew Young, Bishop of Clonfert – a tiny Romanesque cathedral in beautiful remote Galway – who seems to have spent most of his time hanging out at Trinity College in downtown Dublin, where, when he wasn't pondering on the evidences of His providential purposes as Professor of Natural Philosophy, he was known for his playing on the lute.

But it was through my mother's father, who died over ten years before I was born and whose ring I had now inherited, that I acquired my sense that parsoning was the simply the family business. I had been raised on stories of his work in the Potteries in the first two decades of the twentieth century, where, as a missioner priest, he had built up a parish from scratch. There were photographs of him around the house, along with his roll-top desk, his music box, a stack of his prayer books, an old cassock – which I would try on with my father's barrister's wig and go prancing around the house like a Hallowe'en monster – as well as a framed testimonial presented to him by his parish in Hanley on his departure from the Potteries, hanging in the loo. I may not have had a particularly insistent personal vocation to the ordained ministry but, when it came to chosing a professional training I did feel, well, why not?

Actually there were a number of good reasons why not. As the Diocesan Director of Ordinands pointed out when I went to see him following my interview with the bishop, I needed more than a genetic inheritance to convince the Church I was truly committed to its work of public witness. Besides, he added, the world had simply moved on from the days when the youngest son took holy orders as a matter of course. *What sort of fantasy world do you honestly think that you are living in, young man?* I could hear him wanting to ask. Instead he said, 'Shall we bring our concerns to the Lord in prayer?'

Like someone writing cheques he knows will bounce, I bowed my head and mumbled sundry banal petitions about the need for guidance and clarity. It was then I decided I actually needed to put some money in the number one God account. Some days later I went to a Christian bookshop opposite Christ Church Cathedral in the centre of Oxford and spent an hour skim-reading a shelf of how-to books about prayer and spirituality, which seemed to be mainly about the need for perfumed candles and comfy cushions in one's search for those 'moments of stillness' in the 'hurly-burly of modern life'. It was all depressingly fluffy and confected, making the 'dark night of the soul' sound more like a romantic medieval nobleman riding out of the pages of Malory than a period of doubt and searching. I went and bought a fairy cake from the café instead. Before I left the shop I stepped downstairs to the loo, where, washing my hands, I stared grimly at one of those posters of babies with chocolate all over their grinning faces, the caption reading – I suppose ironically – 'Cleanliness is next to Godliness'. Why, I wondered, did this sort of wholesome Christian cheer always make me feel like randomly wringing necks?

Thinking about it later, I'm sure it was *then* that I lost it, at that sink. Was it the soap that washed it away? In fact, it was actually ten minutes later, crossing the High Street, that I first realised it had gone. I panicked and swore and panicked some more. I went back to the shop, retracing my steps, staring furiously at the pavement. I turned my pockets out and looked in my bag, several times, absurdly. I hurried to the spot in the library where I had been working that morning. Over the next few days I put a notice in the paper and in various shop windows. I notified the police, and stopped by at some city jewellers, just in case. But by then I had begun to accept what I had known immediately. I had lost – through some act of unforgivable dereliction – a ring that had been passed through my family, between clergy, literally handed down, for the better part of two centuries. Like sand, it had slipped through my fingers. First damaged by the jeweller, now gone from me. I had become the weak link.

A couple of months after I had received the brush-off from the bishop I was invited to supper in Spitalfields. A friend of mine was passing through London on his way back to New York and a dinner party had been arranged in his honour. When he gave me directions to the address of the house in Princelet Street where he was staying, he got a little confused about the names of the streets and the order of the turnings and quickly began to orientate me in relation to particular Spitalfields sights and recognisable landmarks.

'You turn off Bishopsgate when you see the church at the end of the road, with the market on the left and a fire in front . . .'

'A fire?'

'A bonfire, a big bonfire on the car park in front of the market. Apparently homeless people burn pallets there to keep themselves warm at night. When you see the fire you'll know you're in Spitalfields.'

As I turned into Brushfield Street on a rather wet spring evening the black smoke from this curious bonfire stained the light drizzle and gusted in the faces of the men who were gathered around it. They stood there, staring into its embers, apparently willing it into flame. I wondered whether to take a closer look, to join the watch, but, aware that I was already late for my dinner engagement, I decided to press on. I arrived as food was being served.

The evening was spent in high spirits. There was quite a lot of self-conscious Spitalfields talk, camp gossip about the restorers and gentrifiers of the Georgian houses, arch references to the Bengali 'natives' on Brick Lane, ironic mimicking of cockney market banter:

'Where's the loo, Paul?'

'Right-hand door at the top of the *apples*.'

We spoke knowingly about how Spitalfields was a typical inner-city neighbourhood, experiencing the familiar contemporary shift in land use from 'light industrial' to 'residential' and 'retail'. The same process of gentrification that had brought loft-living to New York's Greenwich Village or made the Jordaan in Amsterdam – the area of the city in which the Huguenots had once settled – such fashionable districts seemed now to be visiting this suburb of eighteenth-century London. With its steady proliferation of design studios and New Georgian residents, Spitalfields looked set to become equally trendy.

Paul, who was employed by the Spitalfields Trust to manage its day-to-day conservation work in the eighteenth-century houses of the area, was, in his own way, part of this very process, an agent of gentrification. For Paul, Spitalfields was not so much his home as a backdrop against which he was able to entertain his friends and style his life. Apart from his work locally with the Spitalfields Trust, he was also busy writing a book about Tuscan hill towns and establishing his career as a freelance journalist.

After eating we went for a walk. We started off along Brick Lane, passing its numerous Bengali restaurants, stopping for a packet of cigarettes from the Taj Stores. Waiting outside, I was struck by the busy energy of Brick Lane, an immigrant community apparently getting on with its own life, marching to its own bangla beat. Paul pointed out the sometime Huguenot chapel, now a mosque, with its Venetian window and gable-end roof and told us of the Trust's concern about the fate of its interior, the panelling and so on, in the hands of its present occupants. Heading off towards the Bethnal Green Road, we passed Truman's brewery (with its 'important 1740s front') and then looped round into Commercial Street, already congested with lorries queuing to make their delivery to the wholesale fruit and vegetable market. I peered through the market gates at the rows of stands, still bolted closed, and wondered at this most resonant of cockney settings. With the porters' barrows propped against the wall, I was reminded of scenes from *My Fair Lady* and *Oliver!* and other popular evocations of Victorian London.

'Of no particular architectural interest,' said Paul, 'except possibly the Horner buildings, the residential bit round the eastern perimeter. The rest will come down with the development, in any case.'

'The development?'

'When the market moves and the site is cleared for offices.'

We had returned to Princelet Street and Paul said he had one last thing to show us. Unlocking the door of the building next to his own, he led us into a dark and rather smelly hallway. From the hall we entered a back room . . . a meeting hall of sorts . . . a church? . . . a synagogue! As my eyes adjusted to the darkness, I could just make out the Hebrew inscription around the rim of the balcony. Now disused, the synagogue still retained an air of prayerful melancholy, an accumulated longing for a lost world. A *bimah* – the wooden construction, like a mobile box-pew, from which the scroll of the law is read during the service – sat in the middle of the floor, and against the back wall, behind an elevated platform, there was a cupboard, like a built-in ward-robe. Was that the Ark, I wondered? Did it still contain the scrolls? Carried away by my mood of slightly brazen impetuosity, I strode over and opened it.

Looking back, maybe that was the moment that let the genie out of the jar. Certainly I felt a shudder of remorse, that I had been unaccountably disrespectful. Yet, in that instant, I also became uncomfortably conscious that I was somehow implicated in a whole web of violation. Where did this feeling come from? Where would it lead me?

We went back next door to Paul's house. Quite soon after-wards I bade my farewells. I walked back towards Liverpool Street station, passing the market on my right and then reaching the pallet fire, which had now become quite a blaze, at the far side. A few men were still standing there, stoking it, warming themselves, keeping their evening vigil. I walked over to join them. There wasn't much conversation to be had and I was happy simply to share the heat.

'It's the Fire of London,' said one eventually, not apparently to anyone in particular, speaking deeply from within his shaggy beard and beneath his beaten-up old trilby. 'It's the last bit of the Fire of London. They never got to it, never managed to put it out completely, they didn't. We keep it going. It keeps the rats out at any rate.' Then turning to face me, he added, with a slightly mad chuckle, 'You never know when you might be needing a bit of a fire.'

As I crossed over from Spitalfields into the City of London, from one of the poorest parishes of the land into its richest square mile, I turned back to frame, in my mind's eye, these few hunched figures gathered around the fire, this little patch of brightness against the gathering dark.

For months, sitting in the Bodleian Library, studying for my finals, I had felt like one of those great fat bluebottles careering into one pane of glass after another, looking for a way out, that window left slightly ajar. I was swotting, as I had done so proficiently for years, memorising dates and quotes, assembling fickle little arguments about Donne's poetic achievement or

Sterne's narrative originality, just going through the motions. I was somewhere else. I would spend long minutes staring blankly at the books I had spread open before me and wonder whether, like so many unsprung traps, they might suddenly snap shut and swat *me*?

When I had gone to see the bishop he had asked me in a particularly episcopal sort of way – I was sure he had asked this question countless times before and had long since ceased to be remotely interested in the answers given – what it was that excited me most about the Gospel. I had answered that it was the travel opportunities. I was, of course, being facetious. Was I also being accurate? I longed to escape. I may not have felt particularly called by the Almighty to be ordained to the office of priest in the Church of God – the bishop had spotted this – but I certainly relished the idea of disappearing, like some undercover detective, amongst those hidden worlds all jumbled together in this strange and exciting metropolis of London Town. Were all clergy essentially nosy? I wondered.

Nor was it just voyeurism, it was also a muffled awareness of my own lacunae, the potholes in my limited life experience. I was all in theory and in principle. I could rehearse the terms of a debate – I could even generate something of a passionate intensity – but when it came down to it I probably couldn't have given a fig. I not only lacked all conviction, I lacked the very thing that gets the motor started on a cold morning – an indignant awareness of my own need, my own vulnerability. A straight run to university through an expensive private education had enabled me somehow to paper over the broken bits, of which there were many, with an apparent ease. I could do breezy insouciance. It was a sham, of course I knew it, but it was an elegant sham.

If my religion was inherited but not really inhabited, my politics were ill-fitting and oddly jumbled. I knew I should hate Mrs Thatcher, but actually rather admired her. I also liked Michael Foot's shambling intelligence although I didn't really understand a word he said – or maybe I just wasn't listening. Of course the key thing was the market and where you stood on it, whether you were for it or against it. Should it be free and open or moderated by strategic intervention? Increasingly this question, with its suggested weighing of the individual against the collective, its pitting of the entrepreneurial middle class breeze-ins (they were in the process of being dubbed 'yuppies') against the inherited prejudices and privileges of upper/working class *Gesellschaft*, had framed the political discourse over the years in which I had moved towards teetering adulthood. Politics, it seemed, was becoming just economics with egos attached.

My first memory of the *polis* at work had been the three-day week in 1972 – a constant run of exciting black-outs and power cuts – when Mr Heath took on the unions and lost, leaving Mrs Thatcher to finish the job ten years later. Indeed in October 1984, during my first week at Oxford, after battling through the profusion of University clubs and societies at Freshers Fair (did I want to learn how to juggle oranges or join the fight against the Pinochet dictatorship?) I remember sloping off to some fuggy caff in the Covered Market to read in the papers an exchange of letters between David Jenkins, the newly enthroned Bishop of Durham, and Peter Walker, the Secretary of State for Energy. It was an edgy correspondence which focused the deepening disagreement between the Church of England and the Government and rehearsed the arguments which would subsequently resurface in the Church's report *Faith in the City*. I cut it out. The bishop had accused the Government of refusing to care for the poor and of making a virtue of confrontation with the unions in the miners' strike. The Secretary of State had spoken of the need to temper compassion with efficiency. With his slight tendency to go on, the bishop responded by agitating indignantly, 'Surely this implies negotiating with and not destroying communities, groupings, and organisations which have grown up over the years, and which represent, however imperfectly, the legitimate aspirations and hopes of real and valued members of our society . . .'

This is what I thought I saw that first evening in Spitalfields. I saw a place which carried a freight of 'aspirations and hopes' and the possibility of making concrete sense here – in this place

– of a number of abstract notions which had been filling my head over the previous few years. Throughout that final term I kept encircling Spitalfields Market in my imagination, just as we had done that evening on foot, casing the joint, bringing to mind the image of those few hunched figures gathering around the pallet fire. I found myself ordering up from stacks books about the East End when I should have been studying Defoe's *Journal of the Plague Year*, and poring over volume 27 of the Survey of London with its detailed architectural drawings of the Georgian terraces, when I should have been revising my Augustan poets.

At lunchtime on June 11th 1987, between my Shakespeare paper in the morning and my History of the Language paper in the afternoon, wearing my regulation academic dress of dark suit and white bow tie, looking like I had just stepped off the set of some costume drama, I slipped down to the local polling station in North Oxford and, standing like a penitent in the confessional, I cast my protest vote. It was the first time I had voted in a general election. Quite what I was protesting against I wasn't entirely sure. But later that night, as Mrs Thatcher stood on the steps of 10 Downing Street and promised 'to do something about those inner cities', I was already one step ahead of her. I was already plotting my passage into E1.

When you fall in love with a person or a place or the prospect of some major undertaking, what, in fact, is going on? Where does the sense of driving compulsion come from? Something stirs inside, a sense of fit, but also one of potential, although of course it's more immediately exciting than that – it's potential with a glass of bubbly in its hand, an enticement of possibilities, as urgent as the flooding tide. You need suddenly to know all there is to know about her, or there, or it – whatever it is that holds you in thrall. You necessarily become an anorak, a little obsessed. That's how I was begining to feel about Spitalfields. I was on for a bit of townspotting.

It was following the Fire of London, back in 1666, that the market traders who had previously gathered outside St Paul's Cathedral were cast out of the City gates and forced to pursue their business where they wouldn't clutter up the narrow streets with their sprawling stalls and undesirable hangers-on. Some came to Spitalfields, which, by contrast, has always been welcoming to all sorts of comers and goers and itinerants: the passing trade upon which the survival of its fruit and vegetable market at one time depended.

At the foot of the East End of London, sandwiched between Bethnal Green and Whitechapel, within easy walk of the river, it has always been permeable as an area, a point of entry, somewhere you can find a niche for yourself. Unlike the City, Spitalfields has always been open to people wanting to get a toehold in society: immigrant communities, economic and political refugees, the very poor. It is what the sociologists call 'a zone of transition'. And since its earliest days as one of London's first industrial suburbs, probably since 1683 when Charles II granted a royal charter to sell 'flesh, fowl and roots' to John Blanch, a silk throwster from Somerset, Spitalfields Market has been at the heart of this hospitable community.

If, then, the area has always been open to society's most vulnerable people (until the late seventeenth century the City disposed of its rubbish there), it has also been amenable to individual ambition, a place of opportunity, a place to get that first footing before moving on. As markets tend to undermine the existing networks of rights and privileges, so market wealth tends to be new wealth, and Spitalfields is unsurprisingly full of rags-to-riches folklore. Take, for example, the story of Robert Horner, who began his working life as a market porter and ended up, in 1875, buying the market leasehold. Or the story of Fanny Marks, who started on Brick Lane with a barrel of herrings and ended up a millionairess. Or of Billy Ocean, the singer, who used to go into Wolman's, the chemist on Brick Lane, to buy throat lozenges. 'This was when he was a nothing,' remembers Sam Wolman, 'when he worked for a fella, a tailor or a presser, off of Brick Lane and he used to come in here and say he wanted to write songs, to sing songs, and I used to pull his leg and tease him something rotten. And then the next thing I knew he was having hit records, he was on Top of the Pops. Well, it just goes to show, doesn't it . . .'

Even William Hogarth, in the eighteenth century, seems to have drawn on this particular Spitalfields mythology in his series of prints 'Industry and Idleness'. These depict the fortunes of two apprentices along their respective career paths, the one to his enthronement as Lord Mayor of London, the other to his execution as a common criminal. In the first print of the series they are shown, side by side, a couple of trainee weavers at their looms in Spitalfields. This is where the story starts; it is also where their paths diverge.

Since its emergence as an economic community in the late seventeenth century, Spitalfields seems to have been a place of lively entrepreneurial endeavour. Maybe because of this, it has also had an uneasy relationship with Authority. Indeed, the parish was formed, in 1729, as part of the established Church's explicit attempt to impose some sort of Anglican order on the raggedy Nonconformist multitudes of East London. Until this time the hamlet of Spitalfields had been part of the larger parish of St Dunstan's, which offered just one church and two makeshift 'tabernacles' for churchmen. It had, however, at least nineteen meeting houses for Dissenters. What was needed, according to the Parliamentary Act which promulgated the parish's creation, was 'better instruction of all Persons . . . in the true Christian Religion'. This was a view held also by Christopher Wren. When, in 1671, he came down to Spitalfields to inspect the scattering of houses which had sprung up along Brick Lane, he was left with the impression that they were 'unacceptably farr from any church'. So in came his apprentice, Nicholas Hawksmoor, and up went Christ Church, that soaring masterpiece of political assertion which stands at the top of Brushfield Street and, to this day, overshadows the market.

Unfortunately, Christ Church never really took. The religious history of the area is more accurately told by the building which stands four-square at the other end of Fournier Street, the Neuve Eglise, the one Paul had pointed out to me on our walk around Spitalfields. Built in 1743 as the Huguenot church, it subsequently became a Methodist chapel, then a synagogue and is now the Brick Lane mosque. Like the joker in the pack, it's theologically wild, having been home to the world's three great monotheistic faiths. It has been taken up by each of the successive waves of immigrant communities passing through Spitalfields and rearranged to suit its own religious needs.

Which brings us to maybe the central characteristic of the area. For the last three hundred years Spitalfields has offered a home to marginal groups on the move. Already in the seventeenth century its proximity to the City (and its lack of parish authority) made it attractive to Roman Catholic recusants. Then it quickly became a stronghold for Nonconformity: Baptists settled, Quakers held meetings, subversive plots were hatched within this 'liberty east of Bishopsgate'. And from its earliest days immigrant communities have also settled here. Records of Huguenot weavers, escaping France after revocation of the Edict of Nantes, go back to 1685. The last decades of the nineteenth century saw a large influx of Eastern European Jewry, escaping the pogroms in their homelands and replacing the by then assimilated French weavers in Spitalfields. They in turn were replaced by the Bengalis from as early as the 1950s, and then more rapidly through the 1960s and 1970s. The parish has also played host at different times to communities of Irish, Vietnamese and Maltese, all passing through the East End of London, on the hoof.

Of course, most cities have one or several such 'zones of transition', districts where migrants have settled and have been able to establish themselves before moving on. Some are more self-contained — one might say 'ghettoised' — than others and all certainly change with the changing fortunes of the city. Take, for example, Scheunenviertel in Berlin, the old Jewish quarter in the former eastern part of the city. This was where Moses Mendelssohn, the celebrated thinker of the Jewish Enlightenment, had once lived and where in 1866 the Neue Synagoge was built to serve some of the 28,000 Jews who were then living in Berlin. This, of course, all changed in the 1930s when it became one of the gathering points for deportation by the Nazis. Since the reunification of the city in the 1990s, the area has become home to a cosmopolitan assortment of artists, students and families on low incomes. This, however, is changing again. With the present influx of huge capital investment in the city, Scheunenviertel looks set to become a prime inner-city residential precinct, located as it is so conveniently close to the new centre of German government.

Or take Istanbul's old Galata neighbourhood. Bounded by water on two sides, at the junction of the Bosphorus and the Golden Horn, this district has its roots in a semi-autonomous Genoese trading colony of the fourteenth century. Under the Ottomans, Galata became 'the European quarter', where foreign merchants set up shop and the European powers built their first embassies. For most of this century, however, it has been better known for its run-down houses and shabby back streets inhabited by refugees trying to find their way from Asia into Europe. But times are changing here too: a local architect has recently launched an initiative to revitalise Galata, hoping to save its stock of fine nineteenth-century Levantine houses and promote the area with its own annual arts festival.

Indeed, one need only catch the Eurostar to Paris and walk the ten minutes from the Gare du Nord into the area known as La Goutte d'Or, 'The Golden Drop', to find a district which is similar in so many respects to London's Spitalfields. La Goutte d'Or is described by Zola in *L'Assommoir*, where the poverty-stricken recent arrivals from the south and the centre of the country established themselves in the nineteenth century. In his novel Zola attempts to use the language of the slums, with all its vivid vernacular, with the result that many translations have the protagonists talking like cockney villains, teetering on the edge of idiomatic absurdity: 'You buggering little pansy . . . I'll teach you if you like with a couple of clips round the earhole! Fancy a sissy like you insulting the worker!'

Before her eventual and sadly inevitable demise, Gervaise, the novel's heroine, enjoys a brief period running her own laundry. In the sections of the book which describe this, one has a sense of the rather wonderful self-contained sanctuary afforded by the area. Standing in the doorway of her shop, Gervaise relishes this sense that she is able fully to comprehend her environment: 'The rue de la Goutte d'Or belonged to her, and so did the streets nearby and all the neighbourhood. Standing there she could crane her neck and take in with a glance left and right to each end of the street, the whole scene, people, houses, road and sky.' Certainly the area readily absorbed its poor migrants from the countryside. Until recently the names of the cafés still recalled their presence – Café du Massif Central, Café de Padirac – although the owners now speak Arabic and the juke-boxes play music that was never heard in the Limousin.

During the Algerian War the population of La Goutte d'Or was mostly Arab and the neighbourhood was generally safe for underground soldiers on the run. Money was collected for the Front de Libération Nationale and, with the streets patrolled by French soldiers and armed policemen, there were the occasional reprisal shootings. Now, along with the residents from Algeria, Tunisia and Morocco there are Africans from Senegal, Mali and elsewhere who wish to make this immigrant ghetto of the 18th *arrondissement* their home. Butchers selling '*viandes hallal*' and spit-roasting, along with the ubiquitous chickens, sheep heads and *merguez* sausages, service the dietary requirements of the local population.

Yet, here too, there are posters plastered to the walls of houses now boarded up which seek '*permis de démolir*' and building sites scattered around the area advertise the incipient construction of '*logements*' comprising '*caves et commerces, un niveau de parking, ateliers d'artistes*'. The studio flat, a commonplace phenomenon in nearby Montmartre, is edging its way into La Goutte d'Or.

If, until now, the Gare du Nord and its sprawl of railway track has protected La Goutte d'Or from creeping gentrification, so too has Spitalfields Market provided a buffer to the City's expansion into the East End. With market activity being so unsocial – noisy, dirty and nocturnal – a healthy market requires a physically chaotic space, capable of containing its unpredictable rhythms of inactivity and congestion. With its dirt and its homelessness, its overcrowding and lack of facilities, Spitalfields has, over the last three hundred years, provided such a place. Paradoxically, therefore, the very qualities which caused the City to turn its back on Spitalfields were also those that allowed its entrepreneurial community, with the fruit and vegetable market at its symbolic heart, to function as its own effective 'zone of transition'.

In the 1980s, however, all this apparently began to change. In 1987 the City Corporation put the market site out to tender. A Bill was lodged before Parliament to release the City from the constraints of the royal charter which had been granted three centuries before. In 1989 the Spitalfields Development Group won the contract to 'develop' the market site with a mixture of offices, shops, housing (both public and private), possibly a theatre, some open space and various other facilities designed to whet the appetite of the local community. As a City Corporation hygienist, who was checking the market cellars for dead rats, put it to me one day, 'The City wants the land, so the market's got to go. The City can't go west because that's the West End, it can't go south, because that's the river, it can't go north because that's Regent's Park. The only place it can go is towards Mile End so that's where it's going. It's progress, it's money, it's got to spread itself. From here to Stratford it's all slums anyway so it doesn't matter. They'll knock them down and expand that way, over Commercial Street and Brick Lane. You've got ten people living in one flat down there, no one's going to mind. The people who live there have no say anyway. Public enquiries only delay things, they don't make any difference. We're just little ants. When the government or the City want to do something, they just do it.'

Despite his rather shaky grasp of London geography, there were many people who shared the rat-catcher's anticipation of change, if not the depth of his cynicism. This area, which had existed for three centuries outside the City, a safe haven for exiles and sundry renegades, seemed to be about to enter the newly-defined city boundary. Like many similar areas in other European cities, this amazingly self-sufficient and defiantly higgledy-piggledy quarter of London faced the prospect of radical transformation by forces outside its control. A global market, sustained through computer terminals and the latest advances in information technology was about to replace – literally – a market of barrows, produce and hard cash.

Hardly surprisingly, the people of Spitalfields went into flat spins. The proposed development raised for them the most fundamental questions of ownership and self-determination. Whose fields were these? Everybody looked to the area's history to legitimate their claims and Spitalfields became a community of hugely inventive versions of its own past. Even its name was up for grabs. Some said it was called Spitalfields since it had been built up on the site of the medieval hospital, whereas others said it was named after the spittle the Huguenot weavers would use to lubricate their looms, while others suggested (and this one I found particularly imaginative) that it was called Spitalfields because it had always functioned as a sort of 'spit' into the East End, rightfully, therefore, belonging to the City.

It became clear that there existed here, side by side, a collection of discrete communities which had little to do with one another, beyond the fact they shared the same postcode. A member of the arriviste gentry, having just moved into one of the 1720s houses in the conservation area, might go and buy a pint of milk or a packet of cigarettes from Mr Ali at the Taj Stores on Brick Lane, but that was about as much direct contact as the two cultures enjoyed. The newly restored and finely crafted shutters of the Georgian houses remained, for the most part, firmly closed, as did the minds of many of the Bengalis who would pour into the Brick Lane mosque for Friday prayers. Unfortunately, the same could not be said for the mouths of many of the market traders – the cockneys – whose racist posturing simply beggared belief. Spitalfields seemed to play host to a number of separate universes, which bumped into and off each other, which collided but did not necessarily communicate.

Shortly after it was published, I was lent a copy of Salman Rushdie's *The Satanic Verses*. Partly on account of the debate which proceeded very quickly to engulf it – and quite dramatically so in this mainly Muslim corner of London – I read it with some curiosity. I discovered a book which is significantly about this experience of migration in a world which has become itself no more than one vast zone of transition. Built around a series of startling juxtapositions, it dramatises what happens when identities collide, when characters fall between worlds. Indeed, like another long book, *The Satanic Verses* itself begins with a fall. Rushdie's two heroes, Gibreel Farishta and Saladin Chamcha, come tumbling out of the sky, ejected from a terrorist-exploded 747 (named, incidentally, after one of the Islamic gardens of Paradise, *Bostan*). If their identities were secure in the plane, they are now no longer so. They have entered 'airspace . . . that most insecure and transitory of zones, illusory, discontinuous, metamorphic, because when you throw everything up in the air anything becomes possible'. They land, the only survivors of the crash, to find themselves changed too. Gibreel has acquired a halo, Saladin has little bumps appearing on his forehead: horns.

The book is itself partly set in a fictionalised version of Spitalfields. As 'the slowly transmogrifying Saladin Chamcha' turns into 'a fully developed devil, a horned goat-man', he takes his lodgings above the Shaandaar, a café which is also managed by its Bangladeshi proprietor, Mr Muhammad Sufyan, as a rooming house. From his window on the top floor he has a panoramic view of 'the Street' (Brick Lane); not dissimilar from the view from the very window at which I sat to read the book. 'The street', according to Rushdie, runs from 'up there, under the railway bridge where the National Front used to do battle with the fearless radicals of the Socialist Workers Party' (at the junction between Brick Lane and the Bethnal Green Road) to the 'Jamme Masjid which used to be the Machzikel HaDath [*sic*] synagogue which had in its turn replaced the Huguenots' Calvinist church' (on the corner of Fournier Street and Brick Lane) past the 'non-tint neo-Georgians' with 'their perfectly restored residences' (Fournier Street, Princelet Street, Wilkes Street, Hanbury Street).

And it is here, in the heart of this 'mythological battleground' as the Cockney, Bengali and New Georgian worlds collide, that Saladin Chamcha slowly grows his horns in his attic room on Brick Lane. Moreover, it is from here that 'stories rushed across the city in every direction'. After all, it 'wouldn't be long before that raid on the Shaandaar Café would send the whole thing higher than the sky. Priests became involved, adding another unstable element – the linkage between the term black and the sin blasphemy – to the mix.'

Set partly in Spitalfields, *The Satanic Verses* is, amongst other things, a book about urban life, its apparent lack of any orthodoxies, the international nature of its clash of its cultures, its linguistic patchwork, impurity, intermingling. As Otto Cone, art historian and social commentator, declares in the novel: 'The modern city is the locus classicus of incompatible realities. Lives that have no business mingling with one another sit side by side on the omnibus.' And elsewhere Rushdie has said of the city that it works as a metaphor at the heart of his writing. It seemed to me, then, that Spitalfields, with its competing versions of itself, its juxtapositions of wealth and poverty, its discrete and identifiable communities, was indeed something of a locus classicus. I wondered whether it would be possible to write my way through these various worlds, to check out the validity of Rushdie's working thesis. Did they really have so little in common?

Spitalfields, then, was at a point of fundamental change. Ever since 1683 when Charles II granted the royal charter to the silk throwster from Somerset, Spitalfields Market had been at the heart of this community. Established at a time in the seventeenth century when, across the country, new networks of buyers and sellers were rapidly replacing the previously isolated economies of local consumption and self-reliance was increasingly giving way to the unregulated play of 'market forces', the appearance of Spitalfields Market in the 1680s may be seen to mark a transition to our modern period of capitalist trade. Did its closure, then, in the 1980s and the planned construction in its place of an office development designed to serve the expanding global financial markets herald the transition from this modern period into something else?

I don't know if it was what the good bishop actually had in mind, but about eighteen months after I spoke with him in his house in North Oxford, I had moved up to Spitalfields. It was at the beginning of July 1988. I did, indeed, stay at Toynbee

Hall for a few weeks whilst I found somewhere else to live. Of course I didn't realise it at the time, but that summer I had begun an exploration into this extraordinary corner of London – this zone of transition, this locus classicus of incompatible realities, this mythological battleground – which would take about ten years (almost the exact period that Rushdie was to spend in hiding) to complete.

COCKNEY SPITALFIELDS

On my first day

Vince winked. Jim grinned. Brian chucked me an apple. I reached out to shake Phil by the hand, sort of man-to-man, to seal the deal, and he nearly fell over with surprise.

'As I say,' he said regaining his balance, 'the job pays a hundred and sixty pound a week.'

I froze silent: had I made a terrible mistake in offering him my hand? Surely market traders shake hands occasionally? *Oh my God*, I suddenly panicked: perhaps he thought I was going to hit him.

'You can start on Monday,' he said.

'Monday's fine,' I said, slipping my hand back into my pocket, trying to appear casual. 'See you then!'

It was noon as I walked out of Spitalfields Market. The traders were piling up their unsold fruit and vegetables and sweeping their stands free of the day's debris. A few women hovered around the discarded produce, picking their way through the boxes of blackened avocados and filling up plastic bags with salvaged food. The porters were chaining their barrows to the wall, where they would remain, like discarded props after a performance, until the following morning. Voices shouted across the market to each other and arranged to meet in the pub.

I walked back to my flat in Brick Lane, passing Gilbert and George on Fournier Street. They strode past, with a synchronised step. 'Hello!', 'Hello!' they choroused, on the up beat, and then disappeared into the Market Café. Some workmen a little further up the street were throwing rubble down a chute, rapidly filling the skip below. On the opposite side of the road a woman sat with an easel on her lap sketching the scene. I stood at her shoulder, irritating her into conversation.

'It's the dereliction I like. These old Georgian houses look so much better before they do them up. The shadows are deeper and so much more interesting.'

I left her looking into the shadows and turned into Brick Lane, which, around the mosque, was congested with après-prayer milling about. Groups of men stood together talking and shuffling between conversations, holding hands. Their children waited sheepishly by the school railings beside my front door.

Home again. A two-minute walk from the market which had placed it several worlds away.

At four o'clock the following Monday morning I walked those same streets to my first day's work in Spitalfields Market. This time it was Brick Lane which looked discarded: rubbish kicked into every corner and doorway like flotsam washed up by the high tide; a broken street light flashing for help in some Morse code I didn't understand; a cardboard box of a body asleep on the steps of the mosque. As I turned off Brick Lane and walked towards the market I could hear a grandfather clock striking the hour somewhere behind a pair of Georgian shutters.

The market, at the other end of Fournier Street, spilled its activity over Commercial Street and into the shops which surrounded the Market Café. Greengrocers' vans were jammed into every available space and some were already half-filled with boxes and sacks of produce. On their sides I read the addresses of shops in Hackney, Tottenham, Chingford, Chelmsford, Saffron Walden and Cambridge: the market drew most of its custom from north-east London and beyond into East Anglia.

Approaching the market from this direction, one was confronted by the gabled Arts and Crafts-style Horner buildings which overlooked the Ten Bells pub (formerly the Jack the Ripper) and the monumental mass of Hawksmoor's Christ Church. These buildings, which were in part residential, formed the short edge of a rectangular space which spread out behind them to cover about fourteen acres of land, the heart of a proposed office development. The interior of the market shed resembled a greenhouse, with its steel-framed structure and glazed roof. The traders' stands in the market were set out along a grid of intersecting alleys with the proprietors' names painted white on vermilion boards suspended from the roof above their allocated space. Adjacent to the fruit and vegetable market, along the northern edge, was the flower market with its undistinguished single-storey red brick façade.

From about eleven o'clock at night the parking space between the market and Bishopsgate started to fill with heavy goods vehicles from all over Britain and the Continent and then, when it opened at midnight, they passed from west to east through the three central alleys. It was always a race to get parked up at the front of the queue, so they could be away sooner.

'We get paid for the round trip, not for the hours we spend having to wait,' I was told one night by a driver down from Lincolnshire with a delivery of cauliflowers. He was standing by his cab, sipping hot tea and peering at me through the steam which warmed his face. He grunted unhelpfully at my questions until, finally, outraged into speech, he said, 'Like it? Everyone hates it mate. You can never get in, you can never get in and out. It's not badly designed, it's well designed, whoever built it, but it's just not capable of the traffic what comes in nowadays. It's got to be like the new Covent Garden, you can drive in round that. But you can't here.

'Years ago you used to bring a full load of cauliflowers to one place, now you've got eight or nine drops, sometimes more. You've got to keep going in and out, in and out, all night. You just can't do anything in this market any more. No, I shouldn't think you'll find anyone who's got a good word for this place. Anyway, aren't they moving it to Millwall?'

'Temple Mills, I think. In Leyton.'

'What are they going to build here?'

'It's going to be a mixed development. Some housing, shopping, quite a lot of offices.'

A look of recognition crossed his face. Turning to his son, who had been listening to our conversation from his seat in the cab, he snarled 'Developers', and his son nodded knowingly.

As I walked into the market on my first day of employment, the last trucks were unloading their produce. I squeezed past a lorry with an Italian numberplate and caught a blast of refrigerated air from its rear as a load of peaches were lifted out by a forklift. It was at four o'clock that selling officially started and the second shift of the night began. I presented myself before my new employer, Phil Barry, who told me to help Jim out with the order he was making up.

'Call me Jim, call me cunt-face, call me anything you like. Most people do.'

'I'm William.'

'Is that Big Willy or Little Willy?'

Jim took me round to another trader where we had to collect twenty boxes of avocados.

'We'll have to sort them through first to get rid of the spotty ones. Who wants to buy a spotty avocado?'

'They don't mind us sorting them out like this?'

'They don't like it when the Pakis do it. Well, would you? I mean those Pakis are so fuckin' filthy: you give them a cup of tea and they use it to wipe their arse, 'cos they don't use khazi paper like the rest of us. Did you know that? That's a fact.'

I could see I was going to learn a lot in the market. I wasn't just going to learn how to recognise a healthy avocado or to stack up a pallet. I wasn't just going to learn how to distinguish between melon and melon. I was also going to learn how unpleasant rotting vegetables can smell and how, if you leave it, one bad potato can ruin a whole sack.

It is in the first impressions, the introductions, the How d'you do's, that you sense the collective feeling, because soon, if you stay, you too become part of it. A family smell hits your nostrils in the hall with its distinct odour, but by the time you've sat down in the kitchen with your cup of tea it's become the air you breathe.

Well, at the end of my first day's work in Spitalfields Market, as I sat in my room on Brick Lane and noted down my impressions, it wasn't the community warmth I was struck by, nor the much-acclaimed cockney good humour. It was the hostile suspicion between traders and the unmistakable smell of rotting vegetables.

The way of the market

A pallet is stacked rather as society is organised, with the hard root vegetables at the bottom and the soft exotic fruit on the top. When stacking an order the skill lies in using as few pallets as possible without damaging any of the fruit. You also have to be careful to interlock the boxes, mesh them together, to distribute the weight more evenly.

Jim could shift the fruit in next to no time. He knew the best order to stack the produce and could see the final arrangement in his head before he even started. He showed me a few tricks. On making up a large order of tomatoes, for example, he told me that it was easier to take twenty off a pile of a hundred and twenty than it was to stack up a hundred on a fresh pallet. He was right.

We sold a lot of tomatoes, both Dutch and English. They came in different sizes and stages of ripeness from the very green 'backward' ones to the dark red ones. In fact it was the tomatoes which set the tone of an order. Many boxes of backward tomatoes would suggest a large shop with a quick turnover and a wide range of produce. A few boxes of ripe tomatoes, on the other hand, would suggest a smaller store with a slower turnover, possibly a corner shop, a generalist and not a specialist, a grocer and not a greengrocer.

Some grocers came only once a week, others came every day. With his regular customers Phil would squeeze their arm affectionately, even offer them tea: little perks with which he hoped to ensure their continuing custom. It was for these regulars that I made up most of the orders: Mr Smith of Bow, Mr Copley of Colchester, Mr Bevans from Bethnal Green. For the first couple of weeks they supervised my selection of produce, occasionally returning boxes which they said were 'slack' (not completely full) or 'on the twist' (going off). It was only Mr Smith who always scrutinised my choice of fruits, and he never trusted me to choose his bananas for him. My relationship with Mr Smith deteriorated very suddenly after a pallet I had stacked for him toppled over in transit, his carefully selected produce splaying out all over the road. He clearly felt humiliated.

Jim showed me how to pack the piles closer together, so that this didn't happen. He also showed me how to use the shrink wrap to stabilise the stack. 'Shrink it, just shrink it,' he'd say impatiently as if I were a half-wit. Then, 'You college kids, you've got piss-all common sense.'

Jim had left school as soon as he could. He had gone straight into the army and when the Falklands War came he was sent out to fight for Queen and country. Shortly after he returned to England he left the army and went to work in a pub in Soho. He became the youngest landlord in London when his boss ran off to Brazil with the all the money and the brewery promoted him to run the pub.

'I had really landed on my tootsies. I could make a substantial bit of profit, especially with all the stolen gear that was coming over the counter: TVs, videos, cameras, Barclaycards, American Express cards, passports, travellers' cheques. I could phone up my contacts and in half an hour they would be slapping notes right down on the counter in front of me.'

Then when he got married and had a little boy he and his family moved out of the pub and went to live in Barking. His job in the market suited him well: he was energetic, enterprising and familiar with the operation of the black economy. He also shared the traditional cockney scorn for the upwardly mobile:

'This is what all you yuppies eat,' said Jim, stacking a box of starfruit on the top of an order for the catering department at Kensington Town Hall. 'That's what all you poncing pricks that are moving into Spitalfields like.'

'So what's the trade in exotics like here?' I asked.

'It's good. We don't do much macaroon though, only a bit of mango.'

'Macaroon?'

'That's right, macaroon. Wog-fruit. Macaroon means coon means coloured. Understand? So when we're talking about a load of macaroni we're not talking about pasta, OK?'

Out of all the people I met in the market, Jim's remarks were the most overtly racist, his language was punctuated by the most frequent obscenities, his manner the most casually insulting. With his feet splaying out as he walked and his hair cut to within a centimetre of his scalp, Jim personified Bovver. He paraded his prejudices like a collection of medals. Sometimes, however, I caught a whiff of self-parody.

'Why do you want to work in the market, anyway?' he asked me. 'I would have thought that a clever dick like you that has a degree and the rest of the old bollocks could get a job teaching fuckin' Fergie and Andy's kids to go and talk English proper like what I do.'

If not as tutors in elocution, many of the traders did, in fact, earn an extra bob or two on the side. Working in the market at night meant that they could work elsewhere during the day. The black cabs lined up in the carpark so that when the porters had finished driving the vegetables around the market, they could do a few more hours driving people around London.

'When I finish in the market I usually go and put a few hours' work in down the undertakers',' said Jim. 'It's me that knocks up the boxes for the stiffs. It's good money. Quick too. It doesn't take ten minutes to knock up a box in the old chipboard. Then when you've put a bit of spray on it, a bit of lacquer, and when you've stuck on the plastic laminated handles, you can make it look like the real fuckin' McCoy. Then off it tootles down the Chapel of Rest, where them *pine lickers* do their bit, before it gets *brown bread and toasted*, before they stick it in the old furnace.'

While Jim knocked up his coffins during the afternoons, Vince did his car-boot sales and Brian cleaned cars. Brian, in fact, wanted to leave his job in the market and develop his car valeting business, to resuscitate it, to make a bit of go of it. He had come into the market when he lost his lease on the previous premises and his business collapsed. The work in the market had attracted him because it left him free in the afternoons to keep a few jobs going. And when Phil took him on there seemed the possibility of promotion, perhaps even of a partnership. But the strain on the family had been too great and, well, he said, the market, it was no good as a place to work. It changed you. It hardened you.

It was because Brian was leaving that Phil had employed me in the first place. He needed someone to take over the morning delivery of fruit and vegetables, which Brian had been doing for the last six months. The delivery van was a diesel-fuelled Ford Transit, with wing mirrors like elephant's ears, prominent but not terribly effective. Tuned into Capital Radio, with an A–Z on my dashboard and a van full of fruit and veg I would set out three days a week on my North Circular tour of London.

I left the market with the day's delivery at six in the morning, guided out of the car park by the car minder. 'Come on, come on, come on!' he'd shout as I reversed into the stream of forklifts and grocers' vans. 'Come on, come on, come on', you'd hear him shout all morning, so that it became a noise rather than a phrase. Then, with a final farewell look up Brushfield Street towards Christ Church with the sun rising behind its monumental bulk and beyond it over the streets of East London, I would turn, cross the boundary and exchange market congestion for city congestion.

I was new to driving. I had learnt in North Oxford where the only traffic I was likely to encounter as I turned in the road and reversed round the corner was a patiently purring Volvo collecting its boys from the Dragon School or another learner driver under instruction waiting to do a similar manoeuvre. And so, on passing my test, I was eager to graduate into a bit of genuine urban congestion.

Driving my market van involved three areas of mastery: 'The Journey', 'The Arrival' and what can be loosely termed 'Relationships on the Road'. This last aspect included such diverse lessons as 'How To Lie to the Police about the Tax Disk', 'How to Intimidate Smaller Vehicles into Giving Way' and 'How to Make a Third Party Insurance Claim when You've just Smashed into the Rear of a Parked Vehicle'.

Brian was my tutor. His *bons mots* helped me sort out my attitude. Driving, he explained, was all to do with bravado. Size of vehicle determined control of the road. When you're bigger, you bugger; when you're smaller, you suffer. I asked where the blind spots were and was aware of sounding rather effete. You don't worry about blind spots, he scoffed, it's their job to see you, it's your job to be seen.

As we chatted in the van, Brian punctuated the story of his career in the market with the traffic lights down the Euston Road. Accelerating on to the Westway and quickly changing lanes, he told me how he had been shunted from one job to another. Employed as a sales assistant, he had been manipulated into doing the delivery round. Then after six months of driving the truck he had decided to leave the firm. We came to the Acton Junction and turned off the M40.

Our first delivery was at the Makro Store in Acton. We queued in the unloading bay behind appropriately large loads of Persil Automatic and deep frozen fish steaks which were being forklifted from the heavy goods vehicles into the checking-in bay. The key figure in the whole operation was Danny, who drove the forklift. Danny sat majestic upon the forklift, whilst we drivers huddled together exchanging routes and porno-graphic magazines and tried to catch his eye. Brian told me that Spitalfields fresh fruit and vegetables got priority, but I left it to him to press our case. After about an hour of eye-catching, unloading and checking-in we were back on the road again.

On the North Circular Brian told me how he had been brought up in Manchester and, as we passed over Staples Corner and the roots of the M1, how he had sometimes thought of going back. But 'home is where you make it', he reflected as we waited in a traffic jam at Potters Bar for the police to remove a group of gypsies who had gathered in a siding. After delivering the remainder of the load to the Makro Store in Enfield we headed back to Spitalfields. It was on the return route that I was offered some strategies for dealing with the market.

'Phil will screw you if you give him half a chance. First he'll ask you to start half an hour earlier and to leave half an hour later and then you'll be working Saturdays and then he'll want you to do deliveries south of the river. Before you know it he'll be stealing your toast. You mustn't take it personally, it's just the cockney way, the way of the market. What you've got to do is sit your ground, don't give him the opportunity to take advantage of you. Block him.'

I was having difficulty with lane discipline at the North Circular junction and Brian, seeing this, told me to go ahead and straddle, to use my width and weight and straddle, that I wasn't driving a Mini Metro, I was driving a four-and-a-half-ton truck.

We crossed the North Circular and drove down the Cambridge Road towards Spitalfields and the City. As we crested the hill before turning down the Green Lanes, I could see, framed by the Tottenham gas works and the high rises of Haringey, the Nat West tower, erect like an immense executive biro.

We cut through Haringey, Highbury and Hackney and then turned east for Shoreditch and Spitalfields. Capital Radio had replaced our conversation until a road repair forced us to take a diversion and Brian's reassuringly pre-emptive route instructions became uncertain. Maybe I thought I was back in Oxford manoeuvring my driving school Mini Metro round my obstacle-free route. Maybe it was just because I forgot to straddle. But what with the terror of an unfamiliar street pattern and a certain steering wheel mismanagement, I found I had made contact with a stationary vehicle.

'It happens every day,' said Brian cheerily nudging me out of the cab, 'just don't say it was your fault and don't sign anything. You must never admit liability.'

Limited liability

Some would say, and certainly my friend Steve would argue, that this refusal to accept liability, or only to do so as part of the contractual small print and then strictly in inverted commas, was a sure sign of our times. Given the fact that our lives were so thoroughly shaped by the exigencies of the international market, by our participation in the endlessly complex networks of global exchange, how could we possibly expect the buck to stop with any one country or single institution or individual? (Or so the argument went.)

'Point being,' said Steve, 'truth is simply the story we chose to believe in, the version we find most congenial. You demythologise the world, you deconstruct the story, and what do you find? You find absence, a not-presence. Our lives are cultural to the core. And because different individuals within different communities don't necessarily share the same cultural assumptions, the telling of social history is always going to be a contest between a variety of stories, where truth is plural, a struggle – a negotiation, if you like.'

Steve and I had been at university together and whereas I had found myself mooching around Spitalfields with vague ideas that I wanted to write about the area, he had gone straight into the City after graduation, with his shiny suits and his business cards and his direct-dial extension, and, even in those days after the forebodings of Black Monday, seemed to be earning ridiculously large amounts of money. Having been brought up in Romford he had returned to his parents' home after university, and was saving up to put down a deposit on a flat he had seen in a converted match factory in Bow. That he had gone into the money markets hadn't surprised me. His grand-father had worked as a trader in Billingsgate Fish Market, his own father sold insurance and his brother, who was a few years older than him, had set up a business flogging fitness equipment to gyms, health centres and boxing clubs across East London. Besides, Steve could talk. And could do so at great length, with persuasive authority, about practically anything.

Although he had only been working as a broker for a little over a year, already he seemed to be involved in the most energetic wheeling and dealing, helping to move substantial sums around the system, buying or selling at the flick of a switch and then immediately, in a way that I felt defied commonsense but which he assured me was financially very creative, buying back his 'sell' or selling on his 'buy'. As he explained to me, the deal itself was the whole thing. And, in any case, it was all 'paper entrepreneurialism', by which I assumed he meant the gaining of theoretical profits without having to trouble himself with the details of actual production.

'It's all to do with confidence. If you think you're going to be prosperous then you'll make money; if you hesitate or hedge or if you panic, your position will slide and you'll lose money. It's as simple as that.'

In retrospect, at the end of 1988, before the 1989 housing slump, it may well have seemed as simple as that. Like many others he was still reaping the rewards from that series of structural reforms which took place in the City of London throughout the 1980s, which are often referred to as the Big Bang and which culminated in the Financial Services Act of 1986. Of course, what was happening in London was just part of the complete reorganisation of the global financial system involving both massive decentralisation as well as the creation of a number of financial conglomerates of extraordinary power. By 1986, global deregulation, made possible by a system of instantaneous telecommunication and its corollary, an accelerated mobility of funds, meant, for the first time, the formation of a single world market for money and credit supply. 'Banking', suggested the *Financial Times*, 'is rapidly becoming indifferent to the constraints of time, place and currency'.

Naturally these changes had a profound effect on the property market. In the eleven years between 1976 and 1986 the average capital value of one square foot of commercial property in the City rose from £200 to £800. By the end of 1987 it had risen again to a staggering £1,200. These prices, combined with the fact that developers had generally underestimated the massive additional volume of accommodation made necessary by the new type of large open area dealing floors, explains some of the excitement which the Spitalfields Market site generated in the world of property speculation. This sudden increase in the value of the property market following deregulation in 1986 was only matched by its equally sudden collapse little more than a year later.

But in 1988 Steve was full of enthusiasm for the changes in the City and for his own prospects on the markets. 'When the history books come to be written,' he said, 'the Financial Services Act will be seen as one of her greatest achievements. No doubt about it.'

There was perfunctory applause at the other end of the pub.

I wondered what was going on. A group of solitary drinkers turned on their elbows and, clasping their drinks, swirled their beer disconsolately. At the table by the door a young Indian lad handed cigarettes to his mates, none of whom looked much more than sixteen. At the pool table a couple of men, possibly traders from Spitalfields Market, resumed their game, offering knowing strategies to each other and grunting reluctant encouragement: 'try sending the black boy home', 'you'll need to open her up a bit, if you're going to put pink away', 'nice one, John, nice one'. And at the far corner of the bar, bang next to the jukebox, a group of City gents, colleagues in fact of Steve's, sniggered a bit, swaggered a bit and then began the elaborate ritual of buying a round of drinks.

'Come and meet the boys before the next dance,' said Steve, crossing over to join them, leaving me a little puzzled about this reference to dancing. I was then presented with a succession of names like 'Basher' and 'Whizzles' which sounded like the cast list of a P G Wodehouse novel and hands which all offered a uniformly confident clench. They had just come on from a Indian meal at one of the restaurants along Brick Lane and were full of schoolboy humour concerning the possible effects on the gut of a vindaloo curry.

'OK lads, who's farted? Own up! Whoever's farted has to buy the drinks.'

I fell into conversation with a man who went by the name of Nogs. Asking him about his job, he said he worked in 'venture capital formation'. And what did that involve, I asked. Looking at me as though to gauge my level of ignorance, he began with first principles. Capitalism, he said, was growth-orientated. A steady rate of growth, he said, was essential for the health of a capitalist economic system, since it was only through such growth that profits could be assured and the accumulation of capital be sustained. OK so far? Yes, I said, I'd got that much. He continued: this need for dynamic growth would necessarily produce, however, periodic phases of 'over-accumulation', phases when there would be a glut of commodities, idle productive capacity and high unemployment. One way to absorb such excesses of capital and surplus labour, such 'over-accumulation', was to switch resources from current consumption to long-term investment, yet the capacity to make this switch (he was beginning to lose me) depended chiefly on the availability of credit. It was here, he said, that there arose the need for the formation of what he called 'fictitious capital', that is capital that had a nominal money value, yet no real correspondence in terms of real productive activity or physical assets. Had I got that? He could see that I clearly hadn't.

I had, however, clocked about the 'dancing'. His instruction was interrupted by a young woman, clearly a stripper, who had appeared between us, shaking a glass full of coins, collecting her 'tips'. We both scrabbled in our pockets awkwardly for change. 'Thanks,' I said lamely, dropping in some coins, 'what's your name?'

'I'm Bernadette, darling,' she said, moving off round the bar.

'So, what do you do?' Nogs asked me, changing the subject.

'Oh, I'm working in the fruit and vegetable market,' I said.

'Best place to start,' he said, 'the best traders in the City started in fruit and veg. It teaches you how to keep a head full of different market positions and how to hold your own.'

'No, no,' I said, seeing his confusion, 'I'm doing a delivery round. I drive a van.'

'He's going to write a book about Spitalfields,' interrupted Steve, who had appeared at my arm and was taking up my cause, 'It's going to be a sort of travel book. A journey into the East End. It's going to be all very postmodern.'

The music had started up and the striptease was about to begin again. Bernadette pulled herself on to the stage and, rather languidly, began her routine. Conversations withered in mid-sentence. Beer glasses were held suspended between table and mouth. And as one piece of lycra after another fell from her body, comments were passed between Steve and his friends as though between ventriloquists' dummies.

'She's a bit rough, don't you think?'

'Not my idea of a good night out.'

'How do you rate her liability?'

'Definitely not liable.'

'Definitely a case of limited liability.'

'That's for defs.'

Long pause, and then 'Nice,' said Nogs, 'very nice.'

A category mistake?

Later, I began to think *Yes!* Maybe what I should be writing about Spitalfields was precisely such a 'travel book'. This is, after all, the era of the global village. With international travel so easy and commodification so thorough, why bother flying thousands of miles and then journeying hundreds of miles by boat to visit some desperately remote village of Sylhet in order to get a taste of its culture when it had so deliciously recreated itself in this corner of East London (and also so conveniently close to Liverpool Street station)? Moreover, with the various competing communities in Spitalfields fighting their corner in this mythological battleground, why not delight in its very fiesta of urban intermingling and interaction? Here, one surely had the added excitement of watching vastly different cultures leak into one another (as Salman Rushdie once said) 'like flavours when you cook'?

This certainly seemed to be the case for Vicky and Mike, two daytrippers I met in one of the tandoori restaurants along Brick Lane shortly after the evening with Steve and friends in the pub. They had travelled up from Esher that morning and were enjoying the full Spitalfields experience.

'We've had this trip on the cards for a long time and then there was this feature in one of the supplements last Sunday all about Brick Lane and we thought, well, why don't we give it a whirl – isn't that right, Mike?'

'That's right, Vicky. Well, you know how it is, we like to do something a little bit different now and again. I was expecting it to be somewhat ethnic, shall we say, but crikey, it's like a miniature India! It's wonderful!'

'Nothing like what we're used to, or course. I mean it's just a completely different world. Like those saris! Wonderful! We actually thought they'd make quite nice curtains, didn't we?'

'Yes we did. And this afternoon we thought we'd head down

to Petticoat Lane market and pick up a bargain, do a bit of haggling, well it's traditional isn't it, a typical cockney carry-on?'

Certainly the area had been finding its way into the papers and on to the television with increasing regularity. While I was living on Brick Lane I came home to find a Canadian film company pointing its equipment at my wrought-iron railings. 'Excuse me, but would you mind keeping out of the way,' said the testy art director as I made for my front door. 'We're trying to capture the sense of Dickensian squalor,' he went on, smothering my door with Coke cans and crisp packets from a nearby dustbin.

More often than not, however, the articles painted a picture of a community in crisis, facing incipient meltdown. Hardly a week had gone past without some reference to the dawning of the End Time in Spitalfields. With headlines such as 'The Battle for Spitalfields', 'The Pinstripe Shadow over Brick Lane' and 'Save Spitalfields', there was a distinctly apocalyptic flavour to much of the coverage. Reviewing an exhibition of photographs at the Bishopsgate Institute called 'A Farewell to Spitalfields', Colin Ward in the *New Statesman* mourned the passing of this highly successful 'zone of transition' and in his colourful account of Brick Lane in the *Illustrated London News*, Henry Porter suggested that redevelopment threatened to 'stifle this community's unique spirit'.

'In this idiosyncratic pocket of London,' he writes, 'property prices will rise and the Asians will be profitably winkled out of the Georgian houses. The sweatshops will disappear and the Bangladeshis will lose that first important entrée into British business life. Conditions may well improve as the buildings are gutted, refurbished and "conserved", and the councillors and town planners will almost certainly congratulate themselves on the achievement. However, it is certain that all this will be accompanied by a loss of spirit. Brick Lane will look and feel much like any other part of town.'

At the very moment Spitalfields appeared to be discovering its identity, producing a variety of versions of its past with such determined self-consciousness, it also seemed to be threatened with extinction. Previously subsumed into Whitechapel or Bethnal Green, Spitalfields, in fact, had only really begun to identify itself as a locality in its own right from the 1970s. So what was happening in this place? Could I capture this 'unique spirit' before it was too late? Would I have time to record the dynamic interaction of this competitive community before the cataclysmic interruption of the market redevelopment caused such interaction to cease?

In 1988, this seemed to be the challenge. I saw the book as a celebration of diversity and urban complexity. I intended to do my research by working in the various communities, by entering a little into the area's imagination, attending to its aspirations, running with its fears, eavesdropping on its dreams. Moreover, with the market redevelopment looming, I felt I was writing against the clock.

And to those who told me that writing a travel book about an area little larger than Wembley Stadium was a category mistake, I would be able to tell them, with the use of my foregrounded first person narrator, that at least I had been there at the Fall of Spitalfields, that at least I had witnessed, first-hand, the revolution in this eighteenth-century London suburb, that I filed my reports as a frontline correspondent in this mytho-logical battleground. I would at least be able to tell them that, for one whole summer, I had worked for my *greengages* as a delivery driver in Spitalfields fruit and vegetable Market.

The caricature and the real thing

In fact, reporters and documentary writers have been journey-ing into the East End in search of its elusive spirit, its defiant cockney energy, producing travel books and tracts and works of high-minded campaigning fiction, ever since the emergence of a mass middle-class readership in the late nineteenth century.

Although Dickens had drawn on deeps wells of a native cockney sensibility in his depiction of London life, particularly in *Our Mutual Friend* and *Oliver Twist*, it was Henry Mayhew who, more than any other of his contemporaries, brought the caricature into focus. Striding self-consciously along the banks of the Thames with his pocket notebook and his ear for a telling turn of phrase, he gives us a rogues' gallery of underworld 'characters', both through his *London Labour and the London Poor* as well as in his low-life column in the *Morning Chronicle*.

Yet, in spite of his detailed tables setting out the income and expenditure of his subjects and other such authentic touches of graphic realism, the language that his 'characters' use, as they recite their stories of abject poverty, is richly stylised, full of crafted poetic cadence. With his elaborate parentheses and stodgy moralism one is conscious, moreover, that he is primarily performing for us, his middle-class readership, delighting always in the artifice of his caricaturing pen. One can almost hear his starched shirt creaking as he condescends to listen to the tales of woe (all his interviewees insistently call him 'Sir'). And recording such tales as he does has the effect of simultaneously making them audible, giving voice to their remarkable tragi-comic quality, and also setting them apart as rather exotic and remote accounts of anthropological interest alone.

In his preface, Mayhew gives various reasons why his work is original or 'curious'. He describes the way it 'supplies information concerning a large body of persons, of whom the public had less knowledge than of the most distant tribes of the earth . . . and adduces facts so extraordinary, that the traveller in the undiscovered country of the poor must, until his stories are corroborated by investigation, be content to lie under the imputation of telling such tales, as travellers are generally supposed to delight in.' Such may be our suspicion, yet his 'tales' do, none the less, tell an interesting story and play an important part in the the late nineteenth-century reconstruction of the cockney persona. And what is this persona?

His street folk seem to be outside recognisable structures, beyond the pale of civilisation, their status determined not so much by their relationships with one another and their place in a class system as by their relationship with what they sell, the objects that pass through their hands, the persuasive force of their street-corner sales pitch. Mayhew variously introduces us to 'a seller of penny short-hand cards', 'a street stationer', 'a flower girl', 'a tin-ware seller', 'a blind boot-lace seller', 'a street-seller of rhubarb and spices', 'a crippled street birdseller' and so on. The cockney spirit is clearly to be found in display and the competitive clamour of performing street-sellers: 'All these men state that the greater the noise they make, the better is the chance of a sale, and better still when the noise is on each side of a street, for it appears as if the vendors were proclaiming such interesting or important intelligence, that they were vying with one another who should supply the demand which must ensue.'

It is a short step from Mayhew's street patterers to the music hall tradition, which was in full swing at this time. Take, for example, a performer such as the Great Vance, who, along with his other parts (which included 'heavy swell', 'parliamentary candidate', 'yokel', 'Irishman' and 'racecourse tout') would bring the house down with his rendition of 'Flash Harry', the crooked cockney dandy. A solicitor's clerk by training, he found the law less attractive than the stage, quickly gaining a reputation as one of the best character comedians of the day. In his passion for performing, he acquired something of a reputation for outrageous and surprising showmanship. Indeed, it was during the rendition of one of his most popular cockney songs, 'Costermonger Joe', that he fell dead upon the stage in 1888.

Inevitably enough, an increasing number of commentators pointed to the disparity between the Caricature and the Real Thing. In his column in the *Pall Mall Gazette* in 1882, Andrew Tuer draws the attention of his readers to 'the obsolescence of the Dickens dialect that was still being copied from book to book by authors who never dreamed of using their own ears, much less training them to listen'. One man whose ears were quite definitely trained to listen was the Revd A J D D'Orsey, the Professor of Public Reading at King's College in London. Writing to the School Board for London on 4 December 1882, he complains of his cockney subjects that their 'final consonants are so feebly uttered that it is sometimes impossible to tell whether the pupil says 'life' or 'like' or 'light'. 'H' is constantly transposed, 'G' is dropped and in many cases 'R' appears improperly at the ends of words . . .' Some commentators even went so far as to explain such verbal improprieties by pointing to the peculiarities in the physiognomy of the cockney, remarking, as Mayhew had done, upon his large jaw and, in particular, his failure to deploy it in the service of correct pronunciation. Other dialecticians, less hostile to the cockney's production of his diphthongs and monophthongs, noted the lively persistence of such speech and its tendency to express itself either in cheerful vulgarity or maudlin sentimentality.

Indeed, there seems to be some such split within the cockney's very identity. Just when there emerged this caricature of the jaunty cockney villain, all heart and fists, quick as a flash and nobody's mug, the penny press had also found a market for tales of the appalling squalor to be found scarcely a stone's throw from Fleet Street. And with this new investigative journalism, 'the East End' as a collective concept acquired particular associations. Used to emphasise a contrast with the West End, the term began to be deployed generally in the 1880s and 1890s, often to suggest an unknown underground world within easy reach of respectable London and bandied around by those who came from outside it. The term conjured up a spectacle of depravity and filth. A perceptive correspondent writing in 1888 points out that, 'A shabby man from Paddington, St Marylebone or Battersea might pass muster as one of the respectable poor. But the same man coming from Bethnal Green, Shadwell or Wapping was an 'East Ender', the box of Keating's bug powder must be quickly reached for and the spoons swiftly locked up.'

This generalised picture of the East End was reinforced by the work of novelists such as Walter Besant, who imaginatively recreated the location in his three-volume fantasy *All Sorts and Conditions of Men*. With the arrival of the hack journalist in the 1880s and 1890s (most tellingly portrayed in the character of Edwin Reardon in Gissing's novel *New Grub Street*) there was a dramatic increase in what might be termed the literature of London low-life. Tales of urban degradation offered a ready scoop for the eager journalist. Indeed, many of them built their careers exposing the horrors of the East End. George Sims, author of the tear-stained ballad 'In the Workhouse, Christmas

Day' began a series of articles in the *Pictorial World* on 'How the Poor Live', moving then to the *Daily News* where he continued to highlight the conditions of the East End poor in his new column, 'Horrible London'. It was, however, an anonymous pamphlet written by Andrew Mearns, 'The Bitter Cry of Outcast London', which caused the biggest stir following its publication in 1883 as a penny tract and its serialisation in the *Pall Mall Gazette* later that year.

It was the account Mearns gave of overcrowding, his tales of the forced association between the 'respectable poor' and the 'criminal residuum', that most alarmed his readership. 'Often,' writes Mearns, 'is the family of an honest working man compelled to take refuge in a thieves' kitchen; in the houses where they live their rooms are frequently side by side, and continual contact with the very worst of those who have come out of our gaols is a matter of necessity.' The Royal Commission on Housing, set up in March 1884 by Lord Salisbury, was clearly motivated by both political fear as well as moral indignation: it spent a lot of time discussing the connection between overcrowding, intemperance and sexual licence in the East End. The vicar of Christ Church Spitalfields, the Revd Billing, was called upon as an authoritative witness to give evidence to the Commission and was at pains to stress what he considered to be the clear link between poor housing conditions and immorality amongst the poor of his parish.

The defiantly jaunty cockney caricature was somewhat submerged beneath this profusion of prurient middle-class concern. To the outsider, the East Ender remained a creature beyond the Pale. In 1888, Professor Julian Huxley felt moved to express his profound dismay: 'I have seen the Polynesian savaging and in his primitive condition, before the missionary or the blackbirder or the beachcomber got at him. With all his savaging he was not half so savage, so unclean, so irreclaimable, as the tenant of a tenement in an East London slum.' He seemed to express the sentiment of many of his contemporaries for whom the East End conjured up the image of a nursery of depravity which had been cut loose from the moorings of middle-class respectability.

It was Charles Booth who set out to put the record straight and refute these 'exaggerated statements as to the situation of the poor'. Turning his scientific methodology on the East End as 'the focus of the problem of poverty in the midst of wealth', he submitted his initial findings in May 1887. In spite of his stated intention of challenging the slum-to-slum sensationalism of such publications as the *Pall Mall Gazette*, and notwithstanding the fact that his results were tabulated and annotated into grotesque abstraction, his conclusions point to the fact that the situation was every bit as depressing as the more lurid accounts had suggested. For example, his research suggests that in Spitalfields alone there was a poverty level of about 45 per cent and that for many of this number, 'decent life was not imaginable', i.e. they faced daily starvation.

It was left to the live-in researchers, the men and women who came to the East End to live amongst the people, to fill out this dry statistical data with flesh and blood and ragged clothing. The best known of these was Jack London. Finding himself stranded in London – he was on his way from America to South Africa to give an account of that country after the Boer War – he sold the idea of a travel book about the London slums to his New York publisher. He writes, 'I went down into the under-world of London with an attitude of mind which I may best liken to that of the explorer.'

In the event of it, setting out for his seven weeks of tramping around the streets of 'the under-world' was a good deal less easy than he imagined. Thomas Cook & Son could provide him with instant information about darkest Africa or innermost Tibet but had nothing to say about the East End: 'We are not accustomed to taking travellers to the East End . . . we know nothing whatsoever about the place at all.' Eventually he instructs a rather bewildered taxi driver to take him East and he is dumped outside Stepney station. And it is here, where 'the streets are filled with a new and different race of people, short of stature and of wretched and beer-sodden appearance', that, for the first time, London comes 'face to face with the English lower classes'.

In spite of his stated commitment to the particularities of

poverty and his distaste for the practice of political aggregation, he finds himself painting with the broadest of brushstrokes. His palette, moreover, is decidedly grey. The 'East End' or 'Abyss' – the terms appear to be interchangeable for London – exudes 'a stupefying atmosphere of torpor'; it is 'a huge man-killing machine'; it produces 'a breed of city savages'. The streets are 'slimy', 'spittle-drenched', covered in 'pavement offal'. The men are 'brutalised', 'empty-headed' and 'stupid'. It is a place where 'there is no privacy', where 'the bad corrupt the good' and where 'all fester together'. Even the rain is greasy.

It is hard not to feel that Jack London only tells us part of the story. Like many of his social realist colleagues, he resists the very quality of cockney defiance that runs through the street patter and has shaped the cockney's burlesquing sensibility, his mawkish sentimentality, his breezy confidence. This is nowhere more clearly absent in his travel book than in his account of his visit to Spitalfields. He comes to the area accompanied by a 'burning young socialist', a man 'in the first throes of enthusiasm and ripe for martyrdom'. Passing through Frying-pan Alley, where, stepping over 'a woman with a young babe, nursing at breasts grossly naked', they visit a house in which twenty-odd individuals live cheek by jowl in six rooms with no furniture. After suitable expressions of indignation, they make their way along Commercial Street to Spitalfields Garden, where, in the shadow of Christ Church, they see a sight which they would 'never wish to see again'. On the pavement, by the portico of the church, where the stone pillars rise towards the sky in a stately row, were 'rows of men lying asleep or drowsing, all too deep sunk in torpor to rouse'. The young socialist is aghast and turns to London, 'Oh why did you bring me here?'

We are tempted to ask the same question. In his determination to disenchant, he resists the performing theatricality of the cockney, so beloved by Dickens and caricatured by Mayhew. What about the penny-gaffs, music halls, patent theatres, blood tubs, gothic dramas, routines in the song-and-supper rooms and in the free-and-easies? Jack London seems not to have passed through the markets or beside the barrow vendors or found himself in the middle of a street auction. We have to turn to a hopelessly sentimentalised guidebook by a Mrs Cook, coincidentally published the same year as *People of the Abyss*, 1903, to find attributed to the London poor 'a certain rude, Dickensian, good nature' reminiscent of the 'incorrigible cockney, Sam Weller'. The 'raciest cockney', she adds, is spoken by the costermongers, the street traders. A later description in the *London Scene* fills out this picture: 'In the Farringdon Road you will run across the more traditional cockney, whose astuteness, nonchalance, easy indifferent fellowship, tolerance, casual endurance, grumbling gusto, shallowness, unconcern for anything but the passing moment, jackdaw love of glitter, picaresque adaptability and jesting spirit make up an unique individual.'

This list of characteristics may have been a ludicrous caricature, but it was generally accepted. Cockney culture seems to have its vital roots in this repartee of the street trader. The author of *London's Eight Millions*, writing in 1937, knew this, suggesting that these markets were 'the strongholds of the cockney' and adding that 'in them you will find the bubbling humour and cynical wisdom which are the undying London . . . the cockney is the same yesterday, today and for ever.'

Clearly there was an unsteady, yet important relationship between the cockney and his East End context, the one expressing defiance of the conditions of the other. It was only, however, when I went to work in Spitalfields Market that I began to understand more fully how this great cockney mythology, rooted in the poverty of the East End in the 1880s, could continue to be both powerfully present in the traders' imagination in the 1980s and at the same time oddly irrelevant to the changing world of Spitalfields in which they worked.

Dodges and wrinkles

The close competitive proximity between the different traders in Spitalfields Market gave rise to a banter almost as congested as the alleys which serviced the stands. Collision, both physical and linguistic, was a way of life.

'You know the rules,' replied Wally to the grocer with his cabbages scattered at his feet, 'porters have priority.'

'Porters have penis heads, more like,' returned the grocer as Wally's reversing forklift continued to dodge its way out of the market.

'That particular porter has a pea brain,' capped Phil. 'He's forgot to put the avocado on Mr Charlton's order. Mr Charlton isn't going to be very pleased.'

It was, moreover, this restless repartee, this constant knocking together of one-liners, which held the traders, the drivers, the grocers, the porters, the stackers, the checkers, the Corporation workers, the market police and the paper boy in touch. The whole market participated in its regular round of opening gambits, in-jokes, put-downs, set-ups and pay-offs.

In Spitalfields Market the typical trader presented himself as being a bit tricksy. If you asked him what made a good banana, he'd tell you how to hide the bruised ones; if you asked him about his sales technique, he'd tell you how to undercut your neighbour. To ask about management of the stand was to be told about price and product manipulation.

'There are lots of dodges, loads of wrinkles,' Vince would say, delighting in his own craftiness, disappearing into the middle of another swindle.

That the market was a night-time operation may also have contributed to this quality of endemic shiftiness. It sometimes felt as if thieves had met in the middle of the night to exchange stolen goods: these midnight deals were made with none of the fetishistic attention which often accompanies daylight trans-actions. Often the trader and the buyer would stand facing opposite directions, arm to arm, talking past each other, twitching their prices, shaking their heads, with the occasional cockney interjection, itself a sideways slang.

'How much *bees and honey* do you want for the nectarine?'
'Five.'
'And the *planet of the apes*?'
'Four fifty.'

There was certainly a sense that deals, if not illegal, were somehow shady. Cash, which asks for no favours and demands no explanations, made credit look sentimental. The traffic in stolen goods, from leather shoes to television sets, was steady and regular. Tips for the porters were really bribes: 'They pay anyway, but if they want it out quick, they pay again.'

For a greeting to be friendly it had also to be punitive. You could feel the suspicious hostility when someone called you 'mate', but it was all smiles and pantomime when you were greeted as a 'filthy bastard'. When someone gave you a generous handshake you knew that they were probably trying to steal your watch, whereas a put-down was usually accompanied by a friendly wink. In general, the market was more impressed by mental agility than displays of machismo: one was more admiring of the speed and effectiveness of a salesman's price manipulation than his muscle definition.

Yet this automatic mistrust was, moreover, no simple refusal to take you at your word, but an urgent need to keep you on your toes. With fresh produce and fresh prices coming in every day, the extent to which you could wrestle your buyers into a better deal was also your ability to keep the negotiation in the air, to keep talking.

'How much is this bit of *macaroni*?'
'How much can you get us, you piece of baloney?'
'Three twenty!'
'Three eighty any good for you?'
'Three eighty! It's already on the twist!'
'What! Are you pissed? That's a first class bit of plum!'
'You think I don't know my *tom thumb*?'
'OK, I'll give you three fifty-five, but that's my last!'
'Three fifty!'
'Done!'
'Done!'

Barter slipped effortlessly in and out of banter. It was in this cross between a Christie's auction and a Punch and Judy show that bargains were struck and money was made. In fact, in order for a trader to play the market at all successfully he had first to show himself conversant with this wheeler-dealer rhetoric, this knockabout banter of negotiation. Harry Woods, for example, a farmer from Kent, recalled a conversation he had with one of the buyers at Spitalfields just after the war. It was an exchange which seems, in his own mind at least, to have established his legitimacy to trade.

'When the stuff was very very short we used to send up rubbish then. I remember when lettuce was a terrific price . . . and they was all crowded round the lorry inspecting it when one of the buyers said: 'Got any pigs down there Woody?' – 'No,' I said, 'Why is that?' – 'Well, you could take them home to feed the pigs!' Then quick as a flash, I said, 'No, 'cos I bought them up here for the rats to eat!'

Rather than pleading ignorance of the lettuce's rubbishy quality or offering the buyer his sincerest apologies, Harry Woods had showed himself willing to pull a fast one, capable of a spot of jiggery-pokery. He had given as good as he got and, in doing so, had proved himself familiar with 'the cockney way': pertly defiant, capable of showy self-parody and merrily on the make.

This defensiveness appeared most obviously when it came to the subject of money.

'How's business?' I asked the trader who was hovering beside his potatoes in the alley.

'Quiet,' he said, 'very quiet, it has been very quiet recently.' He said it very quietly, sucking air through his teeth and shaking his head as though to say: 'I've got five screaming kids at home, the bailiffs have been round and my wife's having a break-down . . .' And then, suddenly raising his voice, he shouted across the market, 'Isn't that right, Alf? In ten years' time the only bit of potato we'll be pushing around will be the potato across the check-out at Sainsbury's.'

'How's trade?' I asked the grocer from Bethnal Green who was sneering his way through box after box of souring grapes.

'Not any good,' he said without looking up, 'we've had a shop on Brick Lane for a hundred years and we used to be open every single day of the week. Now we only open on Sundays. No one shops in Brick Lane any more.' Then he looked up and said with evident distaste, 'Unless you want to buy a leather jacket that is.'

Business, it seemed, was always bad. Despite the evident signs of success – the Mercedes emerging from the market car park at the end of the day like maggots from a rotting apple; the mid-winter tan following a two-week holiday in Tenerife – many of the market traders and porters still used the rhetoric of hardship, of just about scraping by.

'I've made a bob or two in my time,' a trader might concede somewhat disingenuously, before idly slipping into a nostalgic account of how it was in the olden days. In fact, there was also a strong sense among the older traders and employees of the City Corporation, the market's landlord, that 'cockney' was something that had happened in the past. Indeed, as the hype for the new market site became more intense, so too did this retrospection. Cockney friendliness seemed suddenly to have become traditional.

Mick Monroe, for example, talked about the market's 'community spirit' as if it were written into some constitution. He had been employed as a janitor by the City Corporation for over twenty years and in that time he had worked in nearly every area of the market.

'I remember the Fruit Exchange when it didn't have the fourth floor, I remember cleaning out them drains before they opened up that fourth floor. I've polished all the floors, repaired the broken windows, done the decoration. I've done cement work in the market. I know the market backwards. I've done practically everything there is to do from the top of the Fruit Exchange to down here in the market bogs.'

Whenever I went to the loo Mick and I would have a bit of a chat. In fact, under Mick's supervision, the market loos operated as a kind of gossip exchange; everyone, from all over the market, would go down and tell Mick their news; where there had been a break-in, who was getting sacked, what had been agreed at the TGWU meeting.

'It's a very sociable place, very friendly place. Marvellous down here, they're all very friendly when they come down. They always stop and crack a few jokes. And I always leave a paper out. You get loads of lads down here that say, 'Hey Mick, have you got a paper?' 'Here you are,' I say. Then, you see, they can read it while they're sitting there. Mind you, they always give it back. Well, that's the sort of place it is. Very friendly.'

Mick, however, felt all this would change at the new market. 'It will be in a good place where the lorries can come off the MII. They'll be plenty of car parks, more than here. More toilets too. But it won't be as friendly. I can tell you that now. It won't be nothing like as friendly.'

Another person for whom the imminent move seemed to have activated feelings of nostalgia was old Tommy Barlow. He had been born in Spitalfields in 1920 and had gone to the Roman Catholic school a few minutes' walk from Brick Lane. The market had always been a part of his life. His school friends would talk about getting a job down at 'Spits' and he could remember his father coming down to the market for odd portering jobs. Most mornings he would come round the market with his brother, picking up any produce that had been left on the roads. 'Occasionally a salesman would kick us over a nice big cabbage when he saw us wandering around with our bag.'

He got married just before the war and moved out of Spitalfields just after the end of hostilities. For most of his married life he had lived in Leytonstone, where he worked as an electrician. His sons, however, had returned to work in the market and, through them, he had remained familiar with its way of life. Although he was now retired, he would occasionally come down to the market to help out at one of the stands, but he really only returned out of a sentimental attachment to the area.

Tommy described Spitalfields Market as a profoundly social place, yet his impressions seemed to be locked in the hey-day of some pre-war cockney golden world, when the market supposedly operated as a local community of small businessmen, a network of friends and enemies rather than colleagues and competitors. Arthur Harding, who worked in Spitalfields as a cabinet-maker, wardrobe dealer and street trader, similarly remembered the market as this pre-eminently social environment. He recalled walking round it as a boy.

'I used to go to Spitalfields Market and collect waste potatoes. A lot of us kids would go together, through the Wheeler Street arch. When you came home from school, mother would say,

'Go and see if you can get some potatoes. Take that sack and I don't want any specky ones.' The market porters were friendly – they would tip the sack of potatoes out, knowing the kids would come over. There were some good cockneys in the market, when they saw us they would shout, 'Here's the kids, come over 'ere.' They were real market people – they knew the kids was hungry.'

Frank Warren, another old market hand, described these days before the Second World War as a constant round of parties and team sports and day trips to the country. These were the days when you had neighbours, not just people who lived next door. And your neighbours were respectable types, proudly patriotic and thoroughly English.

'Not like now. Spitalfields is full of Bangladeshis now. I hate them, I don't like them, they've no right to be here. When I was a lad, it was all Polish and Lithuanian Jews, genuine exiles. They were the people that made the East End what it is, they brought their trades with them, their great tailoring and carpentry skills. But the moment the Bangladeshis arrived they were no use whatsoever, they've just milked the state dry.

'They go from Brick Lane to East Ham and West Ham and they're increasing in number every day, multiplying like flies. They march through London in their thousands, shouting and hooting. I know they're all God's people, but why can't they all stay at home? Who allowed that rubbish to come in? They should go home.'

It struck me, as I was listening to Frank's beer-swilling prejudice, that this cockney mythology was chronically nostalgic. Life was much better in the past, before the war, before the invention of supermarkets and articulated lorries, before the widespread immigration of the 1950s and 60s, before the foundation of the Welfare State. It was hard, don't get it wrong, but better, more friendly. Those were the days when 'real market people' were generous and mindful of their neighbours' needs, when 'cockney' was a synonym for community-spirited.

It was in the context of this strong sense of a community's solidarity in the face of difficulty that those other cockney characteristics could find legitimation. When life had been hard he had been obliged to become a bit sharp, to develop a eye for the main chance. He had had to become a bit of a dealer. He was naturally, after all, a buyer and seller of goods – 'the wandering distributor' – rather than a maker or producer. To make a living, or at least to make ends meet, he had, more often than not, turned to the practice of street trading – hawking, peddling, totting, pattering, costermongering – in fact all those synonymously entrepreneurial and often illegal forms of bargaining and exchange.

In the late 1980s the cockney caricature was clear. He had become the ultimate wheeler-dealer; fly in style, loyal to his friends yet often on the shadowy side of the law, trading off his wits.

A protest almost

In the last hour before it closed, Spitalfields Market would become crowded with a whole army of scroungers, some offering to clear up the stand in exchange for a fiver, others picking their way through the rubbished produce. The Sisters of Mercy, who ran a short-stay hostel for the homeless in their convent on Gun Street, just off the market, would come collecting veg to furnish their stews. A couple of dossers might also appear with a bin liner, which had probably functioned as a blanket the night before, and proceed to sing a few songs, cause a bit of hilarity, before staggering off again with a sack full of cauliflower and cabbage.

It was also when the street-traders – the latter-day coster-mongers – from all the nearby markets, from the Bethnal Green Road and the Whitechapel Road, from Wentworth Street in Petticoat Lane, came to stock up with their day's produce. Gerald, a street trader from the Whitechapel 'Waste', would arrive to cover his barrow with any old job lot or sack end on offer, which he would then wheel back to his pitch opposite the London Hospital. In Spitalfields Market, Gerald was more than just another small-time businessman; he commanded celebrity status, with his huge body and – not unconnected – his notorious capacity for the consumption of lager. One week he announced he was doing a marathon arm-wrestle and got the traders to fill out a number of sponsorship forms. The next week he returned, his chest blown up like a balloon, his wrists like other people's thighs, collecting his dues and claiming entry into the Guinness Book of Records for the longest continuous arm-wrestling bout ever recorded.

'Who won?' asked a congenitally unimpressed trader. 'You or the beer tap?'

There were a number of others for whom the market was a source of casual work or cash. Joan, a stooped and eccentric old lady from Bow, who had taken it upon herself to feed all the stray cats in the East End, was occasionally slipped a tenner by one of the market traders who had been known to 'borrow' one of her cats from time to time, in an attempt to clear his cellar of vermin.

'If the cats die, then the rats'll multiply, they catch the rats while they're small, don't let them get too big. Cats is better than rats, that's what I say, cats is better than rats,' she'd tell you as she emptied a tin of Whiskas at one of her strategic feeding places.

John was another local character who was employed casually by the market. He worked for one of the stands along Fournier Street, keeping the street clean. A tall man, gaunt with nervous energy, his eyes seemed to be constantly straining to escape from their sockets. He was at it from six o'clock in the morning through to lunchtime, sweeping the rubbish into piles with great extravagant strokes of his broom, striding across the junction of Fournier Street and Wilkes Street as if he were on guard patrol. When he talked, it was usually unprompted and nonsensical: passages of scripture, forebodings of the apocalypse, excerpts from a stream of consciousness which, out of context, could sound enigmatically meaningful: 'The old men in the marathon put the young men in the shade. I'm telling you, the old men in the marathon put the young men in the shade . . .'

His father was a Scot, his mother was from Pakistan, and both had deserted him when he was very young. He came to London in the 1960s from India to dig the Victoria Line and has stayed ever since, living for a while in Brick Lane, then moving into hostel accommodation off the Whitechapel Road. The residents of Fournier Street knew him as the man who cleaned the street; they would say hello to him and thank him and buy him cups of tea and even put up with his occasional rages, when he would turn on them with Old Testament fury, shaking his fist, and announce: 'I'm going to kill an Englishman, I'm going to kill an Englishman, I'm going to strap him up and kill him, right here in broad daylight, I'm going to kill him . . .'

And then, having conclusively re-established his status as the local village idiot, he would return his attention, as suddenly as it had been originally distracted, to sweeping the street.

The prostitutes along Commercial Street also benefited from their association with market hours and market trade. At about seven o' clock in the evening, once the commuter traffic had left and before the market traffic had arrived, Patsy, Dotty, Penny and Babs would congregate by the refreshments van outside Christ Church, first for a bit of a natter and a cup of tea and later, as the night drew in, to keep warm. Commercial Street has long been known as a red light district, passing as it does through the noisy and well-lit vicinity of the market. It was from the market that they got most of their trade, in particular from the lorry drivers, many of whom would park for a night's kip around its periphery.

'I've got one man, a driver, he's a regular; I've got this one driver who I've been with a good ten years now,' Penny told me as she checked her lipstick in the rear view mirror of the refreshments van. 'Oh yeah, I've got a few regulars, everyone's got a few regulars.'

Occasionally, however, a new customer would be led down Fournier Street to the sound of high heels clipping resolutely against the tarmac and disappear through a doorway on Brick Lane. Above the doorway was suspended a hoarding, advertising the sale of 'Quality Skins'. The building was shared with a Bengali leather cutter.

Finally, there were the dossers, hanging out around the market, snoozing, begging, stealing each other's beer cans, screaming blue bloody murder. The market, with its noise and surplus of rubbish, gave them a good cover. They would sit around the entrance to the Christ Church crypt, which had been converted into a home for recovering alcoholics, appealing loudly, between swigs of lager, for cups of tea, and effecting in passing pedestrians a sudden quickening of the stride, a determined indifference. They laughed even more wildly at this. Only Gilbert and George, the Fournier Street artists, seemed to command any deference, striding past, with a synchronised step: 'Hello!', 'Hello!' they would repeat in rhythm, before disappearing into the traffic.

Until 1980 the dossers used to gather in Spitalfields Garden, the plot of land on Commercial Street overshadowed by the south façade of Christ Church, immortalised in the Small Faces' druggy lament 'Itchycoo Park.' It was, however, thought to have become so ridden with body lice and dosser-transmitted pestilence, such a 'welter of rags and filth, of all manner of loathsome skin diseases, open sores, bruises, grossness, indecency, leering monstrosities and bestial faces', that it had been closed to the general public. The dossers had to take their body sores elsewhere.

Dave was one of these 'itchy' refugees. He lumbered around Spitalfields with his shoulders bent over, fed up with his swollen leg, his bad knee and the endless urban hike. 'It's been walk, walk, walk, all the time for two days and nights now,' he said as I passed him in the street. Then, resting by the portico of Christ Church, beneath the row of pillars, at the entrance to the crypt, he invited me to inspect his furry tongue and went on to tell me about his pyorrhoea and how he chucked his medicine away.

'I wish I hadn't now, I'm all hot now. No, listen, the doctor said I would begin to itch, and now I'm feeling very itchy. Here, listen, I was down at Saint Bottle Off church [St Botolph's, Aldgate] the other day and I went to the bog and I was going to take my shirt off and I imagined my whole body would be crawling with insects.'

Dave was so used to talking to himself that there was no room for conversation. His manner would be button-holing, a protest almost, the result of so many years of scornful rejection. Since leaving the Merchant Navy, he'd been permanently on the tramp, apart from a few spells in gaol, unable to survive without a disciplining structure. I saw his name tattooed across the knuckles of his left hand, though faded now with age; the marks of a more brazen man. His hair, now knotted and lanky, looked as if it had once boasted the sheen of a freshly lacquered swathe of Brylcreem. His face, blotchy with booziness, was marked by an archipelago of spots across his forehead. His baby-blue eyes would disarm, however, with their guilelessness.

The last time I saw Dave, I recognised his stooped figure dragging a pallet on to the shared fire by the market car park. In the late dusk a few dossers were standing motionless, sculpted figures against the spotlit steel skeleton of the Bishopsgate development. Walking up Brushfield Street towards the City I was struck by the eerie brutality of its office frontier, foregrounded by this perpetual blaze of pallets, kept alight by the homeless of Spitalfields, a defiant statement of contempt for the approach of the City.

The fire would burn at dawn when the car park was congested with grocers' vans and traders' barrows; in the early morning, when the scavengers started picking their way through the discarded produce; in the afternoon when the site was swept and sanitised by the Corporation dustmen; in the evening when the long-distance delivery trucks came to park up round the edge; at night when the rats were out. It would be burning on Sunday morning when the site operated as a car park for visitors to the street markets in Brick Lane and Petticoat Lane, and it would still be burning at Christmas when the gypsies came and camped there, selling their Christmas trees to anyone who'd buy.

And it was against the crackle of that wet firewood that one day I overheard Dave shouting into the wind, maybe at a passing stranger, maybe just to himself, 'I'm telling you, Pentonville's the best place to be. No I'm telling you, Pentonville's the best place . . . I threw a bottle through the doctor's window because he gave me the wrong medicine and I got four months . . . I'm not long out . . . No, listen, I'm going to do the same tonight . . . I don't like it outside prison, I like it inside prison . . .

Pentonville's the best place ... No, I'm serious, I'm feeling really itchy.'

A shift of the wind caused the fire to belch a gust of thick black smoke, opaque against the steely rise of Bishopsgate.

A bit of zippidy

The spread of the Broadgate development along Bishopsgate cast a huge shadow across Spitalfields and its fruit and vegetable market. As a preview of coming attractions, it intensified the sense that the area was changing, that it was about to change beyond all recognition. Sometimes I would notice the older traders in the market looking up at it, at once scornful and bewildered.

Harry Lakmaker, the only banana ripener left in the market, was one of these traders from a different generation. He had entered the market in another economic climate. He spoke thoughtfully, chewing his words as if he was tasting one of his ripened bananas for flavour and texture. 'Of course times have changed. You haven't got the traditional greengrocer anymore. There's no specialisation anymore. The majority of the traders in the market might as well be working in a factory because they know as much as the ordinary factory worker knows. They know as much as the general public knows, which is nothing at all.

'As long as it looks nice in the fruit dish, they buy it. Whether or not it eats nice doesn't come into it. It's got to look nice, not eat nice. They might as well buy wax fruit. We've got idiot greengrocers who think the same thing, who buy on the look of the banana box and not the taste of the banana. It's brainwashing. You could do shit tied up in blue ribbons and you could sell it to them and that's the truth.'

He saw the spread of supermarkets, with their demand for standardisation, as the main criminal in this story of falling standards. 'They want all their bananas seven to nine inches long. Well, a banana is something that grows and it grows on the stem. At the top of the stalk you've got small bananas and at the bottom of the stalk you've got big bananas. You can't tell the stalk: 'I'm sorry but the supermarket only wants you to grow seven-inch bananas.' Anyway I think the smaller bananas eat nicer than the big bulky fruit which in my opinion eats like a turnip.

'But that's the market they create, those are the problems they create. They're trying to make a standard thing out of something that grows.'

Lakmaker had a relationship with his bananas. He knew them, he did not simply reify them into an economic equation, he respected them for their peculiarities. For Phil, however, the produce was there to be manipulated into profit. He would take any short cut he could to 'shift the gear': mixing up old produce with fresh, hiding the 'twisters', storing the soft fruits in the cool box until the very last moment. He made an effort to serve his regular customers with the quality produce and got rid of the rubbish in the one-off sale. With the unleashing of free market forces, purchasing power had become the only authority which commanded respect, while specialised expertise was rendered an unaffordable luxury.

Mac the Mushroom Man, one of the few other market traders to specialise in a single item, had watched the way his own market had changed. 'It's a sign of the times. Everyone nowadays wants a small hard mushroom. You go for a snack in the wine bar or wherever you lot go and you want to see your mushrooms closed and hard. Well, it looks like you've got more on your plate, doesn't it? If you get a big one and cut it up it doesn't look the same. But I'll tell you what: I'd rather have a big flat one any day, because you've got the taste, see, lovely taste.

'Years ago they were all grown in horse shit and they tasted delicious. Now it's all this false manure. They're force-fed, that's why they've got no taste. It's like everything else, everything's frozen, nothing's fresh. Peaches which go bad no matter how good they look when they come in. We only deal in mush here, but they tell me cucumbers are grown by computer. Can you believe it? Cucumbers which are grown in cement by computer!'

Advances in communication networks as well as technology have meant that fruits never really go out of season. Strawberries are no longer associated with high summer and Wimbledon week, since they can be flown in from California in the middle of the winter. With air-freight, Spitalfields Market had become an international meeting place for fruit and vegetables from all over the world.

Affordable travel has also brought with it a taste for foreign foods with the result that you can now display your cosmopolitan sophistication by the fruit and vegetables which adorn your dinner parties. Some consumption is, however, more conspicuous than others. Broccoli is certainly an improvement on cauliflower, but if you really want to impress your friends you serve romanesco. And green mange-tout is frankly a bit passé when you could be getting it purple from Zambia. Even the market traders who dealt solely with exotics disdainfully refered to their fruit and vegetable colleagues as 'the potato people'.

Alongside these upwardly mobile exotics, 'ethnic' produce also sold well. Both were comparatively new to the market. The exotics in particular had only become popular since the beginning of the 1980s and sales were still increasing at around sixteen per cent a year. Rows of wonderful looking ethnic fruits, vegetables and spices lined Commercial Street, on the east side of the market, easily accessible to the Bengali restaurants and stores on Brick Lane: okra, karella, shim beans, root ginger, lychees, passion fruit, jack fruit, sugar cane, sweet potatoes and the ubiquitous chilli.

Talking with this new brand of trader one could hear middleclass aspirations free-marketeering their way through cockney loyalties and rhetoric. When you asked them if they were looking forward to the market relocation the answer came in two stages. 'Oh I'll be retiring before the move,' they'd say, with stagey defiance, winking at their friends, and then, more soberly and confidentially, they would add, 'No, in point of fact, I think it'll work out well.'

Dino had been running his café on Crispin Street for fifteen years and it had been in his family for twice that time. It was always nicely full of steam and chatter; grocers exchanging and comparing prices over their eggs, sausage, beans, bacon, fried slice and chips, from four o' clock in the morning until nine. Dino was hoping to get space in the new market, to carry on his business, but he knew that there were only going to be a couple of allocations for restaurants and he wasn't hopeful. He was looking at his chances philosophically:

'If you draw an ace you are laughing. If you draw the two of spades you aren't. A lot of it depends on the luck of the draw and what comes out of the pack.'

Yet this perky brand of cockney fatalism, which described life as a lottery and espoused a kind of 'carry on' spirit of making do, of just about scraping by, belied a commercial hard-headedness. Dino was also cashing in on the expansion of offices into Spitalfields, opening up a sandwich bar in nearby Artillery Lane to cater to the hordes of office workers. He had called it Mr City.

This mixed feeling amongst the market traders was also apparent in Mr Thomerson, a trader who gave evidence before the committee of four MPs in June 1988, when the Bill to relocate the market was being debated in Parliament. He was curiously contradictory. He had brought before the committee his petition against the relocation of the market, and then found himself trying to explain to the chairman, Mr Howarth MP, why, if he objected to the move, he had already voted in support of it.

'Sir, if I am out of order, tell me, and call the next witness, but at least that is my view – I leave it like that, sir. You can ask me what you like.'

'I am trying to establish what your opinion was and why, if you held a particular opinion, you apparently voted for something which was opposed to that opinion. I am merely trying to find out what is the genuine state of your mind.'

There had been a poignancy in watching Mr Thomerson put forward his views for the smoothly articulate City barristers to dissect. In the formally arranged committee room, with its straight lines of benches and procedural rigidity, he had sounded rambling and incoherent. Like Mr Starns, another trader who gave evidence against moving the market, he had described his loyalty to some nebulous 'atmosphere' which, when pushed, he had been unable to define. It was Mr Starns who had told the committee: 'I do not think you can link efficiency with atmosphere. Markets are not about bricks and mortar. They are about people and that is atmosphere. Efficiency is a totally different thing.'

It seemed that many of the market traders would claim allegiance to some authentic cockney Spitalfields which, they argued, was threatened by the market redevelopment, whilst simultaneously voting to move the market to a site which was more efficient and offered better motorway and rail access. Some would quite happily express the traditional cockney contempt for the arrival of the yuppies whilst simultaneously profiting from their investment and patronage.

More than anyone else, it was Vince who enabled me to see the contradictions inherent in this cockney posturing. On the one hand he had set himself against all authority, all those institutions of middle-class arrival and respectability, employing the shifty banter and blarney of the traditional East End street trader. On the other hand, he was describing an economic project demanding massive investment and risk and probable profit.

One day, as we were driving back from an early-morning delivery in Docklands, with the van bumping up and down the back streets of the newly gentrified East End, Vince gave me his assessment of the coming move.

'Zippidy doo dar, away we go. If we don't get stopped by the Old Bill we'll be back in the market by eight. Then we can fill up with all the leftover gear for a car boot sale this afternoon. If you get the right stuff you can make a packet out of the old car boot. Ha-ha! Zippidy doo!

'So what do you want to know? The move? If we get it right before the move it can only get better after the move. That's what I think, that we have to get it right before. Phil's got up to a hundred thousand pounds' credit in the market already because he can pay it back. He sells the stuff before he's paid for it so he's always got more in his account. As long as he carries on selling, he's always got surplus in the bank.

'See that, that's Billingsgate, the new fish market. That's what Spitalfields is going to be like, the new Spitalfields.

'Where was I? Oh yes, Phil, he's got a good name in the market, a very good name. He can always pay his bills and if you pay quick, they'll give you a discount. If you pay immediately then they're turning the money over the whole time and they don't run up an overdraft. A quick turnover means more money in the system and more money in the system means more money in the old *fish tank*.

'This street is called Narrow Street, it's the start of Wapping, where all the yuppies have moved. See those flats, these places are going for a hundred and fifty grand. That's a lot of money, that's a lot of zippidy doo dar.

'What was I saying? I use Phil's strength, see, my name works quicker because I use his name. I can't afford to do anything disrespectful in the market. I can't afford to give Phil a bad name. I wouldn't do anything distrustful like buy stuff I couldn't pay for.

'Shall we go through the City, there's always a good bit of crumpet in the City. What time is it? Ten to eight, they'll all be arriving now. If we use the old hand brake stop, they'll soon notice us, what do you say? If we use the old hand brake.

'Phil, yes, Phil's got respect, see, he's got lots of trust. Like the other day when we were sorting out those yellow melons round at Mr Mays', they didn't check how many we took, did they? They trusted us with them, that's the sort of respect we're talking of.

'See those houses here, the houses round the market, they're all getting ready for when the market goes. They're just waiting for us to move now.

'Here we are, if we just park up round the back here. Then we can load up for the car-boot, shift a bit of gear, sell a bit of zippidy. Ha-ha!'

Curiously liberating

As I walked home to my flat on Brick Lane, rehearsing Vince's rather idiosyncratic brand of spry entrepreneurialism, I began chuckling to myself with surreal delight. I realised how much I was beginning to enjoy this defiant subversive energy, this *stands-to-reason-mate* cockney caper. Just as you can use all those funny French *mots justes* to affect a slightly coy chic – a certain *je ne sais quoi* – I was starting to get this *rub-a-dub* banter working for me too.

I have to say, at first, I had felt constantly as though I were being tricked, that as a magician uses his running commentary to attract our attention away from his mischievous hands, so too Vince and others seemed to employ an irrepressible habit of verbal display to conceal the progress of the deal in hand. Certainly the linguistic assumptions on first going into the market had been as unfamiliar to me as they would have been in any foreign city. More so, perhaps. Urbanity, with its slippery suavity and assorted gestures, is also a cosmopolitan style. But this banter, so energetically anarchic, had felt alien and unsettling. For the first few weeks of my employment in the market I was permanently nonplussed, reduced to blushing silence. I was not used to such straight-up bloody-mindedness: I could demur and beg to differ, quibble and generate wry little expressions of disagreement – but nothing to match the in-yer-face antagonism of so much market banter. Initially it had put me on the defensive. I was all prickle and patronising disdain – in fact, I was rather in danger of doing a Jack London special, with his Intrepid Explorer's account of coming 'face to face with the English lower classes'.

But then I began to chill. Or rather I began to withdraw my distancing projections and join in the knockabout exchanges, the singalongaVince.

'Well, *me old china*, what's all this about wanting to be a *pine-licker?*'

'You mean, why am I working in the market with all you *ice cream freezers?* – I'm testing my vocation.'

'Vocation, what's that then, Willy? Sounds like one of those posh package holidays – "my wife and I are going on Mediterranean vocation" – where will you be travelling to on your vocation then?'

Where indeed? Like those tunes which lodge themselves in your head and then resurface in a completely different context, I found this cockney banter reappearing as part of my own internal conversation, my talking to myself about what I wanted, what I feared, where I felt I was going. Somehow it helped to give voice to a sort of *sod you* defiance which had been sitting in my stomach like an undigested meal, rendering me at times sullen and morose, or unaccountably surly, causing me to explode into sudden ill-temper like an untimely fart. This schoolboy surliness seemed to surface particularly in the presence of bishops, in fact any representative of the Church Hierarchy. Dog collars could do it.

Technically speaking, I suppose I had an Authority Problem. On the one hand I felt the oppressive insistence of my family's involvement with the Church, my inherited calling to the clerical life; on the other hand I was uncertain about what it actually meant for me, how I fitted in, whether I wanted it in the first place. Seamlessly I could move from asking myself, *Do I come up to scratch?* to *Who the hell has the right to tell me I'm not good enough anyway?* without even passing through the headmaster's study. I hadn't spotted how my indignation was caught in a loop of its own contrivance, how I had pressed the 'repeat play' button without noticing.

'The Church is full of tight-arsed gits!'
'Hold on, mate, what's got on your tits?'
'Vicars and bishops, I hate the whole damn hopping-pot!'
'Even J C and the big G – surely not?'
'I want to be a writer, not a priest!'
'Is it really so black or white, so west or east?'
'Priests bind together, writers split apart.'
'What a load of old raspberry tart.'

Chatting to myself in quasi-cockney – or 'mockney' – was, in fact, curiously liberating. I had been used to a particularly understated reverence in discussing matters of the faith, all very piano and sensitive, in which the key thing was not to embarrass anyone with one's talk of God (or rather, 'God'). Disabled by my self-imposed deference, my fear of causing any offence whatsoever, I was left snarling with resentment. Bantering with myself, however, I was able to transform this belligerence into something more playful and communicative, something altogether less chippy.

I still had one other little problem. I hadn't yet told my mother that I had lost her father's — and family's — ring. I wondered how to do this.

'Save yourself the aggro, mate. Tell the old woman it got nicked in the market, what do you say Vince?'

'I say tell her it's been half-inched by a crafty cockney — worth a bit of zippidy that ring — not seen since.'

Market traders posed happily as villains. Theirs was a breezy indifference to propriety, not to say veracity, which I really enjoyed. Of course, it was all artifice: the cockney myth — which was essentially to do with a class solidarity — was itself controlling. As it supplied certain possibilities, it denied others. It contained internal contradictions, it seemed to be wanting different things. I also saw how the frequent outbursts of apparently good-humoured cockney vituperation were as self-consciously stylised and managed as the elegant indifference I had perfected at university. But whereas the end of the latter was a sort of world-weary knowingness, where the self is paralysed in a spiral of ironic self-consciousness, the purpose of the former was to display 'character'. And the market was certainly full of it, vital displays of excess, which pranked and performed, limped and snorted their way up and down the alleys. Above all, it was Spitalfields Market itself, with its chaos and congestion, its history and associations, which had allowed this banter — this myth of a cockney working-class community — to thrive.

As I say, it took me a little while to get into the swing of things. And then when I did, it wasn't quite what I expected.

Initiation

It was a couple of weeks before I was due to finish my employment in the market when Jim first raised the question of my initiation.

''Ere, Willy me old mate, you haven't been done yet have you?'

Then, seeing my confusion, he went on, 'I don't think we've initiated you into the brotherhood yet, have we?'

Well, it sounded, at first, all quite friendly and affirming. I was pleased by the suggestion of acceptance, of having proved my willingness to participate in market life. I had, after all, taken my turn as a stacker, checker, delivery driver and tea boy. I had been swindled by the traders, tipped by the grocers, got drunk with the salesmen. I had been the good-tempered foil for numerous practical jokes which included being locked in the cool box for half an hour and being sent off round the market in search of 'exotic' fruits that didn't, in fact, exist. Nicknames, from 'Joe 90' to 'Fighter Pilot Ponsonby Smythe' had been shuffled on and off my shoulders as if I were a shop dummy. And now, it seemed, I was to face a final and decisive rite of passage: I was to become an honorary cockney.

Jim began generating some support for the initiation on the stand. ''Ere, Phil, Willy hasn't been done yet has he?'

Phil, though less interested, was forced to agree. 'No, he'll have to be done by the end of next week.'

'He certainly will, we'll have to take him round the back and have him done there. What do you say Vince?'

'I say, get 'em off!'

Get them off? Get what off? I began to feel a little nervous, that maybe I didn't want to be an honorary cockney after all.

'Oh, leave the poor boy alone,' interrupted Mrs Curtis, the motherly greengrocer from Bethnal Green, 'what you want to go doing him for, what's he ever done to you?'

Throughout the rest of the week, Jim referred at regular intervals to my approaching initiation. It was the fact that it remained so unspecific that made it sound so sinister. He didn't say: 'I know it's a bit unpleasant old chap but in order that we can really accept you we feel we have to hang you up by your underpants and make you eat raw cauliflower.' By the Wednesday, however, I suspected it was going to entail a certain amount of public humiliation and by the Friday I felt fairly confident that the focus of the initiation was going to be genital.

Over the weekend, as I was working on a strategy for dealing with Jim's threatening advances, I went to find another job. I wanted something which would help me get a clearer picture of how cockney Spitalfields was changing, indeed whether, after the market had moved and the site had been redeveloped, it would even exist. I noticed that one of the pubs along Commercial Street was looking for bar staff and I went in to enquire.

The Jack the Ripper pub consisted of one large room with half-blackened windows. Thick red curtains hung across both walls, ready to be drawn at closing time to shut out unwanted eyes. As you came in through the corner door you looked straight across the room to the bar which stretched the length of the opposite wall. In the far corner was another door, identified as 'private', the entrance to the publican's part of the house. The furniture was reproduction Victorian, lots of rather ornate ironwork and stools upholstered in red plush. Just to the right of the door marked 'private' was a piano, a bit bashed up by years of sing-songs. Around the walls hung a number of Ripper collectables, copies of contemporary newspapers and the teasing letters which he was alleged to have written to the police. On one wall there was a board on which all his victims' names had been carefully painted, a grisly roll-call. The general hum of conversation was broken from time to time by the whirring noise of the fruit machine as it invited you to come and try your luck.

The pub stood on the corner of Fournier Street and Commercial Street, across the road from the market. In fact, as I waited for the landlady by the bar that Saturday morning and looked out through the window, I could see the late-morning preparations for departure down the southernmost alley of the market: traders erecting wire barriers around their stands, the market police patrolling the exits, a few familiar dossers loading up their pockets with discarded produce. I thought I could even see Vince piling up the boot of his Mercedes with unsold fruit and veg, getting stocked up for his car-boot sale.

With Christ Church sitting on the opposite side of the Fournier Street junction and with a diagonal view down Brushfield Street towards Bishopsgate, the pub overlooked a significant crossroads, where City suits brushed shoulders with East End overalls, each dodging the unrelenting traffic on

Commercial Street. On the market periphery now, the pub was set to front the redevelopment once the traders had moved to Leyton.

Just then the landlady appeared, backwards, through her private door, ordering a dog to sit, to sit and stay. She repeated the command several times, ferociously, keeping the door slightly ajar, just enough for everyone to realise there was a vicious animal somewhere behind it (and to allow the pungent smell of cat piss into the pub). Then she came over and introduced herself, offering me a hand full of rings. Her name was Yvonne. She was in her early forties, and her face was grained with misfortune and her voice crackly with years of cigarette inhalation. She spoke with the measured precision of someone who'd passed through elocution lessons during her childhood, the sort of voice which could make itself heard at closing time. Wearing a grey woollen dress which seemed to start out as a sweater and just keep going, with a single ring of pearls round her neck, she had about her an air of déclassé elegance. She took me over to a corner of the room and sat me down.

'What do you know about working in a pub then?'

'I know it's hard work.'

'It's more than hard work, young man, it's graft, graft, graft.'

She explained how, when her husband had died, she had wanted to return to the East End, where she had been brought up. They had run pubs all over the world, her and her Frank, she knew the trade all right, but she had never worked in the East End. Then she saw that the Jack had come up for rental from the brewery and she came to have a look at it. She liked it. She already had links with the area, she told me, seeing as how her father had worked as a carpenter in Shoreditch, where she'd been born, and one of her uncles had worked in the fruit and vegetable market. You couldn't beat the cockney for humour, she said. There was no one like the cockney for bringing a smile to your face, she said. It was historic, she said.

Anyway, she'd moved into Spitalfields in 1987 and had been building up the business ever since. Things were looking good. With all the building work in the area, down on Bishopsgate and soon on the market site itself, she wanted to attract the construction lads, 'my boys' as she called them. Then there was the Ripper centenary, that was sure to bring along a bit of custom. And then, once the market had gone, there would be the City types, the yuppies. All in all, she was doing OK, but she needed reliable staff.

She stopped talking and started to scrutinise me. I shifted my spectacles up on to the arch of my nose and tried to look reliable.

'Can you bottle up?'

'Excuse me?'

'Bottle up, you know how to bottle up, do you?'

Then, 'You know how to clean your taps, I suppose?'

I rearranged my legs, nervously.

'I take it you know how to spill a new barrel?'

Yvonne blinked mascara at me disbelievingly, her lashes curved open like bunches of over-ripe bananas. I began to feel a bit unlikely. She asked if I could get some references and I said, rather shiftily, that I would speak to the manager of the market stand where I was working.

'So you're working in the market, are you?' she said, clearly surprised, 'and they accept you all right, do they? I mean, you don't have any problems with your . . . you don't find they . . . I mean, some of these cockney types, they can be a bit wicked if they think you've got airs, if you know what I mean.'

I said it was just a matter of knowing how to keep talking, how to answer back. I said it was just a case of knowing how to banter.

She nodded vigorously. I got the job.

The final week of pushing fruit and vegetables around the market came and with it the prospect of my 'initiation', my 'being done'. As the threat became more and more unpleasant, I felt increasingly impotent. What could I do? It was like walking into the kitchen and recognising the smell of rotting potatoes, but being unable to find the offending tubers.

And then it struck me that I had heard it before. I'd come across it at school, accompanying the first confused assertions of schoolboy sexuality. It was dormitory talk, what was said when the lights went out, when the desire for sexual intimacy and the fear of rejection knotted together into threats of sexual humiliation. Listening to the language of the market, I could hear it bristling with similarly suffocated homosexual intent: 'screw me', 'bugger you', 'I'll get your arse'.

I tried confronting Jim with rage, chivvying him along with humour, working through the issues with reason. I tried ignoring him. Each time his intimidations returned with wearisome regularity. Then I tried High Camp. When we were next alone behind the Golden Delicious I turned to him and said, 'Give us a kiss, big boy.'

Looks of disbelief. Then, 'Don't you fuckin' *ginger beer* me, you fuckin' back door merchant.'

Campness, with its disregard for depth of feeling, its overt transgression, brought with it an immense freedom of movement. The more I flirted with him, the more Jim ignored me and the threat of 'initiation' evaporated. I finished my employment in Spitalfields Market with gay abandon. I was learning to banter.

A decent pint

Yvonne set me to work in the cellar cleaning up Rottweiler incontinence, whilst Shandy, the evacuator in question, lumbered around behind me, sniffing the air conceitedly. 'He's not very well trained, but he's learning. And he has such a lovely, good nature,' she had told me, reassuringly. Shandy, to my mind, looked as if he could quite easily eat me for breakfast, and I determined to keep on good terms with him.

'He's not so bad,' said Yvonne, 'he'll come if you call him. The only time you do have to watch him is with children, who annoy him, and with Asians. I don't know what it is, it must be instinctual or something, but he'd like an Asian, you can tell.'

Yvonne treated her building workers rather as she treated her Rottweiler, with affectionate tolerance – boys will be boys. A lot of the pubs along Bishopsgate and the City fringe wouldn't allow them in, putting up officious notices in their window prohibiting entry to 'travellers' or anyone wearing 'soiled clothing', not wanting to antagonise their besuited custom. The Jack the Ripper, however, had gained a particular reputation for hospitality. The landlady might be a bit of a battleaxe, with her insistence on clean language and her prohibition on gambling, but she was basically OK, they'd tell me when Yvonne had gone upstairs. She had a heart of gold, they said.

'The men who are on demolition tend to come in looking a bit rough, it's true,' she admitted, 'but the steel erectors, they'll never come here in their work clothes, they'll always have changed. Crane drivers too, they're usually reasonably tidy. Most publicans, you see, tend to think they're a load of yobs that come in off the sites, but in fact you get some intelligent blokes working the building trade; if you listen, they'll tell you some very interesting personal stories.'

Yvonne quickly got to know them all by name, where they came from, where they were staying in London. A lot would be down from the North of England and Scotland, living in bed and breakfast accommodation, separated for months at a time from their families. She let them use the pub phone as a contact number and was happy to pass on messages. In fact the pub became something of an employment exchange, as the Broadgate development moved through its various stages and extra labourers were needed at short notice for particular tasks. One of the foremen, Les, responsible for hiring extra hands, would be in most evenings, holding court and taking on unemployed workers.

Yvonne worked hard at building up the regulars. She knew what they liked and how they liked it, reaching for a bottle of Newcastle Brown Ale or the Guinness tap as soon as they walked through the door. Sometimes she'd take the glass from my hand mid-way through an order and, swirling a cappuccino-like froth into the ale, she'd explain to the customer that I'd only just started and didn't yet know how to pull a decent pint. Then later she'd tell me, 'It's only the yuppies that like their bitter flat – they think they're getting their money's worth if it's dribbling out of the top. But the lads here won't drink it unless you give them a bit of a head, if you don't give them a head they'll ask you to do it again.'

She also started serving an evening meal, a dish a day. 'How many hot pots do we have today?' she'd ask coquettishly, standing in the middle of a group of burly workmen, ignoring the muffled sniggers. Then blinking guilelessly at the *double entendre*, she'd continue, 'You'll have to be patient lads, I can only do one of you at a time.'

Only once was there any trouble with the building workers. Yvonne was out for a while and I was working in the bar on my own, when, at about half past three in the afternoon, the pub suddenly filled up and I was faced with twenty or so steel erectors grumpily downing crate after crate of Newcastle Brown between them. They had come earlier than usual and were drinking more seriously, but it wasn't pay-day and neither was it pouring with rain and I couldn't think why they were there. As one of the regulars came over to the bar to buy another round, I asked him what was up with the drinking session, had they just been given their Christmas bonus or something?

'It's the mate,' he replied, matter-of-factly, 'he fell off.'

Steel erectors who fall don't hurt themselves, they kill themselves. His mates had quit work in sympathy, drinking themselves morose, knocking over their drinks, sliding gradually into a torpor of inebriation. Their massive bodies were hunched around a couple of tables, occasionally shifting forward to stub a cigarette out in a central ashtray, a shared fondue of fag ends.

At some point in the afternoon they had started to play cards, which I only noticed when I went over to wipe their tables, thinking nothing of it. It was only when Yvonne returned, horrified at what I'd let happen, that I realised what was going on. They weren't just passing the time with a few hands of gin rummy, as I'd thought, they were betting their wage packets into each other's pockets, crumpling five, ten, twenty pound notes resentfully into one another's hands. The glum reticence of earlier in the afternoon had been replaced by little eruptions of seething fury, as the debtors wrestled to control their anger and made increasingly vociferous accusations of foul play and calls for retribution.

Then one of the younger men, a scaffolder, suddenly stood up. He crashed his drink down on the table, grabbing hopelessly at the steel erector who had pocketed most of his cash. There was a general explosion of limbs and fists. Yvonne was not having it.

'You can all get out of here, right now!' she yelled instantly.

Everybody seemed to think this was a reasonable request and cheerfully bundled out of the door, clearly invigorated by the fray.

'And don't you bloody well dare go and fight outside my pub, giving me a bad reputation,' she screamed after them, waggling her fist.

It was George who cleaned up after they'd gone. Muttering and laughing to himself, he went round with a bucket and a mop, saying how he knew it was going to happen, how he could see it was only a matter of time before someone hit someone, before there was a bit of aggro. When you had been in as many fights as he had, you just got a feeling, a second sight, an 'intuitivisation', call it what you will.

George had a disreputable charm about him, with his thinning black hair greased back, as it probably had been for the last thirty years, and his rounded face covered with an unruly growth of beard. When he smiled, which he did sometimes simply for the effect, crucial teeth were missing.

He was employed by Yvonne 'to keep an eye on things', a sort of odd-job man turned bouncer. He kept the ashtrays clean, he brought the empties back to the bar and stocked up with bottles from the cellar. Most importantly, however, he provided a benign presence around the place, chatting amiably to strangers, suggesting to the regulars that they might have had enough to drink, which they didn't mind coming from George, because he had usually had too much himself. He wasn't paid, but he had free drinks and food and was allowed to keep his own glass, with his name printed across its base, under the bar. During the mornings he worked in the fruit and vegetable market and was paid by the day, cash in hand. Sometimes Yvonne would operate as his bank, lending him a few pounds against the following day's wage, or keeping his money safe over a holiday period or a weekend.

George would always mind Yvonne's corner of the bar. It

was here, close to the entrance to her private part of the house, near the phone, the till, the regulars' slate, the jar of fruit-machine tokens and near the box of Jack the Ripper T-shirts and the various other bits of Ripper paraphernalia on sale for tourists, that Yvonne would sit, with a few select friends, able to observe the comings and goings of the whole pub.

Down the other end of the bar, near the entrance to the loos and the cigarette machine, sat the old-timers, the 'locals' who remembered the pub before it had been changed round, before the two bars had been knocked into one.

'You see where that window is over there, that's where they used to have the door. You used to have to go through this entrance area, where all the girls would sit, they used to be allowed to sit there and have a drink, out of the cold, like. You used to have to go through this entrance area into one of the two bars, left or right. The bar ran down the middle here and where the bar is now used be a corridor through to the bog at the back. It used to be better in them days, neater.'

When Alf said it used to be 'neater' what he meant was it used to be more clearly segregated, the hierarchies were more obviously delineated, the boundaries could be more easily patrolled. Now you found people establishing their pitches at different ends of the same room. They had to put up with the City suits coming in at lunchtime and the building workers filling the pub out in the afternoon. Occasionally they even had to extract themselves from conversations with American tourists who had ended up, with a couple of dozen other people, on one of the 'Ripper walks' around Spitalfields.

Altogether there was a group of about half a dozen of these self-styled cockneys, all of whom worked locally, in one of the markets or for the egg merchants off Commercial Street. They had their own private feuds but always kept to themselves, occasionally shouting something down to Yvonne at the other end of the bar or disappearing out for a few minutes to put a bet on a horse. In their suits, you could hear them talking shiftily about deals they had struck, the kind of respect they had commanded in some recent negotiation. They expected to be treated with a certain amount of deference. Once empty, they didn't expect to have to ask for you to refill their glasses.

Cyril was one of the regulars. As such he normally stood with the other dealers – they never sat on the bar stools, preferring to prop themselves up against the railing. Today, however, he was sitting down at the other end, Yvonne's end, on his own. His friends were ignoring him, his drunken rantings somewhat at odds with their own covert reticence. He was making too much noise. In an effort to make conversation, he asked me if I liked jazz and started slurping out a medley of sentimental refrains.

'Oh, won't you come home, dear baby, won't you come home . . . I don't care too much for money, money can't buy me love . . . you make me feel so good, you do, you make me feel brand new, ooo, ooo . . .'

He was in his cups, heading for a black-out. As he lurched his way from one chart-topping song to another, I managed to pick up a few biographical details. He had spent seven years in the Merchant Navy. He'd left to get married. He'd worked variously as a watch salesman on the Whitechapel Road and an umbrella salesman in Petticoat Lane. He'd had considerable success as a jazz soloist. He'd sung with Frank Sinatra. He had a cat called Ronnie.

'I'm happy now and that's the main thing . . . I knew them all, supplied them all, but I don't care too much for money, money can't buy me love . . . Am I right or am I wrong? . . . I'll tell you something, the past will never go . . . Am I talking sense or am I talking rubbish? . . . You just can't keep on running and running and running, am I right or am I wrong? . . . I don't care too much for money, money can't buy me love . . .'

His borrowed lines and melancholic equivocations seemed to me to be a ghastly distortion of the salesman's patter, those brazenly manipulative twists and turns of logic favoured by the street-market entrepreneur. It was maybe because his usual drinking partners could hear this parody of the language they habitually used that they had distanced themselves so obviously from his present distress.

'You've got to be real, you've got to be true to yourself,' said Cyril, at which point he slid off his chair, backwards.

It was George who came round to pick him up, muttering

and laughing about how he had seen it coming, and walk him home.

You've got to keep dancing

Yvonne was nostalgic for the lost East End and actively nurtured a sense of its mythical past. Never lost for words, she'd keep the stories of traditional cockney good humour circulating for those journalists who came to report on the centenary of Jack the Ripper's months of Spitalfields terror. 'I've been misquoted from the *Brisbane Gazette* to the *Los Angeles Herald*,' she'd say, with matriarchal grandiloquence to the nervous-looking trainee journalist from the *East London Advertiser*, 'so make sure you pay attention.' In her myth-making she had set herself, both politically and personally, against the yuppies, with their crisp autobank money and their supercilious manner.

'They come in here and order a Pils for themselves and a beer for the lady and when I pour the beer into the beaker glass they say it's not womanly enough. Well, as far as I'm concerned that's the glass we do for the half; we do a jug for the pint and a beaker for the half. Anyway they say no, they say they want one of those curly shaped ones, the type we use for the Ripper Tipple, so that's the one they get. Yuppies! So bloody fussy!

'I'd rather have twenty building workers than ten yuppies, any evening. When it comes to selling beer you want the guys who'll knock it back – with the yuppies it's all pink gin this and pink gin that. They're just not the same to deal with, much more demanding, much harder work. They're not traditional to the area at all, and the Jack the Ripper isn't, by way of tradition, a yuppie pub.'

The pub's name had, in fact, only been changed in the early 1970s from the Ten Bells to the Jack the Ripper (and was subsequently changed back, around the time I was working there, as a result of local protest). The landlords at the time, on discovering that the final victim, Mary Kelly, had last been seen disappearing out of the pub on the night of her death, decided to cash in on the new wave of fascination with this local murderer, and renamed the pub. Its renaming, however, took place at a time when the traditional East End myths – those which located the late Victorian era as a time of social cohesion against all the odds, a golden age for cockney camaraderie – were becoming increasingly open to self-conscious manipulation, tourist attractions almost.

The Jack the Ripper certainly had its fair share of weirdo enthusiasts passing through. Many of these 'Ripperologists' were collating their own file on the Whitechapel murders of 1888, doing their own bit of detective 'research'. Some would come simply to buy a souvenir T-shirt or a key-ring or to try and guess what was in Yvonne's mystery Ripper Tipple. Others would want to talk about the murders themselves, cataloguing dates and locations and rehearsing the autoptic details with gory enthusiasm. Often they would want to float their latest theories, chew the fat a bit over this most grisly of tales. Was it the Duke of Clarence or the Prince's tutor at Cambridge, a Russian surgeon or the preacher who used to give street-walkers poisoned capsules, this prep school master, that cobbler? Everybody, it seemed, was equally suspect.

People's imaginations would rove excitedly over the details surrounding the murders and the conditions of life in Spitalfields at the turn of the century. In the context of this bar-room nostalgia, the very real deprivations of the 1890s became simply a colourful background for further accounts of raunchy cockney cheeriness. I heard stories of stand-up comedians, impersonators, drag queens and the Penny Gaff performers which included singing dwarfs, bearded ladies and other such 'freaks'. One old lady showed me photographs of her mother, dressed up as a pearly queen, performing music hall numbers in the song-saloon of a pub just a little further up Commercial Street. Invariably the older men would describe their drinking associations with Ronnie and Reggie Kray, 'and right gentlemen they were too'.

In fact it was the Kray Twins who had most spectacularly sought to recreate the life of the old East End, to re-invent the world they had been told about by their father and grandfather. They were born into a family which had, for generations, relied on the street market for its economic survival. Their father started out as a second-hand clothes dealer and quickly became known as something of 'a pesterer' in the area, a man with a instinct for buying and selling, whilst his father, Jimmy Kray, had kept a barrow in Petticoat Lane. Their maternal grand-father, John Lee, had been variously a boxer, juggler, street performer, impromptu poet and porter in Spitalfields Market. For old grandfather Lee, Jack the Ripper's murders were almost local happenings and the world of Dickensian villainy provided the context for his childhood memories. It was at their grandfather's knee that the twins had sat during their own childhood, living next door to him in Vallance Road, on the eastern edge of Spitalfields.

As the 'new' post-war East End was in the process of being built up around them, with its LCC maisonettes, its schools and later its supermarkets and its working-class respectability, they continued to live in a pre-war fantasy of shifty wheeler-dealing and fierce underworld loyalties. In this respect at least, their activity was essentially conservative, directed towards the reinforcement of the established social order. Immersing them-selves in the sentimental cockney songs of Queenie Watts, they cast themselves into that most traditional of East End roles, the respectable villain. Tough, smart and with a boundless capacity for entrepreneurial skulduggery, they played it out with obsessive dedication. Pearson, their biographer, writes, 'In essence they were not ordinary criminals but criminal performers, consciously acting out the crazy drama of their lives.'

It was this central importance of performance which intrigued me. I had come across it in the market and now in the pub, and the longer I spent in Spitalfields, the more I realised it was part of the cockney's very identity. Yet I also saw it belied the current realities of Spitalfields life, that it was originally imagined in response to a very different and particular set of circumstances. What would have earlier been seen as humorous bravura was now, so often, little more than bone-headed prejudice. What at one time might have been understood as a loyal expression of working-class patriotism now bore the unmistakable mark of racism. In the prosperous 1980s so much of the cockney performance became ridiculous, so much of its posturing redundant.

Street markets, and to some extent wholesale ones such as the fruit and vegetable market, were, certainly still at the turn of the nineteenth century, good places for the economically vulnerable to make a go of things. Their day-to-day quality, their amenability to the needs of the poor, their busyness, their transgressive energy, all served to make them vital, open places. Yet they were also congested and necessarily competitive. Potential traders would have had to establish themselves, very much like performers on the music-hall stage, by the sheer force of their personality, by their banter and salesman's show. It would have been here, amongst the noisy gabble of the patterers, barking their wares, haranguing with their rowdy sales pitch the narrow thoroughfares, where the musty smell of damp cotton fustian mingled with that of toasted herring – the staple diet of the Spitalfields poor – that this love of performance came into its own.

Yet one only had to walk through Brick Lane market on a Sunday morning to see how things had changed. Every Sunday morning that part of the Lane which lay between the railway bridge and the Bethnal Green Road was taken over by an encampment of stalls and an army of apparently nomadic traders, pitching for sales amidst the shells of the burnt-out houses and the warren of passageways and warehouses which intersected the railway arches. Around its fringes, these individual traders would arrange and rearrange a few desultory objects across a towel maybe, or even directly on to the street: they were selling what seemed to be the barely purchasable clutter of some impoverished bed-sitter. But talking with these 'traders' one realised very quickly they weren't stereotypical cockneys; rather they were students from the London College of Furniture wanting to supplement their grant cheques, or maybe a family from Barnes selling old junk out of the back of its Volvo.

Then, as one moved nearer the central trading area, the running sales patter from a number of stalls would compete for one's attention – and money – with the numerous street musicians. A man with a stall loaded with fruit and veg, maybe even Vince from Spitalfields Market, might be generating a bit of interest.

'Taste it, eat it, do yourself a favour. Quickly, quickly, before the police get here. It's all got to go, all you've got to do is eat it, that's all, you don't have to ask no questions. Open your bags ladies, you're taking something home here. Everybody's getting excited here, everybody's getting excited. Quickly, quickly, ladies, do yourself a favour.'

In the 1890s, according to Arthur Harding, Brick Lane was considered one of the best places for the recycling of stolen property: 'My mother used to sell the clothes we pinched from the church sales. She used to sell it in the Lane.' In the 1980s it was the spurious possibility of a black-market bargain which pulled in many of the shoppers as they greedily piled up their bags with produce.

Sooner or later as I wandered round Brick Lane market I'd bump into someone who would try to sell me something: a man with a carrier bag full of playing cards, another with an overcoat of watches hanging from the inside lining, a third with a supermarket trolley full of Christmas poinsettias (in January) or chocolate Easter eggs (in May). I remember talking to one old man, selling needles for twenty pence a box, who said he was on his way to Covent Garden. He said he was going down to the West End to play the cockney, that he wasn't stopping for long at Brick Lane today.

'I'm off to Covent Garden this afternoon, for a spot of dancing and larking about, to earn a few bob. Look here, I've got my funny hat and funny nose and I've got my steps all ready and I'll be off this afternoon. I've done it down here before, jigging around, but I don't feel too dancified today. I think I'll have some dinner and then settle down and do it up there, this afternoon. I don't need the money, but I enjoy it. Besides you've got to keep going, haven't you, you've got to keep dancing. People will miss you when you've gone.'

And he was right. It was what the punters wanted.

Although demographically, politically and socially it was a complete nonsense, the presence of an authentic cockney Spitalfields remained a very strong myth. And Yvonne at the Jack the Ripper was simply cashing in on this wave of interest. Despite her expressed antagonism towards the yuppie clientele, they remained its primary consumers and she was careful to stock up with wine and keep the draught cider on tap, 'just in case'.

The facts of life

It was on the final Friday of my employment at the Ripper, which also happened to be the centenary of Mary Kelly's murder, that an American television crew came and set up its equipment to produce a short features segment for a New York station. Before the dishy Selina Scott arrived – she had been billed as the guest presenter – the camera crew trawled Spitalfields for footage of darkened alleys and shadowy passageways. They said they had been filming various street markets around Spitalfields and then at the pie and mash shop on the Bethnal Green Road. They said they had been looking for the authentic East End.

When Ms Scott was ready and the filming started, Yvonne put on her customary sing-song tape, a compilation of traditional cockney choruses. They panned across the room, taking in the assorted decorations and the crowded bar, closing in gradually on the decanter of pinkish liquid beside the ice dish, the Ripper Tipple, as the knees-up strains of 'Fings Ain't Wot They Used to Be' rattled on in the background. Cut to Selina Scott, who, with consummate professionalism, completely ignored the gathering crowd of spectators to deliver her on-camera scene-setting intro.

'So here we are in the heart of London's East End, the home of the cockney, known the world over for his friendliness and sense of fun, for his loyalty and laughter . . .'

I looked around the room at this 'home of the cockney': Les from Newcastle, deep in conversation with his Geordie steel erector mates in the far corner; George wandering around the pub emptying dirty ashtrays into a bucket; Alf and Cyril propping each other up at one end of the bar, Yvonne adjusting the volume control down at the other; a couple of City suits arranging their empty beer bottles on the table by the door; a few students trying to wash away the recurring taste of curry with a pint of lager; a group of about thirty WI members following one of the Ripper walks.

'. . . It's hard to imagine,' continued Selina Scott, 'that exactly one hundred years ago this same area was plunged into nightmarish fear as Jack the Ripper stalked these very streets, leaving behind him a bloody trail of horror, hatred and hysteria.'

Selina Scott began interviewing Yvonne, who told her some familiar stories about the area and shed a few crocodile tears at the passing of the market. She then moved down the bar towards me and positioned herself beside the Ripper Tipple. Filling a glass, she swigged a couple of mouthfuls, taking particular care not to smudge her lipstick. Then turning on me, she asked if I knew the ingredients. I had just enough time to enjoy my moment of glory before I saw Yvonne frowning serious admonition at me as though to say, 'You tell her and you're sacked.'

'I'm afraid it's a trade secret,' I said, projecting my voice towards the sound box, paying particular attention to my careful consonant definition.

'That's another thing the cockney is well known for,' she said, nodding in my direction and toasting the camera conclusively, 'he's a crafty old devil.'

And so here was I, an outsider researching the area, being presented on American television as the archetypal insider, Flash Harry himself. But maybe this was just as it should be in the fragmented and depthless postmodern global village, where being a cockney was simply one part to be played in an urban theatre of many roles. Moreover, throughout the 1980s, just as these 'traditional' East End communities were disappearing, either through the City's expansion or because they had finally made it to the suburbs, we had been presented with the soap-operatic world of television's *EastEnders*, with its emphasis on

the intimacies of street culture and its portrayal of the con-
tinuities of working-class existence. As this myth strained at the
economic and social realities of the area, it was both generating
and sustaining a world-view necessarily at odds with the multi-
racial, multi-cultural facts of life in the East End, and particularly
in Spitalfields.

And so what were these facts?

Firstly, despite its 'bob or two' rhetoric, Spitalfields Market
had produced a number of millionaires. In fact it no longer
made sense to talk of these traders as working-class. The new
men in the market were young and mobile. They had moved
geographically outwards, deserting Spitalfields, and socially
upwards. In 1930, for example, the local population had
contributed over half the total number of market employees; in
the late 1980s only a handful live locally. They had exchanged
the salesman's traditional white overall for a barbour jacket, an
E1 address for a house in the country, complete with heated
swimming pool and a new conservatory. They may still have
had occasional 'Cockney Nights' down at their local social club
and have looked forward to their pie and mash, conveniently on
sale at the local freezer-centre in hermetically sealed, micro-
waveable cartons, but were these the products of a self-conscious cultural nostalgia rather than a vital community? Was this
not heritage rather than living history?

Secondly, even though Yvonne would rail against yuppies,
claiming traditional cockney status for her pub and loyalty to its
'regulars', there could be no doubt that passing trade was on the
increase in Spitalfields, the sort of customer you would see once
and never again. As a rule, he tended to be a bit upmarket and
mobile, the sort who preferred his sherry sweet and his beer
bottled. In fact, the White Hart, a few hundred yards up
Commercial Street towards Shoreditch, had recently opened a
separate wine bar within its premises, already looking towards
the City expansion, with both the landlord and his wife keenly
anticipating the market's departure.

'Although we love the market and we love the people, to me
it's going to better the area when it goes. At the moment it's a
slum. I live here but it's still a slum. There's a complete

imbalance in the people here, in actual fact, we're in a minority here,' she said referring to the Bengali majority.

And thirdly, a statistic: it was estimated, in 1990, that 4,500,000 people had passed through the whole complex of street markets in Spitalfields. These were mainly shoppers, from outside the area, some of whom were office workers, quite a few of whom were day-trippers and tourists. As Judy Goldsmith, from the East End Tourism Trust told me, 'The biggest draw to Spitalfields is definitely Petticoat Lane and the other street markets, followed by Jack the Ripper. They come looking for bargains or just to enjoy the noise and colour of the area.'

Cockney culture, it seemed, had become big business in the 1980s. Even the dossers around the fruit and vegetable market had changing expectations. Whereas Spitalfields used to be the place they ended up, after a few years of tramping around the West End, it had now become a point of arrival. They came from all over England attracted to the conspicuous wealth of the City fringe.

'There are blokes my age driving around the City in Porsches, that's what she has done for us over the last ten years, that's the sort of thing that can happen now,' said a nineteen-year-old Glaswegian admiringly. He had come to London to make it big but had ended up sleeping rough for the previous three months.

With the 'hope value' for development already pushing up property prices, the Sisters of Mercy on Gun Street were also planning a quick escape. They saw the demand for free handouts declining as the area became encircled by workers from the City's financial services. Similarly, the bottom was set to fall out of the market for the Commercial Street prostitutes.

In the meantime the dossers continued to collect their bowl of vegetable soup from the nuns in Gun Street before wandering over to the fire in the car park, throwing on the occasional pallet, turning the embers into defiant blaze, raging their apocalyptic fantasies into the wind and the rain. They would tell you once more how they had kept it burning ever since the Fire of London, a glowing reminder of the event which caused the original market's expulsion from the streets of the City into Spital Fields, outside the City walls. Soon, however, this fire was to be permanently extinguished by the combined efforts of a group of planners, property developers and some thirty floors of office chic.

GEORGIAN SPITALFIELDS

I didn't have any buckled shoes

Roast beef, sirloin steak, boiled bacon, salt beef, roast lamb, corned beef, cold ham, pork sausages, bacon and eggs, roast chicken: the menu at the Market Café was chalked up on a blackboard, propped up on a chair. There were no prices, there was no waitress. To the uninitiated, it was not, in fact, very clear how you were supposed to get together with your chosen chunk of meat. And if you dared to ask Phyllis, standing behind the counter, steaming up the tea, whether there was a vegetarian option, she'd curl her lip with mock contempt and reply, 'Prunes and custard.'

The fact was, market traders liked their meat. They would pack round the seven formica tables, enthusiastically foul-mouthing each other and carving up their dinners. The walls of the café were painted pale orange and were without decoration, apart, that was, from a hand-scrawled notice announcing the details of the next TGWU meeting for the market porters and a poster offering a reward for the safe return to one of the Fournier Street residents of a missing tabby cat. Radio 2 could be heard coming from among a pile of opaline dishes stacked up beneath the counter. The cash till, above the dishes, was locked into a No Sale position. The clock, above the till, was set fifteen minutes fast.

The Market Café was run by Phyllis and Clyde, sister and brother. Phyllis was quite definitely front-of-house. Winsomely petite, with her hair just-so and her cotton pinny colour-coordinating with her skirt, she pampered her favourite customers with the leanest cuts and the freshest tea. But she also kept you on your toes, did Phyllis, capable at times of the most withering indignation, bringing about the most fearful falls from grace.

'I came here three years ago,' said a market trader, coming into the café for a couple of pints of milk one morning, 'and I hit it off with Phil immediately. But I'll tell you what, there was this salesman that came on to the stand from Covent Garden and he had an attitude problem – that's how they are from Covent Garden, I don't know what it is, they think they're above you or something – anyway, he came in to buy the teas and maybe he didn't say please or thank you, but Phyllis took an instant dislike to him and if she doesn't like you then that's it, she'll cut you completely dead, ignore you completely. It's either good or it's bad with Phil, that's how she is.'

Clyde, on the other hand, stayed backstage. As you went through to the back kitchen to choose your lunch, he'd greet you shyly and take your order, thanking you several times for your custom and once again for helping yourself to a cold drink from the refrigerator. He would have been cooking since four in the morning, preparing butties and roasts for the market traders, so that when, at one in the afternoon you came in for your lunch, he was getting ready to close up shop and go home. He'd always take time, however, to recommend the choicest joint or discuss your preference for veg.

The Market Café on Fournier Street, just opposite the blackened rise of Christ Church, was, all in all, an unlikely institution. Locked into the time bubble of its sixties decor and its unsocial market hours and jealous of its net-curtained obscurity, it had become, bizarrely, the meeting place for New Georgian Spitalfields, the conservationists' caff. Or as Alexandra Artley observed in the *New Georgian Handbook*, a witty account of the cultivated eccentricities of this group of people, 'Next to Hawksmoor's portico is the Market Caff. The Pop-Baroques like it because it is Authentic.'

It was, therefore, to the Market Café that I went to begin my investigation into the New Georgian Spitalfields. I reckoned it was the best place to hang out, to get to know the key protagonists. I would sit there for hours, pretending to read my newspaper or do the crossword, straining to hear the gossip on the neighbouring table. I began to get a sense of the regulars' routines, which days they took an early lunch, when they came and went. I got on to nodding terms with a few of them.

One morning I went in for a cup of tea. The café was unusually empty. Phyllis was serving one of her regular Fournier Street customers, a young man dressed in a tweed jacket and dark corduroy trousers. I stood behind him at the counter.

'I'm not saying anything,' said Phyllis, tapping her nose confidentially, 'but I think I know what might have happened to your tabby cat. I'm not naming names,' she said, peering over our shoulders at the empty room, 'but I think I've got a fair idea of who's got it.'

'You think you know where he is?' he encouraged.

'The market traders,' she said, steaming up the water, 'they take the cats for the cellars, you know, they sometimes take them down there for a couple of weeks at a time.' Then, swirling the bags round in the pot, she whispered conclusively, 'It's the rats.'

As I passed his table, I stopped and introduced myself. Julian Humphreys peered from beneath his ginger hair, reached out his hand and said he was very pleased to make my acquaintance. I sympathised about the loss of his cat. I suggested that he speak with Joan the cat lady, that she might know what had happened to it. In fact, I said I'd ask her for him, if he liked. He gave me some details. The cat, he said, was called Hoxton, after the area just north of Spitalfields. He said he'd first seen it there, soon after he had arrived in Fournier Street, when he was going for a walk. The cat, having followed him home, had stayed ever since. I said I'd keep a look-out. He thanked me for my concern.

Joan, of course, knew exactly where it was. She'd been feeding it cans of Whiskas ever since she'd come across it, with the other strays and runaways, up behind the back of Bloom's Restaurant on Whitechapel High Street.

Hoxton's return was much rejoiced over. Clyde baked a welcome-home pie. Phyllis took down the poster. I was invited round to Julian Humphreys' house for afternoon tea.

He took me up to 'the red room' on the second floor and left me to enjoy the gloriously timewarped interior while he went to fetch the tea. Clearly candlelight was the chief, if not only, source of lighting, with a couple of waxy sconces above the chimney piece and a number of brass candlesticks deposited strategically around the room. The panelling, which was painted a peony red, gave a feeling of unfussy elegance, with the dentil course being the only piece of fancy embellishment. In front of the window, which overlooked the street, sat a sofa which was strewn with various tapestries. The floor boards were richly stained and comfortably wonky. The walls were cluttered with architectural prints. The whole room seemed poised uncertainly between the 1720s, when the house was built, and the present day.

When he returned with the tea tray, Julian explained how, over the course of the 1980s, he had completely restored the house. For the first few months, after having moved into Spitalfields in 1979, he had shared the house with a handful of Bengali jeans manufacturers, its previous occupants, as it continued to operate as their factory. Though structurally sound, apart from a fire in the garret floor which had left the roof in need of total restoration, the house was in a terrible mess, pitifully uncared for. Immediately Julian set about co-ordinating the repair work himself, using the carpentry skills he had learned at the London College of Furniture and financing the work from loans, grants and a small amount of capital.

He had moved to Spitalfields because he enjoyed the house – its age, its simple elegance – but he was clearly also drawn there by the fantasies of New Georgian fogeyism. Spitalfields was the sort of place he could rough it with style. In Spitalfields he was able to set himself at one remove from the vulgar realities of the market-place. Although the fruit and vegetable market redevelopment threatened to remove this seclusion, the area retained, for the moment, its quality of fashionable dilapidation. Like the other Fournier Street residents Julian had seen the grace through the decay, the quiet grandeur of the houses within the squalor of their surroundings. Drawing inspiration from the area's eighteenth-century origins, he saw himself as part of a pioneer community of artists, fashion designers, cabinet makers, wood turners, photographers, musicians and writers.

Julian cooked. That is, he would make his house available, three or four times a week, to groups of between six and twelve people, who wished to dine, by candle-light and to excess, in the manner of the eighteenth century. He called his restaurant 'an ordinary', the name given to a contemporary eating house, a dining room with a set menu and a fixed price list, half-way between a private club and an inn. Julian bought and prepared the food; his partner, Ashley Russell, a jobbing actor, would dress up in full eighteenth-century livery as the footman and wait at table.

I continued to see Julian and Ashley in the Market Café from time to time. Through them I also met some of the other residents of Fournier Street, members of the *arriviste* gentry. I came to know these new occupants of the Georgian houses in Spitalfields – the Neo Geos – as a loosely-knit association of convivial toffs.

Over breakfast in the Market Café I would watch as they left their houses for work in the morning and dodged their way through the traffic towards Liverpool Street station. Nimble John Gaze (single-fronted, 1720s, Fournier Street) would skip lightly across Commercial Street on his way to his shop in Piccadilly where he sold Russian icons. He might wave to urbane Michael Gillingham (double-fronted and pilastered, 1726, Fournier Street) who also dealt in antiques and had been one of the first of the 'pioneers' to take up residence in Spitalfields, back in the late 1970s. Soon to follow would be Eric Elstob (single-fronted with domed doorcase, 1726, Fournier Street) heading off to his job in the City. Or maybe Gilbert and George, (single-fronted, 1750s, Fournier Street) striding past, in synchronised step. 'Hello!', 'Hello!' they'd chorus, on the up-beat, to a passing market porter, before disappearing into the traffic.

In a little while, Ian Lumley (single-fronted, 1718, Princelet Street) might come past in animated conversation with Dan Cruickshank (single-fronted, 1727, Elder Street). Both Mr

Lumley and Mr Cruickshank were members of the Spitalfields Trust, the organisation which established itself in 1977 to save a number of Georgian houses from destruction at the hands of property developers. One would often see them in the area, stopping outside a house under repair, maybe to inspect the re-pointing or to pick their way through the skip, only to exclaim in horror at some architectural insensitivity, stamping their feet excitedly and throwing their arms about in uncoordinated movements of acute distress.

Inside the Market Café, Phyllis would usually be giving us her commentary on the morning news. Charlie Brandt (single-fronted, 1723, but rebuilt in the 1790s, Wilkes Street) might be doing the crossword, while Anetta Pedretti (double-fronted, 1706, Princelet Street) sat in the corner, deep in composition, tapping her latest thoughts on linguistic philosophy into her portable computer. Ms Pedretti would write her books in the Market Café between four and nine o' clock in the morning. Lacking central heating in her house – as well as windows – she found that this was the easiest way to keep warm.

I was still working at the time in the Jack the Ripper pub, now renamed the Ten Bells, on the corner of Fournier Street and Commercial Street, but wanted to change my job. I had come to see how the myth of 'cockney Spitalfields', which had been fab-ricated in the late nineteenth century, was now no longer appropriate as a way of describing Spitalfields culture. It had become at best a popular tourist attraction, at worst a morbid restatement of class and racial prejudice. And now I wondered whether the New Georgians' claim to be the legitimate heir to Spitalfields was any more compelling? Were the arguments they put forward in opposition to the market redevelopment, in par-ticular their insistence that it would overpower the human-scale domestic architecture of the area, any more persuasive? And did anyone care?

As these thoughts were going through my head, Julian Humphreys appeared beside me. He asked if he could join me. We exchanged notes on the weather and the news headlines and the conversation just dribbled on in a rather typical way until eventually Julian interrupted.

'The point is,' he said nervously, 'Ashley's just been offered this job. In some film. Well, he wants to take it. It means, of course, that he won't be able to help with the dinners. The point is, do you want to be my footman, at least for a while? At least while he's working on the film.'

My immediate thought was that I didn't have any buckled shoes.

'Yes,' I said, slightly bemused, 'I'd like to.'

A dispute in the props department

Julian put the word out in the Market Café that a friend of his was looking to move into Spitalfields (by which he meant New Georgian Spitalfields). He let it be known, in passing conversations up and down the street, that he had an acquaintance seeking accommodation in the neighbourhood. He even dropped a little note through the door of the assistant secretary of the Spitalfields Trust wondering whether the latter might be aware of any congenial residents who happened to be looking for a charming young tenant. And then, a week or so later, he introduced me to a neighbour, a dramatist called Rodney, who lived a few doors down Fournier Street, in a house which seemed to fuse the 1720s and the 1970s into a very particular experience of New Georgian psychedelia (rooms of meticulously restored panelling which had then been painted silver, purple rugs, PVC cushions in the window seats) and who said that I would be most welcome to move into his top-floor flat.

I brought over my bits and pieces, my wardrobe of roles, from Brick Lane and settled into this eighteenth-century weaver's loft, this garret to end all garrets. Looking across the Georgian rooftops of Fournier Street, past Christ Church on the corner of Commercial Street, over the Horner buildings of the fruit and vegetable market and towards the emerging office frontage of Bishopsgate, I contemplated how I had, indeed, moved up in the world.

And sideways too. I was becoming suspicious of what lay behind this talk of the city as a 'locus classicus of incompatible realities', an exciting juxtaposition of worlds, languages, signifiers, voices, registers, performing egos. I had already seen the way a cockney mythology, drawing on a particular reading of late nineteenth-century East End history, was being used to shore up the edifice of an outdated working-class identity. Was it not possible that this determined attempt to reinvent the early eighteenth century in New Georgian Spitalfields, this hankering after a Golden World of the 1720s, indicated a similar loss of direction amongst the so-called 'gentry'? And if this were the case, then wasn't this 'mythological battle' in Spitalfields, this competition between rival versions of the area's past and destiny, simply a continuation of historical antagonism by other means? Wasn't postmodern 'frisson' simply boring old class conflict in fancy dress?

It was only about seven o' clock in the evening, but already a few lorries had pulled up along Commercial Street and their drivers were gathering around the tea van outside the church. A crowd of Ripper walkers had spilled out of the pub on the corner and were making their way up the street. Through a pair of shutters I noticed candlelight flickering across the walls of the first floor room of the house of an opposite neighbour. I could also see Gilbert and George in their living room, enjoying a glass of wine (the bottle had been placed on the window ledge, presumably for refrigeration), and then felt slightly shifty when George spotted me peering down at him as he came to the window to fetch the bottle. I wondered whether Steve, my University friend now on the trading floors of the City, would be round the corner in the Seven Stars pub, where we had met before.

He wasn't. In fact, the front bar was rather empty. A few sullen-looking youths filled the tables round the edge of the room and a group of City types stood around the bar chatting up the 'exotic dancer'. I went through to the back bar, apparently a floorshow-free zone, and sat down at a table in the corner with my beer and my peanuts, continuing to reflect on this move from Brick Lane to Fournier Street, from Cockney Spitalfields to New Georgian Spitalfields. It occurred to me that despite the apparent conflict between these two versions of the area, which may or may not have had its roots in residual class antagonism, both communities were, in fact, likely to gain from the market redevelopment. Certainly, when the office development was complete, the conservation area in Spitalfields would be seen more clearly for what it was, a remarkable stock of early eighteenth-century town-houses, more remarkable for its proximity to an international banking centre.

Increasingly the notion of Spitalfields as a collection of discrete communities, all at odds with one another, seemed to belie a shared economic interest in the eventual redevelopment of the market site. The differences between these communities, more apparent than real, were surely exaggerated by the current interest in notions of heritage. Wasn't this conflict between 'Cockney' and 'New Georgian' Spitalfields more like a dispute in the props department of some costume drama than a fundamental clash of interests? In deconstructing these respective cultural stories was one not simply left with the naked and rather sordid reality of market forces reigning supreme? And if this were the case, what makes a community give an account of its past which seems to be so at odds with its economic future?

I went through to the loo which was situated rather trickily by the 'stage' in the front section of the pub. As I was passing the bar I was spotted by the dancer making her way round the pub, collecting her tips, wobbling rather unsteadily in her stilettos. I felt in my pocket for some small change, rather as one does in church before the collection plate arrives, not wishing to draw attention to one's carefully concealed meanness. She came to stand beside me, steadying herself with one hand on the table, smiling encouragement.

'A little tip for the floorshow?' she asked.

'Oh yes, of course,' I said, dropping in my desultory collection of coins.

'Thank you,' she said, following their course into her glass.

'It must be difficult dancing with those on,' I said, nodding at her high heels, trying to cover my embarrassment over the money.

'Not really, love,' she said. 'Anyway, it's the shoes that make it striptease. It all comes off except the shoes. It's not striptease if the shoes don't stay on. If the shoes come off then it's just undressing in some smelly pub in front of a load of filthy old men.'

The evening got off to a bad start

It wasn't, however, my own lack of the correct footwear that proved to be the problem. It was getting my lines as footman sorted out. It was maintaining, for the benefit of the paying guests, the *trompe l'oeil* of New Georgian fogeyism, all snoot and circumlocution, without beginning to sound absurdly mannered. Julian encouraged me to aim for a sort of atonal politeness: formal, humourless, with just a teasing touch of greasy deference. He reminded me that this was eating as entertainment and that I was the compère for the evening. 'Transport them,' he would say, 'just transport them to the eighteenth century.'

Most of our guests were quite happy to be transported – after all, that's what they'd come for. They would already be familiar with the facts of Georgian Spitalfields. They would know that Fournier Street was built in the 1720s and that the houses were originally occupied by Huguenot silk weavers. Some were on the rebound after a purchase had fallen through and would talk poignantly about the house that got away, the quality of its stucco work, the condition of its panelling, the perfectly preserved box cornices in the ground-floor dining room. Others would share notes on the restoration of Christ Church, whose massive rear-end could be seen, sitting sturdy, through Julian's dining-room window. Such guests would display their exquisite good taste, delighting in stories of Georgian restoration, gasping at tales of period insensitivity. 'Barbarism,' they'd declare, 'pure barbarism.'

With these groups my job was easy. They didn't feel at all threatened by my yes-sir-no-sir servility. On the contrary, over the course of the evening we would enter into a sort of unspoken complicity, quite happily indulging each other's pretensions to know the formulae of social gentility. Julian liked these guests, he'd say that they understood Spitalfields, by which I think he meant that they'd been to the right schools, talked the same language.

Then there were the groups which Julian described as being a bit bothersome. These were the ones which refused to submit to the course of the evening, which refused to play up and play the game. They weren't interested in being transported to the eighteenth century. They wanted value for money, they wanted to know why there wasn't any lager and what had happened to the After Eights. They might even ask for more.

It was with such groups that Julian quickly became petulant, critical of their sloppy sense of propriety. Such evenings would take place within a complex etiquette of formalities, in which a gaff, a *faux pas*, some social indecorum might appear from behind any request for water, each selection of cutlery and reference to the food like a banana skin waiting to be slipped on. And when they did slip, Julian would affect horror at their 'complete crassness', such 'unbelievable ignorance'. As I came down to the basement kitchen from the dining room, he would get me to repeat several times over what they'd told me and how they'd said it. Then, as he stood in front of the gas stove in his apron, bringing this pan to the boil, allowing that one to simmer away, he'd huff and puff some extraordinary piece of Spitalfields snobbery, such as 'I mean, why don't they all just go back to the Essex suburbs, where they belong?'

It was hard, however, to take him completely seriously. To what extent, after all, was Julian's New Georgian fogeyism any less rhetorical than the cockney posturing in the fruit and vegetable market and the pub? Surely he, too, was simply hiding behind his lofty early eighteenth-century façade, rehearsing somebody else's prejudice. Certainly his fantasies were shared by the other members of the new Spitalfields 'gentry', dreaming, in their restored houses, of another social world, of a society of old wealth and traditional values, of manners and manservants. And what would happen, I wondered, if these two versions of Spitalfields collided with one another, if the upwardly mobile cockney trader came to make his repast at 'Mr Humphreys' Ordinary'?

Well, one night, several weeks into my employment as footman, I was to find out.

The evening, it must be said, got off to a bad start. Just as we were making the final preparations, waiting for the guests to arrive, there was a loud knock on the door. Rather than pulling the brass bell-pull, located just beside the front door, they had chosen to announce themselves with a knuckle. Julian, unfortunately, took a rather dim view of people who knocked on his front door.

'There are those people who come to the front door and see the brass bell-pull and the word PULL engraved beside it and go ahead and pull it and have the door opened for them, and there are those people who don't bother to look, who don't bother to act on this provision, who just knock, and for whom the door remains unanswered.'

He was in the process of shelling a heap of Colchester oysters. The smell of the sea mixed with the other cooking smells in the kitchen – the vegetable stock bubbling on a back ring, something meaty roasting in an oven, herbs freshly chopped and waiting to one side – and formed a deliciously briny-smelling sort of hot-pot. The mixture filled the basement room and wafted up through the open window, through the grate, breezing up into the street and, no doubt, into the nostrils of the group of dinner guests, who were waiting, like the Bisto Kids, on Julian's doorstep.

'I think we'll just let them stew for a little while,' he said.

Through the window I could see the agitated shuffling of legs, high heels teetering to keep balance. Watches were checked, diaries consulted, bewildered confusion expressed. A member of the party wandered a little further up Fournier Street to see if there were a more obvious entrance to this so-called Georgian Eating House, this 'Mr Humphreys' Ordinary', whatever that might be, which he was sure he'd got down as Number 25.

A further *knock, knock, knock* sounded on the door, but much louder this time, much more clearly knuckled. Julian didn't bat an eyelid. It crossed my mind that, if we weren't careful, we might be left with a pot of soup, a couple of sautéed soles, half-a-dozen boiled chickens, a saddle of roast lamb, a steamy pond pudding, various desserts and cheeses and fruits, let alone a couple of dozen fried oysters – the whole shooting match in fact, and no one to eat it.

When the bell finally did ring, it was pulled with such a last-ditch force that it was still sounding as I passed it in the hall on my way to the front door, and, in fact, only when I had opened the door and greeted the four waiting guests with my customary welcome did it eventually shiver into silence.

'Good evening sirs, madams. The Newbolt family?'

'Blimey! Look at that!' said the older man, pointing in my direction, 'We were beginning to wonder if we had come to the right place, but I take it from your get-up . . .'

'Livery, Bert, it's called a livery,' corrected the older woman.

'From your livery costume, that this *is* the Georgian Eating House. Or do you all dress up like that around here?' he went on, roaring with laughter at the thought of a street full of eighteenth-century skivvies.

'No, you're quite right sir, this is the right place. Do come in,' I said, leading them through the hall towards the smoking room, anxious to get a bit of punch down their throats.

'No wonder you took so long answering the door,' he continued, fumbling his way along the panelling, 'you can't see a bleedin' thing in here. Have you got a power cut or something?'

'No sir, the dimness of the light is due to the fact that we prefer to use the more traditional forms of lighting: gas, oil, candles. May I take your coat, madam?'

'And when the house goes up in smoke I suppose you prefer to use the more traditional forms of fire extinguisher, do you?'

'Shush Bert, come and have a look in here,' said his wife, leaving me in the hall clutching her furs. The other two guests, younger and more at ease, went through to join her. Bert continued to poke around outside.

Mrs Bert settled in a chair by the fire and was joking with the other woman about whether or not they should have come in costume. A *slightly* too tight two-piece harassed her body, its spread of royal Thatcher blue relieved only by a row of rose petals appliquéd across her bead-strewn bosom. The younger woman was wearing a black dress, slit at the side and ornamented with padded bits curving out of the shoulders like inverted commas. They were talking colour combinations. Shoulderpads was saying how she used to restrict herself to black or navy at the office, but how, quite recently, she had been branching out into beige. Mrs Bert said how she loved beige, always had done, but couldn't wear it herself, owing to it being too, how should she put it, too unflattering. I interrupted to offer them a glass of milk punch.

'Milk punch! Oooh, I'm willing to try anything once,' said Mrs Bert, thrilling to the challenge. 'Is this an original recipe, may I ask?'

'Yes it is, madam.'

'Oooh, taste that, Sal, I'm sure there's something a bit naughty in there. Might there be a drop of alcohol in the milk punch?'

'Yes there is, madam.'

'Boys! Come and try some of this. It's delicious and I'm sure it's absolutely lethal.'

'Graham, what are you doing in there? Come and have a taste of this punch,' echoed Sal.

Graham and Bert had gone through to the dining room which they were inspecting like a couple of surveyors: tapping on the walls, shifting the shutters, checking the fireplace for ventilation. Graham was taller than Bert, leaner, fitter. Whereas Bert was paunchily gregarious, humming with affability, Graham had the sharper features of a man working on commission. His suit had the sheen of success. He looked like he knew his way around a balance sheet.

'Punch, sir?' I held out a glass.

'Got any lager?'

'I'm afraid we don't serve lager, sir.'

'Well, I'll just have a Perrier then.'

'Thank you sir. If you'll excuse me,' I smarmed and went downstairs to the kitchen.

'*Perrier*?' exclaimed Julian, scarcely believing his ears, '*Perrier*? Where does he think he is? In some kind of *French bistro*?' he said with a hideously exaggerated accent. 'If he doesn't want the punch, he can jolly well have Thames tap water.'

When I returned upstairs they were talking about Spitalfields. It appeared that Bert knew the area well. He was saying how he'd been coming down here every day for the last twenty years, but that he'd never heard about this 'Mr Humphreys' Ordinary'. He said how he'd been born just a few miles up the Commercial Road, how his Dad had lived off the back of Brick Lane, how he'd gone to school up the Bethnal Green Road, but he'd never been inside one of these old houses. He was interested in a different Spitalfields history.

'This is Ripperland, you know, it's where all them Ripper murders were done. There's a pub on the corner, and if you go inside it you can see all the names of his victims on the wall. A bit nasty, eh?'

'Dad, must you!' cried Sally, but he continued unabashed.

'Some say he was out to get rid of all the prostitutes in the area. Some say he had a vendetta. Whatever his reasons, it's still going on, you know, you still get all the prostitutes coming out at night along Commercial Street. Well, it's historical isn't it? It's traditional. Spitalfields has a bit of a reputation that way.'

I handed Graham his glass of water just as he picked up the conversation. 'It's rip-off land more like. You want to get into property, not prostitution. The house I bought last year in Woodseer Street, off the back of Brick Lane, cost me near on a hundred K. It's already worth about two hundred grand. That's a cool one hundred per cent profit, and I haven't even touched it yet. You just wait, in ten years' time, when they've done up the market and the brewery, this area's going to be a prime residential location. Not just for these New Georgian types, but for anyone who can pay the prices.'

I started refilling their glasses.

'Better save some for Boggy and Georgie,' said Sal, who was hosting the party. 'They should be here quite soon. What time do we start eating?'

'Mr Humphreys serves dinner at eight o'clock, madam.'

'I'm sure they'll be here by then.'

'Very good, madam. Will there be anything else?'

'No, thank you.'

'Madam,' I murmured deferentially, backing out of the door and shutting it gently in front of me.

Standing in the hall, I shuffled my feet on the floor so they would think I was moving off and strained to hear what they were saying. A fazed silence was broken by Mrs Bert, as she whispered, 'Oooh, he's terribly polite isn't he, and hasn't he got such lovely manners?'

Julian was saying grace when I went into the kitchen. As I closed the door, he bent over and placed a dish of meat in front of Hoxton. 'Yum, yum, yum,' he encouraged, 'delicious rabbit, your absolute favourite.'

'Are they all here?' he asked.

'We're waiting for the last two.'

'No we're not. As the Duchess of Windsor used to say, "My guests can wait, but my cook waits for no one".'

I uncorked the wine and decanted it ready for serving. Julian, meanwhile, was warming the tureen with boiling water and seasoning the broth. Shortly before eight o'clock I went upstairs, lighting the candles in the dining room and drawing the chairs up to the table. I put a couple more logs on the fire.

With no sign of the missing couple, Julian invited me to announce dinner. A little cough was enough to distract Sally from her conversation with her mother.

'Dinner is served, madam.'

'Boys,' she said, turning to the others, 'I think he wants us go through.'

As the four members of the group gathered around Julian's dining room table I could hear, through the shutters, Christ Church chiming the hour.

Correct good taste

Christ Church, like the rest of eighteenth-century Spitalfields, was, in the 1980s, upwardly mobile. It looked like it was going to have quite an upbeat future, all set to throw off its image of gloomy decay and dilapidation. As Charles Dance, a local photographer, said, 'Once it's all restored and cleaned up, sparkling and brightly coloured, the way it was originally, with lots of gold and white and cream and eighteenth-century colours – sky blue and coral pink – I'm sure it will have quite a different feeling. It'll be really quite smart.'

Having been closed in 1957 because of major structural problems, Christ Church was rediscovered, twenty years later, by Save Britain's Heritage, which recognised it as one of the best and most neglected examples of English Baroque; certainly the finest of the works of its architect, Nicholas Hawksmoor. In 1978 a group of architectural enthusiasts – they called themselves the Friends of Christ Church – set about raising the money to restore the building to its eighteenth-century plan. It was out of these fund-raising discussions that the idea of an annual Spitalfields Festival, which would take place in the church, was born.

Yet Christ Church was large and contained multitudes. In a typical Church of England way, it was full of people with strong and opposing views, who nevertheless demurred at being quoted ('to be quite candid . . . to be quite frank . . . but strictly off the record . . .'). Broadly speaking, its worshipping congregation, evangelical in style and small in number, resented the way that 'secondary uses' were taking over the church and were appalled by the amount of money required to complete the restoration. The Friends, on the other hand, few of whom lived in the area, saw it more as a venue for their concerts than as a place of worship; they were more deeply impressed by the quality of its acoustics than the depth of its prayer life.

In part this contradiction could be traced back to Hawksmoor's own day and the circumstances which gave rise to the church's construction. With its colossal portico and sheer mass, it is from the outside more reminiscent of an imposing civic hall than a place of Christian worship. This impression is not misleading: in the early eighteenth century it was intended to stand as a clear reminder of state control.

Spurred on by the accession of Queen Anne in 1702, which marked a turning point in the fortunes of the High Church movement, Parliament passed the Fifty New Churches Act in

June 1711. It was through this Act that the Established Church sought to 'Christianise' those townspeople 'in or near the cities of London or Westminster', the Nonconformist multitudes of East London. In the late seventeenth century Spitalfields had been built up only around the two ancient routes which passed through the area, Brick Lane, which ran, as it still does, from Aldgate to Bethnal Green, and Hanbury Street, then known as Browne's Lane, which crossed both Brick Lane and Bishopsgate at right angles. The expanse of land within these intersecting streets was, at that time, little more than a dumping ground for the City. But then in the 1720s, when the parish of Spitalfields was carved out of the larger parish of St Dunstan's, Stepney, the street pattern with which we are familiar today began to take shape. Indeed, there's no doubt that it was the commissioning of Hawksmoor in 1711 to design this monument to church and state power which really marked the beginning of the period of expansion in the area.

Queen Anne went on to appoint a Commission (including Wren, Vanbrugh and Hawksmoor) to oversee the building programme, which was to be financed by a statutory tax on coal. Besides authorising the purchase of sites and burial grounds, the 1711 Act also stipulated that these churches were to be 'of Stone and other proper Materials, with Towers or Steeples to each of them'. It was a happy chance which saw the Established Church eager to promote its political ascendancy in Stepney at just the same time that classical architecture entered its most monumental and self-aggrandising phase. The Commissioners themselves had an even headier sense of political mission, supplementing the requirements of the Act with their own grandiose architectural riders. To steeples they added another substantial external feature, the portico. Also, where possible, they wanted their churches to be free-standing on 'insular' sites; that way they would be seen to their best advantage. Christ Church satisfies both of these stipulations. Indeed, the church probably dominates the neighbourhood as much today as it did when it was first put up.

Inside and out, Christ Church appears to be a simple 'basilican' church, with the nave, chancel and transepts squashed into a rectangular box-like centre, marked out by huge columns which are set on a series of tall pedestals. Yet with the aisles and the clerestory there is also a strong element of Gothic, echoed externally by the spire which soars high above the triumphal arches of the portico. It is, however, the church's scale which most baffles and delights.

'When you look down at the nave from the organ loft your sense of scale comes from the lack of enclosure at the periphery of your vision. You can't get that open-endedness with a camera. Or at least only if you use a wide-angled lens, a fish-eye lens, and then the image is extremely distorted,' says Charles Dance, who has spent many hours experimenting with his lenses in Christ Church. In order to appreciate what Hawksmoor was about, Dance believes, you need to examine the detail, you need to get up close, almost to *lose* your sense of proportion. 'For me the atmosphere of the church comes from the accumulation of detail. It's in the detail that the extraordinary originality and balance of Hawksmoor's vision is to be found.'

It was this vision that the Friends were trying to recover. In doing so, they intended to make good all those regrettable Victorian alterations effected in 1866 under the direction of Ewan Christian, the official architect to the Church Commissioners. As a Friends' publication from 1989 lamented:

'Christian's alterations severely damaged Hawksmoor's eighteenth-century design and radically changed the appearance of the church. He removed the galleries, the box pews and the wainscot linings; he lengthened the upper windows in the north and the south walls; he rearranged the west end; he altered the pedestals to the columns and he removed the old pulpit . . . the prosperous eighteenth-century silk weavers gave way to a variety of less fortunate immigrant populations and the Church found itself in the centre of a severely distressed area.'

The Friends began by repairing the sanctuary beam and then, in 1979, by reinstating the door on the south side of the church. Next they repaired the portico, relaid the west entrance steps and installed cast-iron railings and gates, designed by the church's architects, along Commercial Street. Inside the church, they restored the aisle windows to their original form, in readiness for the reinstatement of the missing galleries. They also removed the Victorian floors and salvaged, from beneath them, substantial remains of the Georgian pew platforms.

Money, naturally, had been a problem all along the line. Through a series of one-off grants and charitable donations they had – just about – balanced the books. Yet, in 1990, the future looked rosier. Fortunately for the Friends, the market developers, as principal sponsors for the Festival and, pending the acceptance of their development proposals, as generous benefactors towards the restoration, looked likely to see them OK. The Friends, in return, were bound to support the redevelopment and use their considerable influence in the architectural world to generate (how should one put it?) sympathetic noises towards the market redevelopment.

All this put Eddie Stride, the rector of Christ Church, in a rather tricky position. He was, after all, the man who, during the first few years of his incumbency, while the parish still worshipped in the chapel in nearby Hanbury Street, would refer to Christ Church disdainfully as the 'building on the corner'. As for the market development, he saw it as being funded by speculative business interests and underwritten by paper money that didn't exist. 'People talk quite happily of credit. As far as I'm concerned, credit is debt and debt is wicked. I don't want to see Spitalfields taken over by this financial empire with money held up as the only thing worth pursuing.'

Moreover, that the developers were possibly to put up the money for the church's restoration caused Stride considerable discomfort. 'This development should provide low-rent housing for ordinary people, but it needs the will to do that. I don't know if the developers have that will.'

This ambivalence stretched to the new inhabitants of the Georgian houses in Fournier Street. 'The new immigrants in Spitalfields tend to be people who have a certain taste, which they share with the people who come to the concerts during the music festival. They are quite likely to be people who won't be here at the weekend because they have another place to go to. Some of the new immigrants have come here expecting to make a killing and they'll leave when they've made it. They tend to be a bit upmarket, I think it's true to say.'

Before training for ordination, during the last war, Stride was a shop steward (his engineering company was later responsible for the parking meters in Fournier Street). It was helpful to know this when talking with him. It helped to explain his rather unnerving stands-to-reason manner. Much of what he said appeared to have several thick lines drawn conclusively beneath it, *quod erat demonstrandum*. 'People say I'm unsophisticated for speaking my mind. People feel that beating around the bush is intellectually respectable. I remind them of what St Paul says in Ephesians 6 about the need to defend oneself against the wiles of the ungodly, "Put on the whole armour of God," and later, "Take up the shield of faith by which you can quench the fiery darts of the wicked".'

We were talking in the rectory, when the bell rang. He went to the front door and let in a couple of overalled men who said that they had come for the table. As they were carrying a large dining room table out to the van, Stride told me how a neighbour had recently suggested that he take one of his bookcases along to a Christie's auction. It was one he'd bought in Eastbourne for £30 some thirty-five years previously and it wasn't going to fit into his new house. Much to his delight, it turned out to be Georgian and went for £1,000. He was hoping the dining-room table might reach a fair price too.

When we returned to the kitchen and our mugs of tea, he'd remembered what it was he found so difficult about this deal between Christ Church and the market developers. 'I've always mistrusted middle-class charm, I still do. It's opportunist. And it's no substitute for virtue.'

It was Michael Gillingham, Stride's eminently charming neighbour, who had given him such handy advice on the sale of his bookcase. Indeed, it had been partly on account of his 'splendid collection of eighteenth-century furniture and needlework' (as identified by the Spitalfields Trust) that Mr Gillingham was such an obvious candidate for the purchase of

4-6 Fournier Street when the Trust was looking to sell it on. He was clearly the sort of resident they were seeking in order to bring these Georgian houses back to life. As an expert in antique organs and their cases, he had also been involved in the plans for the restoration of Christ Church, in particular its very fine eighteenth-century organ.

'Of course, the character of the instrument is now pre-dominantly mid-Victorian, albeit with a clear eighteenth-century ancestry, most obvious in its highly decorated walnut case with its richly moulded cornices and gilt enrichments, truly Baroque in spirit. I must say, though, that when it comes to the restoration, the work of all periods must be respected.'

The same could not be said, however, for the restoration of his own house. One of the first pieces of work he commissioned was the removal of the extension which had been added to the back of the house in the nineteenth century.

'When the extension was removed the house breathed a huge sigh of relief and settled back into its original shape, its sense of natural proportion, which has something to do with the shape of the rooms and the ratio of window to wall,' said Gillingham, referring, in particular, to his handsome façade, with its central door and balancing bays, guarded along the pavement by wrought-iron railings and defined at each end by an impressive Doric pilaster.

Of course, in its ideal form, eighteenth-century town planning was concerned with submerging its varied façades into a single grand design or front, the creation of vistas through an ordered grid of streets, lanes and avenues. Yet in the early eighteenth century, and at the time Fournier Street was laid out, this emphasis on the cool and effortless production of a perfectly proportioned terrace of houses was less in evidence; in the 1720s domestic Georgian architecture tended more obviously to bear the marks of its individual craftsmen than the emerging techniques of mass-production would allow: its ironwork was more likely to be wrought than cast. Take the Rectory, at 2 Fournier Street, which was also built by Hawksmoor and which bears a clear visual relationship to Christ Church, particularly in its distinctive use of Portland stone for the external masonry on the doorcase, window-sills, cornice, parapet and chimney-tops. Here is a building which bridges the gap, in a very particular way, between the monumentality of Christ Church and the elegant domesticity of 4-6 Fournier Street. It is a house with a real sense of architectural propriety.

'Yet there's always rationality behind the way a Georgian house is put together, the way the rooms relate to one another, there's always a pragmatic explanation,' said Gillingham, looking very much the part of the Enlightenment Realist, waistcoated and pocket-watched, comfortably filling his kitchen chair. 'For example, in my own house, the positioning of the two staircases is significant. They would have allowed servants to pass freely about their business without disturbing quality when it came to visit the lady of the house. Of course, this was all lost again in the nineteenth century when the house became hopelessly divided up and the rooms began to be used in a very ad hoc sort of way.'

Much of the work of the conservation architect is spent negotiating a path between the retrieval of the original fabric and its uses, and its necessary adaptation to contemporary needs and building requirements. Julian Harrap, one such architect, has worked on a number of houses in Spitalfields, including 4-6 Fournier Street. Typically, restoration work might include the repointing of fractured brick, the splicing of decayed joists, the splinting and repegging of cracked joists, the relaying and renailing of floorboards, the repair of early iron-work, the strengthening and respiking of the original stair treads and the nationwide search for appropriate hand-made pantiles for the roof covering. The challenge, as Harrap sees it, is to 'make the buildings structurally sound and habitable by modern standards whilst at the same time retaining the interest and quality of the old buildings'.

His workers have a slightly more expedient attitude to the task of restoration. A group of them restoring a house in Wilkes Street described the response of a client to a new sink unit he had bought for his Georgian house. 'When he got it home he said he didn't like it because it looked too new – it was an old house, you see – and so when he went out we went to work on it with our hammers and mallets and spikes and chains and files and sorted it out and afterwards it looked really good, very effective. It had the right feel about it.'

To come across such shameless retro-chic in the rather precious world of Georgian house restoration was surprisingly refreshing. As it was to pick up some local history, albeit second-hand. 'You see that window up there, the one with work being done on its glazing bars, that's where John Wilkes used to preach out of to the multitude of crowds who would stand around listening to him on the street. John Wilkes was an MP, an actual MP, as in Parliament. Whether he lived in that house or whether he just used to preach from that window, I don't honestly know. I just heard it off of that historian who was taking a group of people round the area the other day, Mr Fisherman, someone said his name was, a very knowledgeable fellow. But whether the street got its name changed to Wilkes Street because of him, or whether it's just a coincidence, I don't know . . .'

It's also here, at this junction between Fournier Street and Wilkes Street, where Christ Church and the minister's house sit side by side, that Dan Cruickshank, architectural historian and local resident, also stops when he's leading a group around Spitalfields. It's here, he believes, you can experience something quintessential about the whole of Georgian London. 'This is the only place in London where you can really see the dynamic of eighteenth-century architecture at work, where you've got the monumental stone of the public building contrasting so wonderfully with the more modest domestic brick. It's the only place where you can get that complete vision of what it's all about, the juxtaposition of public and private, the perfect control of scale.'

Is not this, then, at the heart of the New Georgian vision of Spitalfields: balance, control, harmony? As a classical aesthetic, resisting mess and untidiness, it seems to cherish propriety and see the eighteenth century as a repository of correct good taste. Conversely, anything which has its origin in the nineteenth century is felt to be architecturally, not to say socially, anathema. Cruickshank talks of this period of the area's history like a distressing memory which refuses to be forgotten: he acknowledges it, but without affection, and is quick to shift his attention on to something altogether more wholesome and 1720s. Like Commercial Street, which was tunnelled out in the 1870s through the middle of Georgian Spitalfields, Victorian Spitalfields, the Spitalfields which is celebrated in the cockney mythology of the area and is preserved in the traditions of the street markets and pubs, is seen as a betrayal of the area's proper destiny as a residential suburb. The New Georgians see themselves as redirecting the area back to its eighteenth-century roots.

This championing of the 1720s as an era of remarkable social and cultural coherence in the area's history was made most clearly by Mark Girouard in the pages of *Country Life* in 1979. In a series of articles which drew the attention of the magazine's readership to the quality of its architectural heritage and the work of the Spitalfields Trust, he calls for 'the revival of Spitalfields in something of the form it had in the eighteenth century, as an area where people of many types, races and classes can live and work together in a civilised environment and in buildings of humane scale. Such a revival would involve the reversal of the trend which has ruled London since the nineteenth century segregating people in one-class residential areas, far away from their work . . .'

It was a vision which seemed to inspire great passion amongst a very particular group of people. Like the Friends of Christ Church, many of the New Georgians would talk of saving Spitalfields in much the same way that certain clergy talk of saving souls, and with something of the same zeal. Many would want to tell you their favourite tales of improvement and rehabilitation, their most successful 'conversion' experiences and structural renewals. If you were lucky you'd be shown the wounds on their hands where they once cut themselves salvaging a number of discarded architraves from a demolition skip. And in the right mood they would share with you their hopes for the future of Spitalfields, as it so rapidly changed, their fantasies of an eighteenth-century Eden.

Dan Cruickshank was one such man. As a writer of books about Georgian London as well as an editor of the *Architectural*

Journal, he was something of an authority. His knowledge of Christ Church and the stock of Georgian houses in Spitalfields was vast and detailed. His enjoyment of all their peculiarities of design and construction was engagingly apparent as he breathlessly tripped up over his own enthusiasms (for panelling, brickwork, roof pitches and so on and so on), moving in and out of such architectural asides with donnish circumspection. It was said he could recite the 1708–1709 Building Act from memory.

Cruickshank's actual involvement with Spitalfields dates back to 1977 when, along with a group of journalists, publishers and fellow architectural historians, he formed the Spitalfields Historic Buildings Trust. The story of the Trust's first confrontation with the world of property development is a daring and subversive one. It has all the ingredients of high drama: money, passion and a whiff of scandal involving a couple of early eighteenth-century houses in Elder Street which the developers wanted to raze and the Trust wanted to save. With the bulldozers getting ready to move in, the Trust noisily effected its own occupation (what the newspapers delightedly reported as the 'top persons' sit-in') and, during the subsequent legal wranglings, successfully managed to pull the purse strings of some City friends and persuade the developers to change their plans. At the eleventh hour, the houses were granted a reprieve.

Cruickshank subsequently bought his own house in Elder Street, one of the only two remaining Georgian terraces (the other being Folgate Street) which have survived on the Bishopsgate side of Commercial Street. It is probable that Cruickshank's own house, positioned as it is at the southern end of the terrace, was completed some time in 1727. Put up speculatively as part of the housing boom at the beginning of the eighteenth century, it is likely to have been first occupied, either leased or purchased outright, by a member of the rich merchant class. Only in the nineteenth century, with the general 'decline' of the area, would the house have seen multiple occupancy as the prosperous merchants and professionals were replaced by labourers, market porters and dockers, all transient to a degree. This persisted, Cruickshank points out, until the 1970s. 'When I arrived here in 1976 the street was still highly tenemented and the house itself was being lived in by two families and other individuals. It was in a really terrible state with buckets catching water in the attic rooms and ceilings collapsing all over the place. Terrible.'

In fact it was only in the 1950s and 1960s that the former focus of these streets, Spital Square, was destroyed to make room for the market's lorry park. (The one house which survived is occupied, appropriately, by the Society for the Protection of Ancient Buildings and its offshoot, the Georgian Group.) This was where you would have found the houses with grand urban pretensions, rich in plasterwork and exquisite joinery, sporting some of the finest panelling in London. Together with Folgate Street and Elder Street, this used to be the heart of the silk-weaving industry in Spitalfields. Built up as a collection of courts and alleyways off Bishopsgate, on the site of the old hospital priory, these few streets would, in the eighteenth century, have formed a discrete and self-sufficient administrative unit, with Spital Square at its centre. It was known as the Liberty of Norton Folgate.

The idea of the Liberty had caught the imagination of a number of local residents, including Cruickshank himself. 'The Liberty was so utterly contained and rather wonderfully admirable and, from looking at the records that survive, really very well run. It had two charity schools, one for the boys, one for the girls, it had its own courthouse, its own little church, two pairs of almshouses, one for destitute weavers and one for residents of Norton Folgate. It had six night watchmen, a beadle, daily collection of rubbish, sixty-one lights, which is more than we've got today, and a group of notables, of trustees, who were responsible for its overall government. It was a most wonderful, unconscious and informal piece of town planning.'

Spitalfields seemed to have come full circle. Just as the trustees of that eighteenth-century Liberty had guaranteed the area's identity, so too were the members of the Spitalfields Historic Buildings Trust as well as the Friends of Christ Church bringing to the area in the 1980s their money and professional status. With their involvement and patronage, Spitalfields had become increasingly fashionable. It had got itself a name. Those Georgian terraces which remained had been listed and subsequently deemed a conservation area by the council. In Elder Street and Folgate Street there was even talk of reinstating the boundary of the ancient Liberty, of re-establishing the original street plan. Then, with the possibility of the market redevelopment, it looked like something quite creative might be done. For Cruickshank, 'here was this major opportunity of resurrecting the mighty Spital Square, the eighteenth-century heart of Spitalfields. The developers could have put back what was there; it wouldn't have been a cowardly act, it would have been an act of bravery.'

It was not an idea, however, which apparently had any commercial appeal for the developers, who looked set to dwarf the Georgian Group's offices in Spital Square beneath a precipice of high-rise commerce. Despite their support for the restoration of Christ Church, they were not prepared to underwrite the construction of a New Georgian theme-park in Spitalfields. After all, they had their own vision of where the area was going.

A little tricky

'Shall I be mummy?' suggested Shoulderpads, who had taken the seat at the head of the table, and was about to start ladling out the broth. A ring on the doorbell interrupted her. I went to answer it.

'How do?' said the man on the door, walking straight past me, followed by a woman smelling like the perfume department at Harrods. 'We're expected to dinner. Newbolt family.'

'That's correct, sir. If you'd like to step through here.'

'Terrific! Knew it was the right address.' Then, handing me an attaché case and other bits of office hardware, he asked, 'Say, old chap, I couldn't just dump these with you, could I?'

'Of course, sir.'

'Darlings!' greeted Shoulderpads from the dining room, waving the ladle (early Georgian) in the air, 'come in, come in, we thought we'd lost you. Welcome to the Eighteenth Century!'

The man, who was just stepping out of the darkness of the hall, looked around himself, at the table laid for dinner, the candle sconces, the portrait of Jonathan Swift above the fire place. 'A pretty decent-looking place you've found here, Sally babes.'

'Yeah, spooky, don't you think?' said Bert.

'Certainly is.'

'Boggy and Georgie, I don't think you've met my parents Bertie and Joan, and this is Graham, my brother.' There was a general mêlée of handshaking and kissing and squeezing of flesh, until Shoulderpads, wriggling her cleavage into position, remarked archly, 'Boggy works with me at the Union Bank. He's a market-maker and earns an absolute fortune, don't you Bogs?'

'I'm comfortable,' said Bogs in that velvety voice used only by vicars and the incredibly wealthy, 'I'm comfy, let's leave it at that.'

Shoulderpads finished serving the broth and then insisted that the late-comers try the punch, an original recipe, made with brandy and lemon juice and, would you believe it, strained milk.

'Let's go for it,' said Boggy, enthusiastically, 'I'm all for the full ethnic experience.'

Part of the frustration of working as footman was that I would often have to break off half-way through an interesting eaves-drop to collect another dish or decant another bottle of wine. Moreover, there was only a certain amount of attentive loitering I could do without drawing attention to the fact that I was listening in. For long stretches of the evening I would catch only snippets of anecdote, fragments of conversation, the odd unconnected punchline. I had, therefore, to develop a whole series of footmanly errands which legitimately took me within earshot of the dining-room guests: re-arranging the serving spoons on the side-table, placing another log on the fire, peering out of the dining-room window, circling the table to fill the glasses.

Sometimes Julian would tell me to leave the soup tureen on the table, allowing the guests to help themselves to more. On other occasions he would tell me to whip it away as soon as the final bowl was served. It was flexi-time, giving him an opportunity to synchronise the kitchen with the dining room. Today he was running late. He wanted it away.

Julian removed the salmon from the oven and sprinkled flakes of sea salt over the golden scales of sculptured pastry. He then lifted the fish, all eighteen inches of it, and laid it on a bed of samphire, a green sea-weedy vegetable.

I took up the salmon dish. I took up the fricasséed chickens. I took up the creamed parsnips and sautéed cucumbers. The fried oysters. The saddle of lamb. Each dish was met with successively feebler cries of delight and more emphatic groans of disbelief until finally, when I took up the tiny dish of rowan jelly, a complement to the lamb, there was a quiet, palpably enervated, sigh. I had the feeling I had just cracked one bad joke too many. In the early eighteenth century all the main-course food was served at once and the guests would then have proceeded to make a selection from those dishes within arm's reach. The sight, however, of all this food symmetrically arranged around Julian's dining table was enough to silence even the most garrulous twentieth-century guest. Its arrival left sentences trailing away into the middle distance and provided a good opportunity for guests to disentangle themselves from potentially sticky conversations. The meal lurched one step nearer the port.

'Oh heavens, I don't know where to begin,' flirted Shoulderpads, faced with the job of carving the lamb.

'I'll slice her up, if you want,' offered Bogs, taking the carving knife out of Shoulderpads' hand.

'Oooh, careful with that knife, Boggy dear, I'm sure it's absolutely lethal,' tittered Mrs Bert.

'The lad's OK, he's done it before, you can tell he knows his way around a joint of lamb. Aren't I right, Georgie?' said Mr Bert.

'Completely right,' she enthused, 'he's simply *marvellous* with all kinds of meat.'

'I wonder if the serving utensils are original?' said Graham, checking the hallmark on his own cutlery.

After they had piled their plates with food and I had filled their glasses with wine, Mr Bert coughed everyone to attention. 'I would like us all to raise our glasses to Sally. May her next thirty years be as successful as her first thirty, and the thirty after that, well, may the thirty after that be successful too.'

'To Sally – To Sally – Success – Sally – Sally – Success,' everyone chorused.

'Speech!' boomed Bogs.

'You shut your face,' snapped Shoulderpads. 'I say, "Tuck in".'

At her command everyone tucked in and very soon the sound of munching replaced that of talking. I withdrew to the kitchen where I found Julian relaxing in his Windsor chair by the range. Hoxton was curled up contentedly on his lap. A glass of brandy was in his hand. It was at this time – once the rush of plucking and drawing, of basting and braising and browning was over – that Julian settled into more expansive ruminations, considering the future of the business, of the area, of the city, of the nation. Spitalfields, with its shabby dilapidation, had, over the last ten years, provided the setting for his Robinson Crusoe attempt at transforming a wrecked house into a bijou estate, complete with its paid staff (Man Friday) and tradition of hospitality. He had prospered under the economic buoyancy of the 1980s, when money was flush and consumption was ostentatious, and he was conscious of his debts. 'I don't want to hear a word against her,' he'd say with all the briskness of an over-protective nanny. Yet, with his Old Etonian nonchalance, he was also keen to distance himself from the vulgarity of the market place, its emphasis on accountability and performance and consumer rights. Income from the dinners was 'pocket money' rather than a living wage. It was more a hobby than a business. Frankly, it was expendable.

'*Mea culpa!*' exclaimed Julian suddenly, '*mea maxima culpa*: I've forgotten the lemons for the fish!' Juggling the fruit frantically into a dish, he worded his apology. 'Mr Humphreys presents his compliments – you've got to say that, I'm sure it's correct to say that – and requests Miss Newbolt's – no, you can't say that, you don't know if she's married – requests *madam's* pardon for the late arrival of the lemons.' I took them upstairs.

'Terrific!' said Bogs, taking the dish out of my hand before I have a chance to say anything, 'More food! Ah, lemons! Anyone fancy a slice of lemon? I'll chuck them in the middle and you can help yourselves.' The conversation then turned to the subject of Spitalfields. Slowly circling the table with the wine, I remember it as going something like this:

MR BERT: Should think he gets all his lemons from the market, it's not very far to go to get your fruit and veg, is it? I mean it's not what you would call inconvenient. Too bad that it's moving.

GRAHAM: At least he's got the house; these houses will be worth a fortune when the market goes, he'll be laughing then. I wonder how much this place means to him now? It must be worth at least four hundred grand and that's *before* modernisation.

SHOULDERPADS: I think it will be really sad when the market goes, it's got such a lot of character. It's been here for hundreds of years, it will be the end of an era. If you come up to the Ten Bells around lunchtime it's just amazing to see all the rubbish scattered all over the road, whole boxes of avocados, the lot, some really good stuff too. And all the scavengers: it's like something out of Dickens. I'll tell you what I do sometimes, I go up behind one of these West Indian women – there's a whole group of them, housewives with carrier bags – I'll go up to her and say, 'That's a pretty decent pineapple or whatever you've got there,' and I bet you anything you like she'll reach out and give it to me, she'll say, 'Here. You have. You take.' That way I can get the free fruit without even having to bend over to pick it up!

BOGS: That's all very well, Sally, but what I really resent is seeing the church become a playground for all those hobos, smashing their bottles against the walls, urinating all over the pavement, leaving their rubbish just cluttering up the street. I mean, that building is one of the finest examples of English Baroque we have, and to see it in that kind of setting really gets my goat. I'm sorry, I just feel very strongly about this.

MRS BERT: That's OK, Boggy, I'm sure you're absolutely right.

BOGS: Well, to my mind, Hawksmoor you see is the man, he's the absolute man. That portico, its size and strength, just leaves me breathless. It's saying: 'I know what I'm talking about, I know what I'm doing, I have supreme confidence.' Well, I just think he happens to be a genius, that's all.

GEORGIE: I'm afraid I agree with Bogs, Sally, I think you can over-romanticise the squalor. OK, sure, there's the church and a few decent houses and it's certainly convenient for work, but apart from that it's a pretty iffy area. With that hostel for alcos under the church and Brick Lane at the other end of the street, which is basically ninety per cent Pakistani, it's not exactly the King's Road, is it! Frankly, I'm not surprised there are so many eccentrics living around here. What with those creepos Gilbert and Sullivan, you know, the painters, and that American who gives tours of his timewarp house, I saw him on telly the other night, and, well, all this, I mean it's perfectly lovely, don't get me wrong . . .

MRS BERT: Don't worry, Georgie, I know exactly what you mean. Personally speaking, if you want to know my opinion, I find it all a bit pretentious, that's the only way I can describe it. Candlelight is fine for an evening, but it would get me down after a while, it's just not practical.

SHOULDERPADS: You don't want to take this candelabra business too seriously, Mum, it's all a big con really. I went round one of those tours in that American's house, just like this one in fact, and I mean it was OK, but you don't want to look too carefully, you don't want to look too closely. It's all a big fake really, it's all one big DIY job. It's just not real.

I poured the last drop of wine into Shoulderpads' glass and took the empty decanter downstairs. Julian was back in his Windsor, talking to the cat.

'Well?' he asked.

'They said the lamb was just right, the salmon was deliciously moist and the vegetables were cooked to perfection,' I lied. It was in my interests to keep Julian sweet. If he felt unappreciated, he might become punitive, and if he became punitive, the guests might become pissed off, and if the guests became pissed off, I might not get my tip. 'The lemons,' I added. 'They were particularly pleased with the lemons.'

'Hmmm. What do you think, Hoxton? Do you think they're appreciative enough? What's that, darling?' he said, putting his ear beside the cat's face. 'You think they might be a little difficult, do you? You think they could be a little tricky, do you? Hmmm, well, we'll see.'

Pretty standard postmodernist stuff

Nevertheless, on reflection, maybe Shoulderpads was right to highlight the depthlessness of the New Georgian aesthetic, its self-conscious discontinuity with context, its readiness to turn the telling of history into 'one big DIY job'. While the myth of a New Georgian golden age may have been a useful invention for a particular group of people to locate its social aspirations around a notional understanding of good taste, it also bowdlerised history, distorted the past something rotten.

Walking down Fournier Street in the late 1980s, inspecting the cleaned-up façades, it was easy to forget that these same houses would have been put up speculatively by businessmen builders, borrowing against the promise of a building lease and working to fine deadlines. Constructing the house as quickly as possible, they used as many inferior and cheap materials (underburnt brick, corrosive lime mortar walls) as they could get away with. Looking at the obsessional care with which some of the houses had more recently been 'restored', it was easy to think that Spitalfields had been built not as an industrial suburb but as the showpiece of 'Georgian' architecture into which it has subsequently been gentrified. The fact is that it never had any of those swanky Georgian squares, all bloated with self-confidence, which punctuate the West End of London. Spital Square, its single example, although grander than other parts of Spitalfields, was distinctly modest in comparison with its west London equivalents. In general, Spitalfields' terraces were narrow and tightly-packed and were built without concern for vistas or vantage points. Not so much to be looked at as to be lived in, the houses were quickly filled by the prosperous Huguenot weavers.

Even though these Huguenots brought to the silk industry their Calvinistic sense of purpose and enjoyed periods of real prosperity, the business none the less suffered periodic fluctuations, at times plunging the journeymen apprentices into severe poverty. With the ending of Marlborough's wars in 1713, for example, competition from cheap silks which had been smuggled into the country from France threw the English market into confusion. Yet it was the introduction of printed calicoes which produced the most upset.

Despite ineffectual legislation dating back to 1700, which banned the import of the cloth, the wearing of calico continued as a cool and colourful substitute for woollens and silks, not least because it cost a fraction of the price of the latter. The fashion grew and reached a peak soon after 1717, when a slump in the weaving trade provoked the weavers to angry retaliation and a call for a total prohibition. In the hot summer days of 1719 the silk-weavers of Spitalfields, who were feeling the pinch particularly, began to riot. Handbills were posted. 'Must the poor weavers starve?' they asked, as the riots spread to nearby Moorfields and Bunhill Fields, and added indignantly, 'Shall the Ingy [East Indian] calicoes be worn whilst the poor weavers and their families perish?' With calico-wearing women risking verbal abuse – or worse – a group of Horse Guards was sent into Spitalfields, while reserves remained in the nearby Tower. It was only a further Calico Act in 1721, banning the import and wearing of the cloth, which brought an uneasy period of calm back to Spitalfields.

It is clear, from this period of unrest, that life in early eighteenth-century Spitalfields was very unlike the retrospective imaginings of those New Georgian conservationists such as Mark Girouard who longed for 'the revival of Spitalfields in something of the form it had in the eighteenth century' as 'an area where people of many types, races and classes can live and work together in a civilised environment'. In fact, such was the mutual hostility between the master weavers and the poorer journeymen that many of the latter, following the riots, claimed they had even seen their masters' wives, during that long hot summer, arrogantly flaunting the very calicoes they were trying to outlaw.

The conflict between the journeymen and the masters continued in this Georgian suburb of 'balance, control and harmony' throughout most of the century. Indeed, in the very spot where Dan Cruickshank would marvel at the aesthetic composition of the Georgian terrace, at the junction of Wilkes Street and Fournier Street, just opposite Christ Church, John Wilkes, the eighteenth-century radical MP, had roused the embittered journeyman weavers into political insurrection, as I had been told by a twentieth-century building worker. On 27 April 1768 he waved to his supporters from the upper window of the Three Tuns Tavern, outside Christ Church, responding to their enthusiastic cry of 'Wilkes and Liberty!' And in the following year journeymen protest turned into open revolt as Louis Chauvet, a wealthy Huguenot, had 67 looms smashed by some 1,500 angry journeymen in a demonstration against the importing of engine looms from Holland. Shortly afterwards, two prominent agitators were hanged in Bethnal Green. It was only the passage of the Spitalfields Act through Parliament in 1773, which strengthened the barriers against foreign competition and settled the rates of pay, which brought about a measure of cooperation between the journeymen and the master weavers of Spitalfields.

It is very easy to find any such number of anomalous little episodes which threw into question the New Georgian vision of eighteenth-century Spitalfields as a place of 'balance, control and harmony'. Such a reading of history clearly had more to do with the social aspirations of its twentieth-century 'gentrifiers' than the struggles of its contemporary residents. Nor did the discovery of such 'DIY history' particularly surprise me. I was by now familiar with the way that Spitalfields contained a variety of versions of its own past, each determined by the assumptions, implicit or explicit, of its host community.

What puzzled me more was the way that such historical misrepresentation should be presented as being philosophically respectable. The argument seemed to go something like this. Because ours is a fragmented culture, a jumble of incompatible realities, and because there can be no single authoritative vantage point from which to view 'the past', we need, there-fore, to recognise our histories for what they are, an endless struggle between rival stories or competing versions, a collection of 'imaginary homelands'. Rather than offering a window to the past, such histories are more like mirrors to the present, particularly when our strict temporal boundaries seem to blur altogether. Peter Ackroyd, author of the novel *Hawksmoor*, set in the East End and significantly in Spitalfields, has this to say about traditional chronological sequentiality: 'Recent work in cosmology and quantum physics seems to suggest that the 'flow' of time and causation do not really exist – that it is possible, for example, for events of the 'future' to determine the 'past'. Those of an imaginative disposition have known this for some years.'

Certainly Ackroyd 'knew' this in *Hawksmoor*. In this book the author alternates between the eighteenth and the twentieth centuries, between the necromantic obsessions of the architect of Christ Church Spitalfields (known in the novel as Dyer) and the strangely inert detective (known as Hawksmoor) who is investigating a series of murders, in which he, through some curious loop of history, appears to be personally implicated. In its mixing of the historical and the fantastic, and in its extended dream sequences when the narrative horizons seem to disappear altogether, Ackroyd questions this clear demarcation of linear causality.

'For when there was a light there was a shadow, and when there was a sound there was an echo, and who could say where one had ended and the other had begun?' he writes.

Of course, this may all be pretty standard postmodernist stuff, this play between fact and fiction, and it certainly makes for a jolly spooky detective story, but there were those who objected to a depiction of Hawksmoor (the architect) as a crazy obsessive. Gavin Stamp, for example, rose up to defend the honour of this most famous pupil of Christopher Wren from such suggestions of 'sensational and mendacious notoriety'. The real Hawksmoor, he ventured, was a fine upstanding man who had been 'laid to rest in a Herefordshire churchyard 250 years ago'. Not only was he 'one of the greatest of British architects', but the churches he built in East London in the early eighteenth century were 'wonderful masterpieces of the English Baroque' as well as 'tangible gestures against heresy'. Frankly, suggested Stamp, Ackroyd had 'perverted' history, libelling the dead and misrepresenting the architect's proud achievement.

So who was right? Was it Stamp, the apologist for High Church Anglican Spitalfields, or Ackroyd, its revisionist novelist? Or did these two authors simply articulate alternative accounts of the postmodern position? On the one hand, one might argue, there were the 'reactive' postmodernists, the individuals who wished to turn the clock back, to relive the past, or at least a particular version of it. By resorting to the sort of pastiche offered by notions of 'heritage', these 'reactives' would attempt, sometimes quite literally, to buy back second-hand time and in doing so distort authentic memory into an enhanced version of itself, the myth of 'a golden age'.

On the other hand, there were the 'avant-garde' post-modernists who, while recognising that we lived in a frag-mented culture, sought nevertheless to remake the fragments into a new pattern, to reinterpret our position in the modern world rather than shore it up in some fantasy past. These were the postmodernists who wanted to breathe new life into the Enlightenment project, a project that had somehow lost its way this century. Rather than turning the clock back, they were quite happy to dispense with the services of old Chronos altogether, delighting indeed in all manner of sequential juxtapositions, timewarps and anachronisms.

Yet, notwithstanding their differences, were not both these postmodern 'positions', in the end, little more than the lifestyle choices of a number of wealthy and intelligent middle-class residents, who, uneasy about their social status, had turned to the eighteenth century for the trappings of gentility?

The demon of suburbia

I began to see that this story of New Georgian Spitalfields was not just the story of what had happened over the previous fifteen years to a few terraces of eighteenth-century town houses. It was also the story of the emergence over this same period of a sensibility which was at once privileged, dilettante and exuberantly stylish. Defining itself in contrast to the policies (and buildings) thrown up within the post-war planning consensus, it championed the terraced house against the high rise, the inner city against the suburban overspill, a spirit of makeshift and mahogany against that of concrete conformity.

'The fact is, you see, the proportions of the houses are just so damn fine,' John Gaze, a Fournier Street resident, told me. 'Apart from anything, the ceiling heights are just right. The majority of Huguenots were small people like me, so the houses are really designed for someone of about five foot five, or five foot six. You see, you probably find the stairs a little steep – well, they're not for me, with my little legs. I just leap on up, no problem.'

Gaze was one of the first of the residents who moved into Fournier Street for its Georgian proportions. He remembered those early days, the suffering for beauty's sake, with some affection. 'I had no bath, I had to come over to the club every evening, when I closed the shop, to have one. I boiled water to shave in the morning. In fact, it was a bit like it was when I was a child – freezing cold, very dirty – and I spent my whole life filling skips. I loved it.'

There was always, it seemed, a certain camaraderie amongst these early residents, or 'pioneers' as they sometimes called themselves. 'If you're gay, you don't have kids, do you? You don't have a wife to support. You have a certain amount of freedom and obviously, by nature, the majority of our class of homosexuals – middle-aged and quite well-heeled – just love George the First houses! I mean, as soon as I got here, the whole street rallied round with offers of help and cups of tea and there was a terrific feeling of community – "Do come and have a bath in my place!", "Please borrow a hammer!", "Help yourself to some firewood!" and all that sort of thing – oh yes, it was great fun.'

That a group of gay men had settled in Spitalfields was hardly surprising. Apart from the early Georgian architecture, clearly an attraction, there was also its tradition of being an area hospitable to outsiders, tolerant of 'deviance' and eccentricity. Its well-proportioned houses, in urgent need of restoration, were quickly taken up by a body of men looking for a place to pitch camp.

'As far as I'm concerned, Spitalfields is a safe area, I've never had any trouble here. I remember, a couple of years ago, I was washing down the front of the house – it was Saturday afternoon – when I suddenly saw these skinheads walking up the street – it was all "fuckin' this" and "fuckin' that" – with their cans of lager, you know what I mean, and I thought, "Should I get down off the steps and go into the house?" and then I thought, "No! Why the hell should I?" When they got to me they looked up and one of them stared straight at me and said, "The trouble with this place is it's full of Pakis and poofs." "Actually, dear," I said, quick as a flash, "They're Bangladeshis." One of the party laughed, the other went bright red and they were gone.'

Eddie Stride was less easy to humour. Known for his hard-line views on homosexuality, he was seldom backward in coming forward. Gaze first communicated with him, shortly after he had moved into the street. He wrote explaining that, in 1822, his great-great-great grandfather had installed the chiming mechanism, since disappeared, for the bells at Christ Church and that it was his hope and intention to replace it. Stride wrote back to say that it was very nice having a Christian living in the street and that he hoped to see him in church on Sunday. Gaze replied by saying that he was, in fact, already parish clerk at St

Michael's Cornhill and, what was more, his rector was coming round to bless the house and would he (Stride) like to join them? Stride wrote back to say that it was blasphemy to bless anything except a human being and that homes were not to be blessed. The correspondence ended there.

'In fact, we had a lovely service in the weaver's loft. Michael and Donald held a candle each and Father did a marvellous job with the holy water.' He then added, a little impishly, 'It must make Mr Stride's job terribly difficult, don't you think? With half his parish being gay, and the other half being Muslim.'

Gaze became expansive. 'Of course, it will all change so rapidly when the market gets redeveloped. I don't think there'll be many more residential owners around here, it'll be mainly stockbrokers buying and doing up the houses as offices, maybe with some accommodation thrown in. And Brick Lane too will change. It'll be full of chi-chi little delicatessen shops serving the City. The City will just grab the whole thing. Of course, on the money front, I've done very well: I bought for forty thousand pounds in 1982 and I could sell up right now for four hundred thousand. With four hundred thousand pounds I could do very well in Chelsea, thank you very much. Well, yes, it's always at the back of one's mind, one's just waiting to see how things turn out . . .'

Clearly, however, the area still held some charm for Gaze. He told me the story of a friend of his, how he had invited him to Fournier Street for supper one evening and had suggested that, if he really wanted to see Spitalfields at its best, he should arrive by tube at Liverpool Street, come out on to Bishopsgate, turning right into Brushfield Street and then walk up towards Christ Church, passing the fruit and vegetable market on the left. Now when this man arrived at the house, he was – so Gaze reported – 'gobsmacked'. He said he had just walked past a huge bonfire outside the market, crowded round by a group of appalling-looking derelicts. One of them, staring wildly at him, had been pointing this huge black finger accusingly at the sky. The sight had been 'wonderful', 'very dramatic', 'pure Dürer'.

'Alas,' Gaze added, lowering his voice for effect, 'that fire will not be with us for very much longer.'

'But your Spitalfields, has that been saved?'

'Saved. It's a funny word, isn't it, does it mean preserved? Does it mean preserved or changed, I don't know. For me, to have saved Spitalfields means to have saved the fabric of the houses – but I'd like to think we could also have a nice Bohemian community living here, headed up by Gilbert and George. You've got Marianna with her panel paintings, Robert with his wood carving, Simon the potter, Julian and his eating house. You've got Rodney working on his plays, Ricardo printing his silk ties, Jim who makes those funny tables, Charlie the sculptor and then there's Dennis, dear old Dennis. What would we do without Dennis?'

What indeed. Like Julian Humphreys, Dennis Severs was another Spitalfields resident who had decided to make the eighteenth century pay. A Californian by birth, he came to England to go to law school in 1969 and ended up with a horse and trap giving history tours of Knightsbridge and Kensington. In 1979 he bought his house in Folgate Street and, restoring it room by room, wove into its restoration the story of a Huguenot silkweaver's family, following its fortunes through the five floors of his house, over a period of about a hundred and fifty years. Having completed the renovation, he devised a 'tour' of the house, which he would give, or perform, to groups of between six and ten people. As much a social history of Spitalfields as the story of a single family, the tour was also a piece of supremely energetic theatre.

When you arrived at Severs' house in Folgate Street, you were left to wait with the other ten or so people who had booked in. From the outside his house looked like a tourist staggering through customs at Heathrow, self-consciously wearing the national dress, the togs and tassels, of another culture: canaries twittered in a cast-iron cage beside the door, straw covered the pavement, watercress grew as illogically as a hair transplant across the steps, vermilion shutters flirtatiously obscured the ground-floor windows, an oil lamp spluttered its shadow across the road. As seven o'clock chimes, you might notice the letterbox flutter and you'd know he was in there, making a few last-minute adjustments. Then the door was

pulled open and out he came towards you: stocky yet surprisingly nimble, balding, bearded. He twinkled his greeting
playfully. He opened his mouth: North American.

'As we go round the house, please remember every room we
go into is lived in, every bed you see is slept in, every table,
chair, candlestick is used. This isn't a museum, it's my home. I
live here with the Jervis family, master silk weavers of
Spitalfields, and tonight we're going to follow them round the
house, we're going to enter each of the rooms just after the
family has left and before the servants come to clear up.' Severs
talked breathlessly, in a sort of stage whisper, bringing you
sneakily into the conspiracy. 'We'll hear them, we'll smell them,
we might even catch a glimpse of them. We're going to learn a
lot about this family, and who knows, we might even learn
something about ourselves.'

'One more thing,' he said, switching on a rather more
censorial tone. 'I'm an American, I wasn't born superior, I'm
only as good as my job . . . If I explode it simply means that
someone is so full of attitude, so out of tune with what I'm
trying to do that he is preventing me from doing my job.' With
this warning he would let you into his house, take you
downstairs and lock you in his basement.

Severs put you in the basement to soften up your
imagination. It was the storm at the beginning of *The Tempest*,
the wardrobe into the land of Narnia. In the pitch dark and dank
cold of the room, one would hear, transmitted over a pre-
recorded tape, the history of early Spitalfields, how it grew up
on the site of St Mary's Spital, a medieval hospice just outside
the City wall, and how from its earliest days it became a centre
of Nonconformity, where all the Protestant denominations
could get on with the important business of hating one another,
of defining their identities.

The basement experience was not, however, everyone's idea
of a good night out. Some groups demanded to be let out.
Others would be told to go. Indeed, Severs got almost as much
pleasure in throwing certain people off the tour as he got in
performing it. His capacity for pique was legendary. The Italian
ambassador had been shown the door, as had senior politicians

– 'That's right, out they all went.' It seemed that the three high risk groups were intellectuals, interior designers and people who requested to go the loo mid-way through a tour: 'I just send them back to the suburbs so they can get on with rearranging their Habitat furniture.'

If, however, you got to experience the whole house, you would hear the *Roots*-like saga of the five generations of the Jervis family. The story begins in 1685, following the revocation of the Edict of Nantes by Louis XIV and the renewed persecution of the Huguenots. Isaac Jervois, a twelve-year-old boy of a Protestant family, is smuggled out of France in a wine cask and across the Channel. Arriving in London, homeless and penniless, an avuncular weaver takes him on as an apprentice and teaches him the trade. He discovers he has considerable flair for design and quickly makes his mark in the fashion world of early eighteenth-century London. He marries the daughter of a Fleet Street mercer and, in 1724, he buys the Folgate Street house and moves into this emerging suburb of Spitalfields.

Their son, Edward, inheriting his father's Protestant serious-mindedness, works hard and successfully as a master weaver. Courting the aristocratic and extravagant Elizabeth St John, he eventually marries her and gains entry into the landowning Establishment. She gives birth to William, who grows up to squander his father's reputation (there are violent family arguments in the withdrawing room over the question of gambling debts) and insult his father's simple faith with his trendy Romantic agnosticism. In the 1840s William's son, Shelley, struggles to maintain the household against impending bankruptcy, replacing the looms in the garret floor with lodgers in an attempt to make financial, if not woven, ends meet. The family line, and story, ends with Isobel, Shelley's daughter (Isaac's great-great-grand-daughter) who lives out the nine-teenth century and Queen Victoria's reign in spinsterly and eccentric bed-sitterdom.

Through keeping house for his fantasy family, Severs has furnished us with a history of Spitalfields snobbery, the ornamentations and counter ornamentations of social one-upmanship, of a community's attempt to keep up with the

Jervises. We hear of the rivalry between Elizabeth and her neighbour Mrs Stillwell, their terribly, terribly polite disagreements over matters of taste and decoration, their deceptively eirenic-sounding snubs and put-downs. Their social exchanges are arch and niggling: Mrs Jervis regrets dreadfully that she won't be able to join Mrs Stillwell 'at home', having previously arranged to spend these hours supervising the clipping of her canaries' claws; Mrs Stillwell is very sorry to hear that Mrs Jervis won't be coming to tea, particularly since she will be serving Earl Grey's latest mixture, a wonder cure – so she has been told – for chronic dyspepsia.

Elizabeth Jervis moves the withdrawing room from the ground floor to the *piano nobile*, in order to introduce a little more ceremony to the reception of guests. She instructs the footman to parade the visitor with due dignity up the stairs to the the first floor. The room itself she keeps graciously old-fashioned (for the 1770s) with its Stuart ceiling and baroque mouldings. Frankly, she finds the current fad for the neoclassical all rather parvenu. Let Mrs Stillwell follow the fashions, she says, defiantly arranging her walnut festoons, with their distinctive rococo associations, about the room. As she sits in her favourite chair to the right of the fire, with the walls flickering forest green in the light from the scallop-shaded candles and the smell of wood ash from the cinders sweetened by the scent of lavender flowers which hang about the skirting, she considers, with some degree of nostalgia, her mother's aristocratic confidence. Then she thinks of poor Mrs Stillwell, poor, impressionable, breeze-in Mrs Stillwell.

The story Severs told in his timewarp house was one of conflict and reconciliation, of fallings-out and makings-up, of one generation superseding another with its particular concerns and its differing notions of good taste. In Severs' hands heritage became something with internal contradictions and anomalies, something living. Historically, the narrative which accompanied his tour may have been as fanciful as those golden age accounts given by members of the New Georgian gentry, but aesthetically it was far more persuasive. With his excess of imagination, his genius for detail and his skill at depicting in the design of the house the aspirations of its former occupants, he was able to lay bare the social and domestic antagonisms which drove his family forward. By identifying the cross-currents of style between successive generations, his magical mystery tour managed to bring their story to life around a series of vivid incidents and encounters. Definitely more 'avant-garde' than 'reactive', he exploded the idea that 'heritage' needed necessarily to be something static and conservative, something preserved in aspic.

The quibbles and rivalries he dramatised were all, of course, in Severs' head. As with the Jervis family, his own Spitalfields was a Spitalfields of umbrage and one-upmanship, in which everyone was brought together within the endlessly hospitable, endlessly alienating round of gossip and intrigue. Like those earliest dissenting Protestants, who came to Spitalfields as exiles and immigrants, he had come to Spitalfields cocking a snook at Californian suburbia, tilting at dried-up art historians and over-precious interior designers, looking for a home for his own fantasy past. And along with his self-styled Bohemian neighbours, he had found one in the restoration of his early eighteenth-century house. Through bringing it back to life, room by room, he was also able to re-invent himself, to come into his own inheritance, ancestral portraits, family silver. He was able to become the irreverent tearaway son of upper-class Huguenot descent.

As well as a strong identification with the petty rivalries of his Huguenot 'forebears', he had also acquired something of their high-born hauteur. Both Severs and Gaze talked disparagingly about the upwardly-mobile middle classes who passed through Spitalfields in their predatory BMWs, looking to make an opportune property speculation. 'They come up to Spitalfields expecting to see row upon row of Palladian houses,' said Gaze, 'and then they take one look at the filth in the street, one look at the meths drinkers, one look at the prostitutes, before going straight back to Hampstead or Barnes or Chigwell or wherever they come from.'

Severs was similarly dismissive of those who failed to enter into the spirit of his house, who refused to collude in his fantastical account of Spitalfields sensibility. It was precisely those visitors who drew attention to the join between fantasy and reality, who were more interested in the mechanics of the tour – how he did the smells, how he caused the plates to rattle, where the speakers were concealed, where he bought his 'furnishings' – than the spectacle of the show, who were most at risk from peremptory ejection. Sometimes, after they had all gone home, after he had stuffed their cash into his money jar, he would hiss at their miserable suburban ways.

In fact, the demon of suburbia seemed to hover around the whole of this conservation community like a spectre which threatened at any time to overwhelm it. But whence the fear? After all, with their obvious investment in the fabric of Spitalfields, surely both the Neo Geos as well as the Bohemian set, 'reactive' and 'avant-garde' alike, had themselves been primary agents in the gentrification of the area? Having opened it up so successfully as 'pioneers' how could they then begrudge the subsequent arrival of the 'settlers' in the form of middle-class suburbia? Or was I missing something?

Sneer

Indeed I was. I had decided to come clean and tell my mother that I had lost the family ring. I wrote her a letter. A few days later I received a small package from her in the post. A bomb?

I opened it to find a book, handwritten by her own mother about my grandfather, some years after he had died. It was a family document, a collection of fondly told stories and affectionately remembered details. My grandmother had glued together three ring-bound notepads, which she had then covered with wrapping paper, sticking a label on the front, 'John Goodacre, the Story of a Good Man'. Enclosed in the package was also a card from my mother, suggesting that since it appeared I had lost his ring, it was maybe time I found out more about its former owner. She added, not without edge, that were I planning to lose this too, maybe I could take the trouble to photocopy it first.

It was a gracious gesture. But somehow I was unable to

respond in kind. New Georgian Spitalfields, probably the version of the area in which I felt most at home, privileged aesthetics over ethics, beauty before charity. Why should I want to read the story of a *good* man? In my role as footman I had cultivated a sneering anti-suburban archness. I thought I was being urbane and sophisticated. Who was it that said that, were Jesus to return today, rather than crucifying him, we would simply invite him to dinner and hear what he had to say and then make fun of it all?

I put my grandmother's book in a box.

We always say that Spitalfields is Typical Planet Earth

It was Gilbert and George who pioneered the self-made arty aristos of Spitalfields. They first moved into Wilkes Street in the 1960s when they were poor art students looking for cheap digs.

'It was very run-down, just what we needed. The old generation of Jewish landlords would rent you the floor of a building as a workshop,' said George.

'And turn a blind eye to your living there,' added Gilbert.

'Eventually, we got the house –'

'And then the studio –'

'And that's all we needed –'

'The atmosphere was brilliant –'

'We say walking up Brick Lane is more exciting than walking up the Charing Cross Road,' said George.

'We think the trouble around here was largely invented; all that talk of bad racist attacks, it never happened,' said Gilbert.

'Exaggerated, in any case. By people who went to public school, media people.'

'In fact it's very peaceful around here. The Bengalis are not at all aggressive.'

'It's terrific.'

'It's amazing.'

Having seen them often in the Market Café, or passed them on the street, I had approached Gilbert and George one day, explaining my interest in the area, to talk about Spitalfields. They invited me to afternoon tea. 'In case you're wondering,' I was told by a regular at the Market Café, 'George is the one who looks like Eric Morecambe, Gilbert is the one who looks like Ernie Wise.'

Now, I had also seen them on television and read a number of profiles and interviews in the press and was certainly familiar with the way they talked in their peculiar dovetailed sentences, as though they were competing for the same lines. I had assumed, however, that once you sat with them around their tea table, found yourself lounging in their art deco chairs and chewing the fat over a cup of Tetley's, they would relax into amiable chit-chat, bicker fondly with one another over trivial domestic details, call each other by some absurdly cosy pet names. At the very least I expected they would camp it up a bit, unbutton those suits, enjoy a bit of a gossip. Not so, however. Throughout the whole of our tea-time engagement they remained relentlessly serious, didactic to a slightly embarrassing degree, preferring slogans – what they called their 'G & G sayings', such as 'Education is Organised Bigotry' or 'the Force behind all Life is Sex' – to the idle pleasantries of neighbourhood small-talk.

Having met at the St Martin's School of Art in 1967, Gilbert and George launched their career with their performance of the 'singing sculpture', and then, moving into Spitalfields, they developed their distinctive photomontages soon after: mosaics of rectangular images borded by black frames, assembled into huge grids of colour and symmetry, usually containing images of Gilbert and George themselves, proprietorial and besuited. These photo-pieces, remarkably like posters, were bold and declamatory and were often given small, hard and explicit titles such as *London, Hope, Bad God, Cunt Scum, Life, Shit Faith, Class War, True Man, Death* and so on. In 1984 they won the Turner Prize. They have continued to delight and disturb the viewing public ever since.

By appearing themselves in each photo-piece, by making themselves and their manifest friendship the subject of their work, they attempt to make universal what is specific and particular about their life. Starting from the (indeed, post-modernist) position that there is no hidden meaning behind the surface of things, they go on to use their imagination to transform their environment. Spitalfields imagery – Christ Church, panoramic views of the City, scenes from Brick Lane – become in their work merely the backdrop to the newly realised world of G & G. And they encourage us to make a similar journey, pointing the way, through our own particular contexts, to the creation of plural worlds, multiple moralities, in which a person may grow into his own work of art, may follow his own individual aesthetic . . .

It's not, however, a round trip. My attempts to return them to matters of local gossip were categorically ignored, my efforts at small-talk – 'I see the Rector has painted his door red . . .', 'I hear Marianna's organising a poetry and wine evening at the big house . . .', 'Did you get the circular about the extension of the rehabilitation centre in the church crypt?' – were made to look very small indeed.

'We feel we have more of a finger on the pulse of the world than any other artist living, probably,' said Gilbert, remarkably unselfconsciously. 'We are reduced to tears when we realise the world is inhabited by all these desperate people, turning in pain the whole time.'

'We don't feel we need to go to arty dinner parties to learn about it.'

'If you look at the first puddle you see when you leave this house, you'll see your face and you'll see two dead matchsticks, a bit of a dog's jobby, an empty cigarette packet, a weed beside it – nothing is more encompassing than that. It's all there. There's nothing that's not there, in fact.'

'Yes,' I replied rather cautiously, 'you seem to use a lot of Spitalfields imagery in your work.'

'But these are universal images,' said Gilbert.

'We always say that Spitalfields is Typical Planet Earth,' said George.

'Is that why you live here?'

'We live here because we can do what we want here.'

'We're protected from the educated classes.'

'We're free to live on the edge, to push out the possibilities of our art.'

'We're free to influence the future of civilisation.'

'We can think new thoughts. We believe that humanoids have scarcely begun to discover the extent of their powers.'

'We believe, for example, that humanoids, one day, will be able to fly.'

'Unassisted.'

'Well, why not?'

Sensing my resistance, George took a swipe at my 'organised bigotry': 'If we weren't like this we'd be sitting in Hampstead, with a paperback stuffed up our jumpers, talking about Proust.'

He then began another train of thought. 'Life is invisible anyway – if you walk down Fournier Street, you can never remember the colours of the doors or any of the people you meet. It's all invisible, isn't it? We make it all up in our memory.'

Gilbert recognised his cue. 'Every time we walk down the street we get a different view of the church, it's never the same view. The church is always the same church, but our view of it changes the whole time.'

'As far as we're concerned, all life is artificial. As far as we're concerned, the humanoid is a completely artificial idea,' George said and immediately stood up. He suggested that we go upstairs to take a look at the view from their roof-terrace. This is where they went, they said, to see the residents of Spitalfields 'turning in pain'. Standing on the narrow terrace I could clearly see into my own garret room on the other side of the street and made a mental note to relocate my bed along the opposite wall. Gilbert, meanwhile, enthused about the panoramic skyline, pointing out his favourite buildings. George told me about the chimney pots. In the distance we could just identify Hampstead, hazy and secluded. Nearer to home was the Bishopsgate office frontier and closer still the deserted market place. A light drizzle left Fournier Street looking black and shiny and Christ Church a smudgy grey colour. It occurred to me that, with the help of these weird Peter Pan characters, this *folie à deux*, I could just float off into space.

'It's great,' I said, attempting the local conversational style.

'It's terrific.'

'It's amazing.'

One of the most impressive qualities of Gilbert and George is their transparent enthusiasm. They really believe in what they are doing. They may be their own greatest fans, but at least they have put their narcissism to creative use, they have made it pay. And their concerns, as artists, are the big ones: gender, identity, love, life and death, regeneration. If not confessional, their work is certainly rich in religious imagery and theme.

Moreover, taking on the art world on their own terms, theirs is a story of making good, of arrival. Spitalfields has been for them a real zone of transition, a place where they have been free to create their own world, to generate and sustain their phenomenal fantasy life. Working from their studio at the back of the house, a converted rag trade sweatshop, they are artists who have won recognition, if not respectability, for their craft. They are, in fact, not unlike those dissident Huguenots, fleeing France following the revocation of the Edict of Nantes, who were able to remake their lives through their silkweaving in Spitalfields.

We went downstairs. Piling me high with Gilbert and George memorabilia, they showed me out, wishing me well with my book: 'We're sure it will be very beautiful, very amazing.'

A cardboard box had blown up against their railings. Seeing this, Gilbert irritably threw it over into a neighbouring skip. 'What bothers me is when they put it in front of the house, because of the danger of fire, you see.'

'Doesn't that sound a bit like Hysterical of Hampstead?' I asked.

George leapt to his defence. 'In the eighteenth century the street would have been entirely deserted, immaculate; all the windows would have been absolutely sparkling.'

'And we are part of that,' said Gilbert, 'we have enough money to live here in the way we want to. And as soon as money comes in, the area changes, it becomes bourgeois.'

'And that's what's happened in the last ten years.'

'Thanks to her.'

'It's been terrific.'

'It's been amazing.'

'We are the Yuppies.'

The drizzle was light and refreshing. I crossed over the road. As I was peering into one of the puddles by my front door, one of the Fournier Street dossers appeared from a nearby doorway and asked me for the price of a cup of tea. I hurried inside, back into my own world. I had just enough time to slip into something a little more eighteenth-century and head round to Julian Humphreys' house for an evening of waiting at table.

Not without due propriety

As footman, it was my responsibility to set a considered pace to the meal, to encourage a gradual and controlled satiation rather than a frenzied binge. Some groups, unaccustomed to the length and shape of the Georgian dinner, would over-indulge too early, too eager to eat up everything in sight, unwilling to turn down that further glass of claret. Really to enjoy the meal, the guests needed more than greed, they needed stamina and foresight. In fact, the greedy would in the end only suffer the punitive length of the evening, the prodigious amount and richness of the food. The luxury of so much sensual enjoyment needed to remain exactly that: a luxury, a conspicuous *waste* of resources.

Maybe I had been too eager on my eavesdropping tours of the table with the decanter, or maybe they were drinking more rapidly than usual, but for some reason, on the particular evening that Shoulderpads and her family came to dine I found I had used up all the allocated wine by the end of the first course. The port would accompany the dessert, but the second course needed lubrication: I decided to sneak another bottle out of the cellar. Unfortunately, Julian had been counting too. He wasn't going to have any of it: 'I think they've had quite enough to drink.' And that was flat.

So I cleared the plates and relaid the table. Then I went

downstairs to watch Julian dish out the next course. I stood by with the icing sugar and sieve as he turned the Sussex Pond – or Coronary Pie as we called it in the kitchen – on to a silver salver, steaming and oozing in all its suety glory. He then talced it with sugar and I took it upstairs.

Next came the sweetbreads, swimming in a clotted cream sauce. Finally, there were the anchovy whets, little strips of fried bread covered with a single anchovy and melted cheese. As I was passing through the hall *en route* for the dining room, I slipped one into my mouth and hoped I wouldn't have to say anything to the guests with my mouth full of anchovy. Delicious.

While they continued eating, I let the fire burn down in the dining room. I waited in the ante-room. Then Boggy caught my eye and, noticing his empty glass, I guessed what he wanted to ask, so ignored him. A few minutes later I found him beside me: 'Where's the lavvy, old chap?' I told him, but unfortunately that wasn't all. 'I think we could all do with a bit of a refill,' he said, illustrating his point with a wiggly movement of his wrist, backwards and forwards, as though he were sprinkling the floor with an imaginary bottle of wine.

'Indeed, sir, I shall enquire of Mr Humphreys as to whether this is possible.' I went downstairs.

'They want some more wine.'

'I hope you said no.' I returned upstairs.

'Mr Humphreys presents his compliments and would like to remind sir of the incipient arrival of the dessert and, with it, the port.'

Shoulderpads intervened, choking with sarcasm: 'Well, I think we'd prefer to stick with the wine, if that's all right with you.'

'Very good, madam,' I said, feeling increasingly trapped, 'I shall inform Mr Humphreys of your preference for the continued enjoyment of the claret.' I went downstairs.

'They want to stick with the wine.'

'Well, then they have absolutely no idea and I don't want to hear any more of this nonsense.' Then, as I was going out the door, he added, somewhat whimsically I thought, 'Don't they have any sense of proper proportion?'

The conversation stopped as I went into the room and began to try and explain Julian's objection. 'Mr Humphreys is sure you would prefer to proceed to the port wine, which has, in fact, already been made ready for your consumption, as opposed to the claret, which, unfortunately, he has not had an opportunity to prepare.'

'What you mean is he has already opened the port,' Graham translated.

'Indeed, sir.' I felt this might be the breakthrough.

'Well,' sniggered Mr Bert, 'Perhaps I might be so bold as to suggest a place where Mr Humphreys could put the port wine bottle in order to cork it up again.' There was a ripple of laughter around the table, then silence, the embarrassed sort. It was Mrs Bert who broke it.

'Excuse me, but I've been meaning to ask you, do you think you could tell me who is the gentleman in the portrait over here?'

'That's Dean Swift, madam.' The bewigged Swift looked down wryly at the table from above the fireplace.

'Oooh, isn't that lovely, that's exactly what Brenda has called her little boy. And I've always said that it's such a lovely name isn't it, Dean, such a lovely name for a little boy.'

Shoulderpads was folding up her napkin, Georgie was chasing a sweetbread around her plate with her fork, Graham was inspecting a piece of wax that had fallen on to the table cloth. Bert burped.

'Yes, it is madam,' I said in barmy desperation, encouraging the diversion, 'It's a really very lovely name.'

In fact, maybe I should have consulted Swift a little sooner. In his *Directions to the Footman* he provides us with a whole catalogue of artful shortcuts and sidesteps, in particular the importance of cultivating a deaf ear and a blind eye. On the request for more booze he writes:

'Give no Person any Liquor till he has called for it thrice at least; by which means, some out of Modesty, and others out of Forgetfulness will call the seldomer and then your Master's Liquor will be saved.'

He goes on to offer the footman a welter of deceptions, from the most effective way of getting 'everyday the best Part of a Bottle of Wine to your self' to the guilt-free appropriation of a guest's 'Snuffbox and Pick-tooth' and the most tactful way of dealing with accidental breakages. He writes:

'If you have a large Stock of Glasses, and you or any of your Fellow Servants happens to break any of them without your Master's Knowledge; keep it a Secret, untill there are not enough to serve the Table, then tell your Master that the Glasses are gone. This will be but one vexation to him, which is much better than fretting once or twice a week; and [of particular interest to me in present employment] here the Cat will be of great use to take the Blame for you.'

In preparation for the puddings, I cleared the table, removed the tablecloth (finest damask) and relaid on the polished oak. Julian dished out the syllabub, the jellies and the burnt cream as well a goat's cheese, a dish of pears and the port wine. He then went upstairs to prepare the bill (hand-quilled), while I waited in the ante-room, watching the guests wobbling the jellies and playing with the syllabub. Graham got up and poured everyone a glass of port, one for the road. The conversation had turned to thoughts of departure, the best way to get back to Dulwich and Finchley and Cheam.

'How about going round to the Ten Bells for a swift pint first?' suggested Boggy.

'Good idea, I could murder a Guinness,' agreed Graham.

'Haven't you boys had enough?' exclaimed Mrs Bert in mock horror, then turning to Georgie, 'Men, they're never satisfied are they?'

'Excuse me young man,' said Shoulderpads, spying me through the curtain which separated the dining room from the smoking room, 'but do you think you could possibly purloin us the bill?'

'Certainly, madam.'

Payment was always a tense time. Would they or wouldn't they add on that magic ten per cent? Should I quiver a little smile or was it already too late? Usually, in fact, by the end of the meal, you could pretty well guess. Oddly enough, it wasn't the 'gentry', with its apparently old money and older manners, which was the most generous. If they weren't too abstemious to sit at Mr Humphreys' table, they certainly would be to leave a tip. The group, on the other hand, which had flunked out of the etiquette stakes, which had grumbled most persistently about the bad lighting and had asked for extra salt and pepper was also the most willing to include the service. I soon realised that it was this new wealth, this disposable wealth, the wealth straight off the dealing floors of the City, the sort that was in the process of overwhelming the area, which was the most likely to end up fattening my wallet.

Back in 1989 such speculative investment looked pretty unstoppable. The market, having broken free, seemed ready to devour everything and everybody in sight. Appeals to notions of community, although aerosolled widely within the debate about the future of the area, looked helpless to resist its advance. Both 'Cockney Spitalfields' and 'New Georgian Spitalfields' appeared to offer an alternative vision based on their respective class roots, but, in reality, there was no will to translate these golden world fantasies into anything other than stylised cuisine, formulae for interior design or a collection of off-the-peg prejudices. Was there no tradition of solidarity available to us now that we were all middle-class, I wondered? Or were we destined to follow Gilbert and George into eccentric solipsism, a world of our own? And what would happen if we couldn't *afford* to do so?

I brought the coats up, fur and otherwise, from the cloakroom, as well as the various bits of office hardware I had been handed. They had decided to walk down on to Bishopsgate and hail the black cabs there. It was shortly before eleven o'clock and the heavy goods vehicles would be parked up around the market, waiting to off-load their produce. Shoulderpads plucked her rocks from her ears.

As I ushered the guests through the hall towards the front door I took Swift's advice: 'When a Gentleman is going away after dining with your Master be sure to stand full in his view and follow him to the Door and if you have Opportunity look full in his Face, perhaps it may bring you a Shilling.'

I did and it didn't. Nothing was slipped surreptitiously into my palm, nor crumpled disregardingly into my breast pocket. The only exclamation came from Georgie as she nearly tripped over a sleeping body, curled up in a cardboard box just outside Mr Humphreys' door, and that was of surprise rather than delight. No 'goodly vails' tonight.

When I went back into the dining room I found Julian inspecting the scene. He looked about him for a little while, then walked slowly around the room, almost as though he were repossessing it. When he reached the head of the table, the place where Shoulderpads had been sitting, he stopped. Then, reaching out across a plate awash with jelly, he plucked up her neatly re-folded napkin and, with a defiant flourish, he flung it into the air, causing it to flutter for moment above our heads like a suddenly agitated bird.

'Solecism!' he exclaimed, watching it fall back again, crumpled, on to the table.

It was only then that I noticed – probably because it had been partly obscured by the napkin – a crisply folded ten pound note.

'Service!' I said, picking it up and putting it, not, I might add, without due propriety, into my black velvet livery breeches.

PROFESSIONAL
SPITALFIELDS

Gush and Flutter

'Between you and me,' whispered Angie Peppiatt down the phone, 'and this is strictly four walls stuff, the boys here haven't got a clue. They think all they need to do is sponsor a concert, invite a few locals, give them a couple of glasses of Liebfraumilch and everyone's going to go home a happy bunny. It's what I call a Canapé-and-Cocktail Consultation and I can tell you, matey, it ain't gonna work. By the way, did you get an invite?'

'No, I don't think I did.'

'Let me see what I can do. I know they've been juggling with numbers a bit this year, the A list and the B list, I'm sure you know the sort of thing I mean, but I'll have a little word. We must get together soon, in any case, and have a good eyeball to eyeball. Give me a tinkle next week. Come and do a sandwich lunch. Bye for now, kiddo, and take care.'

Angie, for whom strategic indiscretion was a fine art, was able to inspire a wonderful conspiratorial loyalty. Which was just as well. As the developers' community relations officer she needed the full range of PR techniques, every last ounce of gush and flutter, to charm the locals into – as her colleagues would put it – 'getting on board'. Angie herself had got on board in June 1989. Until then, she had spent a career working in and out of politics, from her time as Jeffrey Archer's personal assistant to a spell at Central Office. She was an old school Conservative, a One Nation Tory, as powerfully certain of the rightness of her politics as she was of the callow greed of most of the property developers for whom she was working. She was also a bit of an earth mother in pearls. On the occasions I went up to the developers' office to negotiate my freelance contract with her, she was as likely to question me on the vitamin content of my diet as she was to discuss the finer details of my proposal. Since I had moved to Spitalfields from Oxford I had been angling for a (well-paid) commission from the developers: I would provide a worm's-eye view of the area in exchange for an inside track on their development dilemmas.

With the following morning's post the pleasure of my company was duly requested by the Spitalfields Development Group on Friday 22nd June 1990 at Christ Church Spitalfields to be their guest for the festival's performance of Haydn's *Creation*, and to join them afterwards for refreshments (canapés and cocktails?) at their offices in Bishopscourt.

In the event of it, as we found our way into the church and prepared to hear John Tavener's impressive, yet decidedly uncatchy, *Ikon to St Seraphim*, I found myself surrounded by a veritable conference of professional planners, architects, campaigning activists and sundry other consultants, not to mention the boys from SDG and Angie herself. As the women, mostly wives, teetered and grimaced and self-consciously ingratiated themselves, the men continued to talk shop, pointing their bellies at one another, their eyes scanning the assembling audience. Intermittently such groups would explode into a boardroom guffaw.

During the interval, as we all stood around on the steps of the church and said how interesting we had found the piece by Tavener, I spoke to one man for whom, like many of the other guests, Spitalfields was a singularly 'unique and exciting project'. He had only recently 'got on board', but was fascinated by the 'challenges and the opportunities' presented by the scheme. He saw in the proposed development a means of reforming the modern city, of redefining the urban grain in such a way as to bring Spitalfields into the twenty-first century. His area of specialism? Plumbing.

'You're being consulted on the drains?'

'I'm an expert in waste management and control, yes, that's right.'

'So you've come to sanitise Spitalfields! Don't you think the area will lose something when the market moves, when it's all been cleaned up and redeveloped?'

'No, no, certainly not. We've got to follow this thing called progress and waste management has always been at the forefront of social progress, pulling the chain, as it were. In fact it was only when local authorities acquired powers over drainage, sewage facilities, water supplies and so on in the Public Health Act of 1875 that the process of slum clearance here in the East End really began in earnest. The key event, of course, was the death of the Prince Consort from typhoid in 1861 when public health became a matter for public intervention. Oh no, my friend, the time for harking after some sort of Dickensian squalor is over, we've got to face the future and the future is already upon us. There's no alternative, I'm afraid, the writing's already on the wall, clear as crystal, sure as day.'

The bell called us back to our seats. As we climbed the steps towards the portico, I watched one of the dossers, who had been hanging around the door of the crypt beneath us, polish off his can of lager and, continuing to argue the toss with his mates, relieve himself extravagantly, in great calligraphic arcs, against the wall of the church.

Haydn's *Creation* was sung and performed with great energy. We followed God's progress through his unstinting week of creation, fiat by fiat, and were led, at the end of a lengthy and sustained crescendo, into the momentous choral declaration of the Heavens telling of the Glory of God. The church shuddered with exultation. It would have required a particularly curmudgeonly disciple of Darwin not to feel a little stirred by such a spectacle of God's power and grandeur. The soloists puffed themselves up and did their bit with great vigour, singing into being the entire animal kingdom, with each new creation identifiable within the score by its own particular motif: from great whales and other finny tribes, through herds of cattle and fleecy flocks, to cheerful lions, flexible tigers, nimble stags, hosts of insects and only finally ending up (with the soloist dipping his voice into its lowest register and looking straight, I was sure of it, at Brian Cheetham, the chief executive for the Spitalfields Development Group) with the lowly worm.

After the performance we wandered in small groups over towards the ark that was the developers' centre of operations, the fourth floor of a block on Brushfield Street, overlooking the fruit and vegetable market. Trays of white wine greeted us at the door of the office which, for this evening's festivities at least, had become open plan and open house. Huge, waxy and oddly distended lilies decorated tables covered with fantastic arrangements of exotically garnished bits of lettuce and chicory. Beside the forks and napkins lay clever plastic gadgets which enabled you to attach your glass on to your plate and in this way freed your other hand to reach into your inside pocket for your business card. We shuffled along in a polite queue, piling our plates up, self-consciously trying not to look too greedy, before moving into tentative little groups around the room, in the centre of which, like a giant executive toy, was the architect's model of the redeveloped market.

Drinks parties! What strange and exhilarating occasions! Gatherings where you trade headlines, gossip, potted accounts, where you drop guppies, names, clangers, where thought bubbles crash into each other above your heads as you small-talk your way through several glasses of wine. I found myself locked in tedious conversation with a prospective tenant on the market site and thought how hopeless I was at these things.

I spotted Angie two or three conversational orbits away and no sooner had our eyeballs met than she was at my side. 'Wasn't it superb? I've always said the classical repertoire needs a classical setting, but to hear it in that building was simply inspirational.' She moved a little further into my personal space and, lowering her voice into a confidential whisper, said, 'I've got to do something about Kay, she's lecturing Brian about the state of the rag trade on Brick Lane. This simply isn't the time or the place for that. Besides, he's got to mingle.' And then she was off again, transfixing somebody else's eyeball, oozing with drinks party enthusiasm, throwing over her shoulder, as she went, 'Give us a bell next week about your proposal.' That's the way to do it, I thought, as she disappeared up someone else's ear hole.

I saw my friend Tassaduq Ahmed, elder statesman of the Bengali community, chatting to one of the waitresses and went over to join them: '. . . and another thing we need to ask,' he asked, now addressing the two of us, 'is that if the property developer and the capitalist class has a big slice of the cake, then are they going to share the cake with the community? Because, if they don't share the cake with the community, then they are digging their own grave and it will be our job to push them into that grave,' – pause, staring at me narrowly – 'unless, of course, you are thinking of jumping into the grave with the property developer.' Tassaduq slipped a piece of raw herring down his throat and continued, 'I know, Williams, you have got the good will, but the good will is not enough. The good will needs to be transformed into the effective action.'

'Have I told you about the report I'm going to be writing for the developers, about the needs of the local community and the different ways that the two can build a partnership? I'm a great believer in bringing the community and the developers together so that they can begin to work in partnership.' I was uncomfortably conscious of beginning to sound a bit like Angie Peppiatt.

'You are sure you are not getting into the bed with the developer,' warned Tassaduq darkly, 'because if you are getting into the bed with the developer, then you will have to get out of the bed with the community. You cannot get into two beds at once.' Nor two graves, I reflected to myself soberly, especially when one's scoffing all that cake.

Our conversation was interrupted by the calling of the assembled party to attention. Brian Cheetham was going to make a speech. He thanked us for coming. He talked a little about the importance of the close association between the developers and the Festival and went on to thank singers for singing, players for playing and Richard Hickox, the Festival's musical director, for his advice and enthusiasm etc etc . . . Predictions, he went on, particularly in his line of business, were always rash and experience, if it had taught him anything, had taught him caution, but, having said that, it was his genuine hope and honest belief that, before too long, Spitalfields also would see its very own New Creation. To the New Creation! he toasted. To the New Creation!! we all cheered.

It wasn't to be. In retrospect, it was, indeed, tempting fate for the Spitalfields Development Group to have sponsored the concert at the Spitalfields Festival in 1990 which billed Haydn's *Creation* in its programme. What had started out, in the early 1980s, as a bold and confident statement of the Group's plan to transform Spitalfields into its own version of Eden, had become, dismally, even before that particular summer was out, a sorry tale of loss-making, compromise and temporary use.

Scheming

I was sitting in the reception, waiting for Angie to appear, wide-eyed and apologetic, and lead me into one of the conference rooms, gathering coffee, telephone messages, scrawled memos, letters to sign, as we went. As I pretended to read the *Financial Times*, I heard two voices beneath the high reception desk talking to one another, exchanging bland intimacies between answering the telephone.

'How does my hair look?'

'Fine.'

'It's not sticking out at the back? I didn't have time to wash it this morning.' Phone rings. 'Good morning, SDG . . . I'll just put you through . . . David, there's a call on line three for you.'

'I've seen a bikini I'm going to buy at lunch, it's wildly expensive.'

'What's the top like?'

'It looks really 1960s, all black, very Ursula Andress.' Phone rings. 'Good morning, SDG . . . I'm afraid Mr Cheetham isn't in today, may I put you through to his secretary? . . . Yes, he should be in on Friday . . . goodbye! And the other thing about it is the straps come off.'

'It sounds gorgeous.'

'Of course, I'll never get into it.'

'Don't be so silly!'

'No, I'm serious, my hips!'

Phone rings. 'Good morning, SDG. I'll just put you through
. . . I'm afraid her line's busy, would you like to hold? . . . From
the Quicksand Estate? . . . Sorry, Chicksand – and you'll be in
this afternoon . . . I'll give her your message, goodbye! Well,
personally speaking, I think it sounds divine and of course black
always looks great under water.'

Angie appeared, interrupting the preening girl talk, profusing
her sincerest apologies, 'How about a cup of coff? Gillian, can
you bring some through?'

I followed her into a side room and took a seat at the table.
She said she would be with me in half a tick, that she just had to
give someone a quick buzz, and disappeared off again.

I'd been in this particular room before. Over the previous
eighteen months I had spoken with various members of 'the
team', ostensibly to perform the role of unofficial 'community
relations' liaison, to offer some sort of insight into how people
felt about the development in the various communities that
made up Spitalfields and suggest ways in which the developers
could usefully 'raise their profile' and 'improve their image' in
'the local community'. They recognised that I was in touch with
the vested interest groups in Spitalfields in a way that, by reason
of their role, they couldn't be. While they sat by their fax
machines, I had my ear to the ground, my clippers to the
grapevine. They had commissioned a series of reports, bulletins
from the streets, in which I tried to offer 'feedback', to show
how the development lived in the imaginations (nightmares) of
the people of Spitalfields.

Of course, as I was selling them my services, thinking up all
sorts of fancy rationales for their 'sponsorship' of my 'project',
for their 'patronage' of my role as a 'writer-in-residence', I
realised that, ethically speaking, my position was a little tricky.
Although I was not prepared to demonise the developers, to
suggest that, simply because of what they planned to build in
Spitalfields, they were necessarily the villain of the piece, I was
also mindful of the way their interest in the area – and in me –
was significantly circumscribed by financial considerations.
Most cynically, they wanted me to provide them with

'intelligence' and were prepared to pay for it. For a lot of the time I was prepared to play the game, talk in inverted commas, use this experience of employment to learn more about the way their minds worked, to enter into their world, as I had done elsewhere in Spitalfields. Yet I wondered: would I recognise it, if my involvement with the developers compromised my commitment to the area? What, in any case, was I committed to in the area that would conflict with my employment by the Spitalfields Development Group? These were the questions floating somewhere in my consciousness when Gillian arrived with a tray of coffee and a plate of exquisite-looking chocolate biscuits.

Angie followed shortly afterwards. Having sat down, poured the coffee and told me that I was a good boy for not taking sugar, she sighed deeply, and began. 'Do you ever wonder where we're going, I mean really going? There surely comes a time in anyone's life when they begin to think about the rest of society, when they really begin to think about their values and priorities, if you know what I mean. Well, you know me, I'm a great believer in putting something back into society, taking a long-term perspective, when you cut a tree down, you plant another one type thing.' Angie seemed to be clearing the ground for some significant indiscretion, gunning her chainsaw for some major tree surgery. She continued, 'Between you and me, I simply don't think the boys here have any sense of what's really going on in the community. They talk about the global situation, about the Japanese markets and what have you, but they simply don't have a clue about the element and feeling of goodwill in Spitalfields itself. It's what I call macroscopism. SDG need to sell themselves as a caring developer who want to use their scheme to rehabilitate the fabric of a very deprived area. What do you think?'

Developers always seemed to talk about their proposed 'scheme', with its (unintended) suggestion of devious subtlety, of a plan pursued secretly for personal gain. Although this was not necessarily always the case, I also found it hard to see developers as particularly committed agents of social philanthropy. Maybe what I frequently failed to identify was the vision thing, a consistent commitment to an identifiable version of the area. What did their golden world look like? Thankfully Angie wasn't really wanting a response.

'You know as well as I do we've been having a few difficulties with local groups opposing the scheme in recent months,' she continued, 'what with the Save Spitalfields Campaign slowing us down as we went through the committee stage, upsetting the progress of the Bill through Parliament. And then we had all the problems with the architects, having to lose Richard, taking on the American architects, having to renew outline planning permission. And now with all the hullabaloo in the press about the new scheme, it looks like the plan may be called in by the Secretary of State, which would of course be a disaster in terms of timing. What nobody seems to realise is that it's the same minority interest group in total cahoots with one another which seems to be behind all the bad publicity we've been receiving. Tell me, William, what do you know about the Spitalfields Trust?' This time she appeared to want an answer.

'Well, I know Dan Cruickshank. I know they care a lot about the Georgian houses. And I know they don't think very highly of the latest redevelopment plans.'

'Have you seen this?' said Angie, handing me a copy of a letter, addressed to Brian Cheetham, on the Spitalfields Trust notepaper and signed by its secretary, Douglas Blain. The air was suddenly thick with perfume and intrigue. I skim-read the letter:

'It seems to me we must now face the fact that negotiations for the development of the market have now entered a new phase. We have got beyond the stage of cosy confabulations. Those involved must place their cards on the table. Our position is that, whilst we were prepared to overlook the politics of Richard MacCormac's sudden departure from your design team, we cannot ignore the subsequent deterioration in the quality of what you are proposing.

Those members of the Swanke Hayden Connell practice whom we have met are charming and personable. David

Walker, in particular, we found particularly persuasive in discussion. It is therefore surprising as well as tragic that they have so manifestly failed to respond to the special needs of Spitalfields. Their proposal shows no sense of history, or even of style. What they have put forward is in almost all respects boring, and where it is not boring it is ugly.

If it is still important to you to try and carry people with you, rather than rely on the appeals procedure (which could in any case prove a trap, I fear) then I am afraid the only way you can restore the company's credibility is by sending Swanke Hayden Connell back where they came from, and appointing someone of real talent – preferably of genius – to sort out what looks like becoming one of the most expensive planning muddles of the age.'

'The fact is,' said Angie, when I looked up, 'that Douglas Blain and the Spitalfields Trust are seen by many as being divisive with their policy of gentrifying the houses in the area, of creating what I like to call a 'have and have not society'. I notice their objections to the scheme are on purely aesthetic grounds. They talk about the way the plan lacks 'style', how it is 'ugly' and 'boring'. I think we have a real opportunity to get mileage out of being seen as 'community developers', of offering a true example of inner city development for the nineties and after – we must be seen to be a community development for all, not just the minority groups.' There was a momentary pause in her strategy formulation. She leant across the table to offer me some more coffee. 'It would be good to bear this in mind in your report on the area. I don't know if you ever come across the Spitalfields Trust people in your travels?'

'Occasionally. I know which houses they live in.'

'All I know is we've got to make this development work for the whole community. It's got to be a flagship development into the next century, a truly mixed-use development.'

'It's certainly a challenging project,' I said lamely, feeling slightly weighed down by subtext.

'Now, tell me, William, would you like me to organise some sort of advance payment? I know Brian's signing cheques on

Friday, he's got quite a few to do. But leave it to me, I'll see what I can do.' Angie stood up. She was ending the conversation. 'I love this area,' she said, leading me towards the reception desk, 'so full of character, so full of colour, it's been a real road to Damascus type experience working down here.'

As we were walking down the corridor we met Tim Budgen, who had been involved in the development plans from the beginning. Known in some quarters of Spitalfields as 'the ferret', he was responsible for 'site assembly', identifying the owners of different plots of adjacent land and, in an attempt to construct a single development site, making offers they found it hard to refuse, though often did. Tim had also offered to take me through the early history of SDG's involvement in the area. We arranged to meet. Angie and I said goodbye at the lifts. As I was waiting for the door to close, I heard the telephonist at the reception desk ordering a taxi, giving SDG's address.

'Bishopscourt, Artillery Lane, EC1,' she said.

'E1,' corrected the other one, and then, when she had put the phone down, continued, 'What, of course, we need in Spitalfields are some half-decent shops. You have to go into the City for everything, Boots, Smiths, Miss Selfridge. The nearest Knickerbox is at least ten minutes away, over in Liverpool Street station, and if you want anything a bit sexy . . .'

With a little tug the lift dropped towards the ground floor.

Genuinely fairly straight people

Before the Spitalfields Development Group finally took to the high seas of massive speculative borrowing to fund its building plans, before even its numerous consultants and experts and specialist negotiators had 'got on board', even before the drydock construction of SDG itself as a consortium of the three different property developers (Balfour Beatty, Costains Construction and the London and Edinburgh Trust), there was Tim Budgen. In fact, Tim Budgen existed before the deal was even a sketch on the back of an envelope and when it became so, the envelope was his. Or so the story goes.

'I see myself as a sort of Helen of Troy, launching a thousand ships,' said Budgen, heaving the ring-binders full of correspondence on to his desk, slightly flushed, his lips moistening into a grin, just this side of a leer, removing his jacket. 'It was in December 1984 when I came in to see Peter Beckwith, who was then the chief exec of London and Edinburgh, about the Spitalfields project. We had a couple of meetings, you know the sort of thing, informal explorations, and talked around a few possibilities. He was interested and made me the project manager, put me on a retainer and asked to see if myself and a colleague [John Linford, now deceased] could get the deal off the ground, persuade the traders in the market to move, find a suitable relocation site, test out the water with the City Corporation, the owners, and get the ball rolling with Tower Hamlets.'

There is an unabashed clarity to property developers' strategy. The favoured way to the bank is always the most direct. Detours or delays are expensive and to be avoided, if at all possible. If it's people, with their unpredictable resistance to change, their opportunistic foot-dragging or downright bloody-mindedness, which tend to get in the way, to slow things down, then it's money, with its capacity to sweeten and enlighten, to turn opponents into allies, which is brought in to smooth the path.

'It was around this time, in the mid-1980s, that we were always being pressed for what they call planning gain. Well it's really a way for local authorities to get extra benefits, payment in kind if you like, in return for planning permission. It's a bit of an unknown quantity really, a bit of a horse-deal, I mean I don't know if there are any yardsticks, I've never come across any . . .' Then swerving away from a rather too uncomplicated sounding pragmatism, he checked himself, somewhat reluctantly conceding the principle at stake, 'No, I suppose the argument is that if the developer is going to benefit from planning permission, then the community has the right to gain from it too. I think on the whole, it's true to say, we've been happy to pay it, if it speeds up the process, prevents a delay, that sort of thing.'

For Tim Budgen, tied to the fate of the development by the terms of his retainer, his vision of Spitalfields was circumscribed by the terms of a possible deal. His account of the history of the development, of his involvement with the area, was a succession of talks about talks, of edging, expedience by expedience, towards a clinching agreement. His file offered a chronological and minuted account of presentations, discussions, proposals, packages, consultations and submissions, all intended to win support for the development in both the City (which owned the land) and Bethnal Green Planning Department (which had responsibility as the local authority). Indeed SDG took every available opportunity to show what reasonable people they were.

'We even wrote to the Prince of Wales asking him to get involved, saying what a lot of planning gain we were going to provide for local people, and so on and so on. And we received a reply, let's see, here we are, with a nice royal coat of arms: "His Royal Highness was most gratified by your taking the trouble to write to him and asks me to send you his best wishes." So now we had the Prince's best wishes. Can't say it did us a lot of good.'

One might be forgiven for thinking that SDG wanted to be all things to all 'on-site and off-site client groups'. Certainly they emphasised in all their publicity material the fact that what they were proposing was a 'mixed development', one with which they hoped to excite 'a community of uses: shops and houses, cafés, restaurants, offices and open space, all setting a new standard for environmental planning'. But scratch a property developer and you don't find an environmental planning officer, present him with a development site and he's more likely to reach for his pocket calculator than for his handbook on the greening of cities. However innocently SDG may couple 'offices' together with 'open space' in their publicity material, when it comes to the architect's drawing board, one is more likely to see offices joined to more offices.

What then to do with those offices was a problem that each of SDG's successive architects had to face. Following its deregulation in 1986, the City wanted lots of offices, naturally enough, and the developers were happy to oblige, given the fact that offices command higher rental values than shops and houses or cafés and restaurants. Yet not everyone was so delighted about this. The opposition came first in the architectural press and proceeded, via sceptical feature articles, into the morning papers. The developers had not reckoned on the fact that there were more architectural journalists and well-connected Georgian enthusiasts per acre in Spitalfields than anywhere else in London. For rather different reasons, local activists, particularly those involved in the housing and social needs of the Bengali community, were similarly unconvinced by the merits of the proposed schemes. Suddenly, something called 'the local community', with its various voices, demanded to be heard.

Richard MacCormac, a resident of Spitalfields and also for a number of years a leading light in its conservation group, was cannily hired by SDG in May 1986 to lead its architectural team when it was submitting its original bid. He offered the developers the cachet of local residence and his unquestioned commitment to the conservation of the area. He also brought to the design his considerable learning as an architect – he taught at the faculty in Cambridge – and his concern to redefine the place of the office within the debate about urban planning. In essence, he questioned the North American presupposition that the only way to represent commerce in architecture is by building tall buildings. In his plans for Spitalfields he aimed to build the offices in such a way that they were not simply objects in and of themselves, but that they were interlocking structures, framing a central circus where, so he argued, the commercial presence would become the space itself.

Behind his specific thinking about Spitalfields lay a concern about the way cities had retreated from their public spaces, especially since the eighteenth century. On this matter, about which he spoke with some passion, quoting authors to read, citing sources, convoluting himself with various philosophical notions, MacCormac is programmatic. 'The space and activity of the city must assert itself as the public domain which office space encloses and protects and the office as a social organisation must find characteristics in itself which make it more city-like.'

There are those who say he was doomed from the start. Certainly it transpired that he and the developers didn't speak the same language. On his resignation, MacCormac suggested that his position had become untenable, that he had become trapped between irreconcilable interest groups: 'I was being pressed by the client to be more commercial, while the community and the local authority wanted me to be more social in content.' Budgen, never one to agonise too excruciatingly over conflicts of interest, summoned up his straightforward property developer financial realism: 'Richard had all sorts of clever ideas and I'm sure he was a good architect, but he frankly didn't understand the sort of constraints we were working within and in the end it was probably best we parted company.' Meanwhile, SDG went ahead and imported some good old North American presuppositions into its scheme in the form of the architectural practice Swanke Hayden and Connell.

David Walker, the architect from the American firm who was managing this project, was, you might say, more realistic about the requirements of the scheme. He knew how many beans make five, how many hundreds of square feet of office make a dealing floor: 'Richard's vision of what Spitalfields should be was not consistent with the vision that was held by the more powerful players among the developers and the City and the planning department.' A distressingly charming East Coast American, Walker made his British predecessor look shambling and surly by comparison. He wasn't afraid of calling an office an office, in fact he delighted in doing so, delighted in his bold claim to architectural 'authenticity'.

'For me the challenge is not to respond to some yearning for the past – I don't believe architecture should simply duplicate the forms of the past – nor do I have some utopian vision, an idealised version of what the future might be. As an architect you have to accept that you can't change the world, but what you can do is make something unique, something authentic for what it is. I'm not troubled by the fact that the offices in my design present themselves forthrightly, I don't think you need to cover the offices which are 'bad' with housing which is 'good', that's not a point of view that I'm particularly troubled by. I believe a building looks beautiful when it's straight-forwardly representing what it is and not pretending it's a steel building when it's a stone building or such like. I believe you've got to follow the grain, you've got to respect market forces, that the market works just like gravity, you can't ignore it.'

You had the feeling that Walker, like some persuasively articulate art student at his degree show, could talk endlessly and with dazzling enthusiasm about his intentions and theoretical assumptions. You also had the feeling that, like such a student, he was more excited by the formal qualities of his project than by issues connected to its effect on those around him, by considerations which were aesthetic rather than ethical. 'Spitalfields presents me with a 'design task', it's a balancing act, the apex and the fulcrum and the turning point for a huge number of questions which as an architect I need to address: is it going to be in the City or in the East End? Community architecture or City architecture? International or parochial? High rise or low rise? Single use or mixed use? All these questions and more, many more . . .'

Such as American or English? Little did SDG anticipate such headlines in the architectural press as 'The Yanks are Coming' and quite such resentment at this prospect of a transatlantic operation amongst the New Georgian lifestylers.

'No, I mean, the press obviously gave them a hard time, but I always found them pretty decent sorts to deal with,' said Budgen, conceding what was clearly, in retrospect, a tactical mistake, 'always very professional'.

But to a property developer that is after all what matters: professionalism. And that is what SDG had in black attaché case abundance. They just couldn't work out why the community was so awkward and unpredictable. As Chris Harris, one of Budgen's colleagues, said, 'We happen to believe that we are genuinely fairly straight people. We are honest people – always remembering that we have shareholders and we have to make profits – and we want to talk. But as far as we can see there are fifteen guys, all of whom think they represent the so-called local community. It's horrendous, plus the fact they don't trust anyone.' This was a complaint echoed by Budgen, in one of his more lamenting moods: 'If you offer money, they say it's bribery; if you don't offer money, they say you don't care.'

Surely one might even feel moved to pity by this sorely misunderstood man, with one eye on his retainer and another on his planned kitchen extension, particularly as we watch SDG, trying its hardest to make an honest killing, gradually get crushed between the City's demand for office space, Bethnal Green's planning consent delays and the community's resistance to the very fact of development?

One of the first suburbs

The quarrel between developers and planners, between those with their eye on short-term speculative gain and those labouring to build the New Jerusalem, is an old one. It goes back, in its current form, to that period of massive expansion in the eighteenth century when London, shaken up by the advance of the market economy and the emergence of a vigorous mercantile class, was on its way to becoming the largest city in the western world. The original market in Spitalfields dates back to this time, when, following the granting of a royal charter, it began to trade in the 1680s.

As Palladian design became the fashionable thing after 1715, a system of related town-planning ideas evolved to complement the order of this new type of façade. Put simply, this meant more symmetry, less spontaneity. The planners wanted to see the construction of an ordered grid of streets, avenues and lanes, either opening out into vistas or interrupted by squares, crescents and circuses. Balance and uniformity were the watchwords, although often, in fact, not the reality. In much of the rapidly growing city the amount of control necessary to discipline construction along these lines was simply not available. Like today, those developers who underwrote the building programme were more concerned with getting a speedy return on their outlay than with the laying out of street patterns according to some strict Palladian aesthetic.

Speculative interests also effected the quality of the building work. The houses themselves were often thought to be technically unsound. Isaac Ware, in his *Complete Body of Architecture*

(1735) lamented this apparently shoddy approach and called for stricter control over working methods: 'The Greeks and the Romans built for succeeding ages . . . our people are not so sanguine in their hopes, and therefore not so solid in their structure . . . It is certain the present methods of running up houses in London, not only disgraces us in the eyes of strangers, but threatens continual disasters. Till such a control shall be laid upon bad builders by public authority, those who have more skill and integrity should distinguish themselves from them by their work.' Controls were indeed laid on such builders, most particularly by a succession of Building Acts which sought to restrict the unregulated excesses of this new free-market economy.

At the same time that this major expansion of London was taking place, there were also significant shifts in the intellectual concerns of the age. The two currents of change were surely connected. As the 'market' reality became an inexorable one, with new networks of buyers and sellers replacing the old economies of local consumption, so too concern with the old order of ultimate purpose was replaced by a new interest in the problems of cause-and-effect relationships, of contingency, of temporality.

Setting aside the medieval view of creation and history, which had the will and purpose of God at its centre, these eighteenth-century thinkers set themselves the task of identifying what was eternal and immutable in the maelstrom of upheaval and social change. They wished to develop some sort of objective science or universal morality, to spot the logic within this apparent proliferation of chaos. They believed that with the emancipation of the human spirit from the pressure of dogma, superstition and tradition and with the purposeful exercise of the power of human reason, it was only a matter of time before the evils that had enslaved men and women in the past would be conquered. No longer would the holy city be a gift from God, rather it was to be the final triumph of the science and skill of the enlightened peoples of the earth. The doctrine of progress, of social perfectibility, was born.

Following the fire of London in 1666, when most of the medieval city with its higgledy-piggledy timber-framed houses was razed to the ground, a great opportunity presented itself for the reconstruction of London according to these emerging Enlightenment principles of order and uniformity. Moreover, as building technology shifted its operations from wood to brick, from hand-wrought individual structures to a system of greater standardisation, there came also the means to construct this version of heaven on earth.

Many were hopeful. In his novel *Hawksmoor* Ackroyd puts something of this energetic aspiration for unity and order into the mouth of the contemporary architect Christopher Wren when, in his address to the Royal Society, he says: 'This is a learned and inquisitive Age, Gentlemen, a prying and laborious Age, an Age of Industry: It will be a beacon for the Generations to come, who will examine our works and say, It was then that the World began anew.' And new metropolitan elegance was certainly eye-catching. Around 1700 Celia Fiennes writes of how she found 'London joyned to Westminster . . . it makes up but one vast building with all its suburbs.' Twenty years later Daniel Defoe is commenting on the remarkable speed of urban construction: 'New squares and new streets rising up every day to such a prodigy of buildings that nothing in the world does, or ever did equal it, except old Rome in Trajan's time.'

The planners were certainly clear in their commitment to the future, to their building of a better tomorrow, particularly through the busy laying out of 'new squares and new streets'. Yet they seemed resistant to the very reality of city life, its necessary muddle and multiplicity. In their habit of seeing the city simply as a problem to be solved through the rigorous application of scientific method, and the enforcement of planning legislation, eighteenth-century town-planners were curiously anti-urban.

Uniformity of design, though pleasing for some, was experienced as oppressive by others. Take John Gwynne, for example, whose influential *London and Westminster Improved* was published in 1766. On the construction of Mary-le-Bone parish church he has this to say: 'If it had been rebuilt in a magnificent manner and well placed it would have answered the purpose both of a commodious place for worship . . . and at the same time would have broken the line of new buildings, which as they at present stand give no better idea to the spectator than that of a plain brick wall of prodigious length.' Though a dissident voice in the eighteenth century, his perspective offers a valuable corrective to the notion that all contemporary commentators were sympathetic to the use of grid-iron symmetry in urban design. Clearly one man's geometric order could be another's 'plain brick wall'.

Did the 'plain brick wall' aesthetic not mask, however, a deeper anxiety about the discontinuities of urban life? Richard Sennett, author of a number of books on the growth of the modern western city, believes it did. The eighteenth century, he suggests, had very mixed feelings about the version of nature visible along the streets of the metropolis – the horse dung, the rivers of domestic slops, the decomposing vegetables, the rotting flesh, all the indications of poverty and disease – and was ready to use any means at its disposal to impose some sort of artificial shape on this incoherent townscape. If God had created the country – so the argument went – then Man had made the city, at best a necessary evil, at worst a grotesque perversion of the natural (rural) order of things. Even Adam Smith, champion of the city as the motor for his free-market economy and the source for the wealth of nations, was contemptuous of its idle taste for luxuries, for 'vanities', for the fripperies born of envy and display. The underlying assumption to much of this thinking was that cities were, quite simply, morally as well as physically *unhealthy* places.

One way the planners tackled this problem was through the separation of wealth from squalor, the healthy from the diseased. Until the eighteenth century all different sorts of people had lived alongside each other, mixed together in the jumble of streets in the capital like bubble and squeak. But with the expansion westwards, there developed a whole new pattern of social segregation in which the hierarchy of rank was stamped on the topography of the city in much the same way that postal codes divide it up today. Addresses assumed increasing importance. Identifying a trend which continues to this day, the *Spectator* magazine commented on how London was fast becoming 'an aggregate of various nations distinguished from each other by their respective customs, manners and interests'. It was in the eighteenth century that the West End/East End division first emerged.

From these earliest days, then, the 'problem' of the city was not so much solved as displaced by these planners. In their eagerness to 'clarify' the muddle of city life, for reasons which were commercial as well as social, they engineered this split between the rich and the poor. This is in evidence, moreover, not only in the laying out of whole districts, 'ends' of town, but also in the development of much smaller patches: the terrace, the crescent, the mews, the row and most particularly the square. As Sennett writes, 'Given his anti-urban prejudices the Enlightened planner set about to remedy the defects of the city through creating unities and the primary urban form to use in creating unity was the town square.'

Yet, as with the new suburbanisation of London – the dividing up of the city into 'good' areas and 'bad' areas – the town square created its unity precisely through its ability to exclude, to keep out. One can see this happening in Spitalfields. Spital Square was laid out in the heart of Spitalfields and became, in many ways, the focus of this Georgian suburb, certainly its residential showpiece. Not only were the houses much grander than any others in the area, but they were also arranged in such a way that reinforced their status, overlooking one another, the one drawing attention to the other's magnificence. And having been built for the newly prosperous mercantile community, the square managed to preserve its exclusive identity throughout most of the nineteenth century, despite its proximity to both Bishopsgate and Spitalfields Market.

In 1733, when the eastern side of the square was being completed, Robert Seymour's edition of Stow's *Survey of London* remarks that, 'In place of this hospital [St Mary Spital], and near adjoining, are now built many handsome houses for merchants and others'. In 1842 it was described as mainly inhabited by silk manufacturers, 'the humble operatives living for the most part eastward of this spot'. Only in 1891, with the establishment of a girls' school in the square, is there any suggestion that it was losing its attraction as an exclusive residential quarter.

The bollard, or 'post' as it was then termed, played a key role in the fortunes of this particular eighteenth-century square: its seclusion was chiefly maintained by the strategic placing of obstacles to through-traffic. Judicial bollarding at the northern and eastern ends of the square kept the chaos and congestion of the market at bay. In 1742 the right of the lessee at 34/35 Spital Square to create an effective through-way to Fort Street was restricted to a foot passage blocked against wheeled traffic by, yes, more bollards. Further bollards were introduced at the eastern entrance of the square in 1789 in order 'to prevent danger to the inhabitants of Spital Square from the driving of Cattle and Carts and Horses through the Opening'. Then, in 1821, Mr James Tillard replaced these old bollards with some nice new iron ones, which were themselves only finally removed during the First World War.

All this bollarding, the forerunner of modern day security fencing, preserved the privacy and 'unity' of the square until the early years of our own century. It kept it zoned as a residential quarter, largely free of the comings and goings of humble tradespeople and the unwelcome interruptions of passing traffic. This is, of course, what those responsible for its construction had intended when, in the second decade of the eighteenth century, the square was laid out. Imposing on the street plan an architectural form with clear boundaries and impressive grandeur, Sir Isaac Tillard had clearly wanted this part of his estate to be a confident statement of his faith in himself and in his family's future. In its order and neat symmetry the square set itself almost defiantly over and against the muddle and mess of the newly opened market nearby.

Yet, in the end, Spitalfields Market drove its way through the bollards regardless. In 1917, Robert Horner, the market's lessee, had them removed, at his own expense, to relieve the congestion in the neighbouring streets. The bollards were put into safe storage by Stepney Borough Council, pending their possible reinstatement, which, of course, never happened. Once the bollards had gone it was only then a matter of time before the square went too. In the 1920s the eastern side was purchased by the Corporation of London – under powers granted it for the extension of Spitalfields Market – and then pulled down to widen the street. The western and northern sides of the square were subsequently demolished in the early 1930s to clear a site for the Co-operative Wholesale Society Fruit Warehouse. The remaining house on these sides, number 15, was demolished in 1952 under a 'dangerous structure' order.

If the planners created their urban idylls by blocking out potentially disruptive elements, in doing so they also unwittingly created comparable pockets of urban squalor. In the old city, before the great fire, poverty had clearly existed, but not in such homogeneous zones, not in such an exclusive way. During the course of the eighteenth century, however, the full-on 'slum' was invented, posing a persistent problem to successive generations of urban reformers. Then, as middle-class perceptions of poverty shifted in the nineteenth century, from seeing it as an indication of personal torpor into seeing it more as the product of social and environmental circumstance, the urban planners came into their own. With poverty as the irresolvable problem of the city in the modern period, those responsible for planning its future shape saw their task as nothing less than a redemptive one.

The theorists tended to swing one of two ways. Either they favoured the high-density city, with the focus of urban life in the centre, or they argued for the low-density city, with the dispersal of people out to the suburbs and beyond. Often they disagreed. Usually the one took up a position in defiance of the other. Each, however, claimed to be exercising the voice of reason, of scientific empiricism.

The low-density city, with its roots in William Morris's writings, was first codified by Sir Ebenezer Howard in 1898 in his book *Tomorrow: A Peaceful Path to Real Reform*. He put forward a programme which involved the building of the Garden City, offering, as he saw it, the best of all possible worlds. Yet, like his eighteenth-century predecessors, the vision was essentially anti-urban. Quoting Ruskin with approval, he explains how his chief aim was 'the spontaneous movement of the people from our crowded cities to the bosom of our kindly mother earth, at once the source of life, of happiness, of wealth and of power'. In its neat form, Howard's programme was pure poetry, an unrealisable dream, yet it continued to exert an important influence on subsequent generations of urban planners, such as Lewis Mumford and Clarence Stein in America and Sir Patrick Abercrombie in Britain.

As chief author of the *County of London Plan*, published in 1944, Abercrombie was a key figure in the plans for post war reconstruction. Singling out the East End for special study, this was seen as a once-in-a-lifetime opportunity to reorganise this area on a 'rational' basis, which, in short, meant the 'sweeping away' of all working-class housing. Basing his report on Howard's model of the Garden City, he and his colleagues suggested the construction of 'terraces around open quadrangles and lawns' to replace the overcrowded tenements. Those people they couldn't accommodate in these quasi-cloisters would be moved to satellite towns. Fortunately, the grand plan for the East End never materialised, although its assumptions lingered and when Spitalfields and its environs did actually come up for redevelopment in the 1970s the old arguments resurfaced. The people were told that there were too many of them living in impossible conditions and that the only solution was for them to be moved out of the area.

Le Corbusier, meanwhile, had put forward his own city plans in 1918 in *La Ville Radieuse*. Formulated, to some extent, as a reply to Howard's Garden City programme, Le Corbusier attempted to articulate a corresponding vision of high-density urbanism through his enthusiasm for high-rise towers. He described his creation as the Garden City made attainable. 'The Garden City is a will-o-the-wisp,' he wrote, 'Nature melts under the invasion of roads and houses and the promised seclusion becomes a crowded settlement . . . The solution will be found in the "vertical garden city".' In his drawings his towers soared above the lush arcadian landscape, reminiscent of an artist's impression of Canary Wharf set amidst the cosy domestic streets of the Isle of Dogs.

In their different ways, both Howard and Le Corbusier

defined the boundaries of the post-war building boom. As modernists, they were not unlike their Georgian predecessors creating 'unities' through simultaneous concentration and exclusion, bollarding in and bollarding out. Wielding their professional status, they and their colleagues were willing to unleash schemes of grotesque imagining on the unsuspecting people of East London. Then along came Jane Jacobs, writing as a consumer and not as a planner or developer, to challenge their assumptions root and branch. In the opening paragraph of her book *The Death and Life of Great American Cities*, she is unequivocal: 'This book is an attack . . . on the principles and aims that have shaped modern, orthodox city planning and rebuilding.' Rather than *building* the ideal city, she argues, it surely had to be uncovered, revealed almost. It was a matter of pruning, rather than planting out. As spirituality turned inwards in the 1960s, so, it seemed, did the new planning orthodoxy. Setting herself against the huge redevelopments of the 1950s and 1960s, which in any case were rapidly coming unstuck, she championed the local initiative: the need for small blocks, diversity in street life, mixed uses, old buildings, overlooked spaces, interrupted vistas and any proposal which followed the fine-grain of the city rather than the logic of large scale modernist 'regeneration'. Looking around herself in New York, her question was always: 'What makes this part of town work and this part not work?'

The challenge Jane Jacobs offered the planning community in the 1960s was, in some ways, not unlike John Gwynne's complaint against Mary-le-Bone terrace in the 1760s, that despite the virtue of its unbroken symmetry, it was, to the local resident, little more than a 'plain brick wall of prodigious length'. Power, money, influential people, the professional academy may all have a vision of what is best for the city; it is not necessarily the same, however, as the one expressed by those who actually have to inhabit this dream landscape. What is scientifically feasible, even logically desirable, is simply not always the case. What the planners plan does not necessarily square with what the people want. There is a gap between the drawing-board version of the future and the way things actually pan out.

This inevitable gap seems to point to a paradox at the heart of the project of Enlightenment rationalism. In the eighteenth century the new scientific methodology seemed both to provide a mechanism with which to order the whole of nature but also, at the same time, to question the very possibility of arriving at any absolute truths. It seemed to offer the promise of a total explanation whilst simultaneously depriving the explainer of the authority necessary to propose it. Whereas the orderliness of inquiry appeared to demand an equally orderly symmetrical nature, the very process of empirical study required the pulling to pieces of the evidence, the atomisation of reality. As for the planners, instead of recognising the necessarily contingent and regulative nature of their schemes, they tried to mould the city according to their twilight imaginings. They interpreted their own dreams in a literal way. Until the eighteenth century, from Plato's *Republic* through Augustine's *City of God* to More's *Utopia*, the ideal city had certainly been designed in intricate and loving detail, but always to show up the one we inhabit, the actual city, to be in some way fallen and degenerate and to inspire it towards some sort of possible regeneration. They were never programmatic in the way that Howard and Le Corbusier (and indeed Jacobs) are programmatic. Nor, indeed, were they so banal. Whereas our actual cities are dark places, full of ambiguity and delight, these post-Enlightenment fantasy cities tend to be places of anodyne contrivance.

This gap between what the professionals envisage and what the city allows was very obvious in the debates that circulated in the late 1980s about the possible futures of Spitalfields. On the one hand there was Richard MacCormac with his heady modernist plan for the appropriation of the office block into the fine grain of the area. On the other hand, there was David Walker's defiantly unapologetic proposals for offices *qua* offices, postmodernist almost in his retreat from the scheme's wider context. Meanwhile the Campaign to Save Spitalfields from the Developers opposed all plans to impose a false City 'unity' on the diversity which they saw as the area's chief characteristic. And with the Prince of Wales also charging around Spitalfields on a series of fact-finding tours, these local concerns about the planning process were revisited again at the Great Debate in November 1989 at the Victoria and Albert Museum where, through his allies, the Prince posed the provocative question: why should the future of our cities be left to the experts? Somewhere in all this one also needs to find a place for the poet Iain Sinclair, townspotter *par excellence*, whose fictional account of Spitalfields and the East End, his depiction of a world of relic-strewn, spirit-infested disintegration, acted as 'an inverted parody of future-orientated urban planning' (in the words of Patrick Wright) and usefully reminds us that it will all end in tears anyway.

With its origins as one of the first suburbs of eighteenth-century London, Spitalfields carries in its history the hopes of this Enlightenment city as well as its inherent shadow-side. Scientific rationalism has generated in this area, partly through the planning process, the very divisions it sought to eradicate in its pursuit of clarity in urban design, zoning, separation of uses, the maintenance of unity through exclusion (bollarding) and control and so on. In *The 100 Mile City*, his account of the changing face of the post-industrial metropolis, Deyan Sudjic suggests that these debates in Spitalfields 'run along one of the most unstable urban fault-lines in Britain' where 'two utterly different worlds [the City and Brick Lane] which live in the closest proximity entirely fail to meet'. It is precisely because of this apparent *impasse* that the question of how the planners, the developers and the people talk to one another is of such crucial importance.

Too many questions

Where Tim Budgen and the Spitalfields Development Group failed, the Spitalfields Trust, and in particular its secretary, Douglas Blain, succeeded. He managed to elicit from Kensington Palace an endorsement of the Trust's work in the area, which, given His Royal Highness's tendency to circum-locute, was positively glowing. In a letter which accompanied the Trust's publication of *The Saving of Spitalfields*, at the end of

1989, Prince Charles congratulated the 'hard-working achievement' of the individuals of the Trust who had managed 'to reverse the decline of the most intact early Georgian streets in London'. He added, pointedly, that 'Publication of this book comes at a particularly appropriate time to coincide with the current proposals for major new development schemes around Spitalfields, and the questions raised for the future of the existing community and the setting of the Georgian streets.'

'Drafted, of course, by us,' said Ian Lumley, assistant secretary to the Trust, snatching the letter playfully from my hands, searching for his keys, mumbling to himself how he must have had them to let himself in, finding them in the pocket of his incredibly tight-fitting tweed jacket, pulling open the window of the Trust's office in its eighteenth-century town house in Brushfield Street and tossing them to someone waiting below. An eccentric Irishman who had proved his commitment to the cause of historic building conservation by sitting in a cement mixer in Dublin as part of a campaign to prevent the demolition of that city's quays, Lumley brought to the day-to-day manage-ment of the Trust in Spitalfields a certain unpredictable charisma. Meanwhile, he found its trustees, mainly worthies from the City and the West End, steely and understated by comparison with their Irish counterparts.

But they certainly knew how to run an historic buildings' trust. With the publication of *The Saving of Spitalfields*, the Spitalfields Trust was able to mark this achievement and draw attention to its continuing role in the area as a pressure group. Having its roots in glorious opposition to a property developer's plan of demolition in 1977, the Trust was clearly wishing still to maintain an initiative in the face of SDG's proposed redevelopment of the market. As well as skilfully deploying its contacts in the worlds of the media and high finance, the Trust had also managed, over the years, to catch just the right tone of defiant indignation in its press statements, newsletters and occasional publications. In this way it had been able to stake out and maintain its position on the moral high ground.

So, for example, in the newsletter which was put out shortly before the publication of its book we read of how the Trust unequivocally stated the Bengali community's cause in the face of the impending office development: 'The housing and employment needs of the Bangladeshi community must be paramount. There is a particular local demand for large housing and a need for affordable workspaces to sustain the rag trade, which must be satisfied.' And, as though that weren't championing enough, the newsletter continues darkly, 'Once a major office scheme is allowed, an overspill of land values into the surrounding area is inevitable. There are practical problems as to how locally affordable workspace can be created, and controlled rents maintained.'

Such censorial finger-wagging might seem rich coming from an organisation which had presided single-handedly over the gentrification of Spitalfields for the previous ten years, but question the Trust's integrity in these matters and one is likely to receive a 'robust response', as they say. When, for example, an article appeared in the *Guardian* which accused the Trust of 'winkling out' its Bengali tenants and of pursuing the restoration work at their expense, the Trust, leaning on the editor with threats of litigation, demanded and received an apology.

Yet could such defensive self-justification not mask less clear-cut intentions with the Trust? When I pushed Lumley on this he was cagey, as well he might have been, knowing my interest in getting an angle on the Spitalfields Trust for the SDG, my 'sponsors'. So I tried a different tack. I asked him which the properties were that the Trust had needed to clear of its Bengali tenants, before restoration work could begin.

'Before my time,' he said, 'ancient history. But you could try Fournier Street, the big house.'

Now 'the big house' on Fournier Street is number 27, larger and finer than those adjacent to it, with a wide three-storeyed front with five windows closely spaced in each upper storey and, on the ground floor, a central doorway flanked on the right by two windows and on the left by one window and a passage opening to the back premises. The Survey of London reports that it was originally leased on 14 December 1725 to a successful merchant weaver called Peter Bourdon and subsequently to 'a weaver of silk mixed with worsted', Obadiah Agace. The house remained apparently in private ownership until it was taken over as 'The London Dispensary' in 1829 and organised for the provision of free medical attention and medicines.

Isobel Barker, one of the oldest parishioners of Christ Church, whose family had run a dairy in nearby Wentworth Street, remembers Nurse Wright – 'kindness itself' – taking a room on the top floor: 'They gave you medicines if you were poor, you went there and saw the doctor and he gave you a free ticket, a prescription, I suppose.' 27 Fournier Street continued to act as the London Dispensary until 1946 and the arrival of the National Health Service, when it was sold again and occupied at first by Jewish tailors and later by Bengali leather cutters. 'I can remember an incident,' says Barker, 'when they went in to do Miss Wright's room up, to take a partition down, and the builders refused to work because it was full of bugs! But the bugs were everywhere in the East End, it was all bugs in those days!'

If only the bugs had kept the builders permanently at bay. Once the Bengali tenants had been relocated it was only by careful, one might even say forensic, 'opening up' – that is, brushing down the floors after the old linoleum had been taken up – that the Trust was able to identify the position of all the missing partitions. Yet the rewards were great: they also discovered the locations of the door openings (given away by water marks in the boards) and even the exact size and shape of the architrave mouldings, neatly traced in dirt where it had become encrusted against the skirting boards.

Although the Trust's newsletters give a blow-by-blow account of the architectural delights to be found in number 27 Fournier Street, its fine carved door case and most unusual staircase with 'barley sugar' balusters, its ornate chimney pieces and moulded cornices, its dado rails and door architraves, they only record in passing the fact of the relocation of the rag trade tenants, their so-called 'winkling out', into premises on Heneage Street. So I went round to the house itself to see if the present occupants could shed any further light on this episode. A young man, dressed all in fashionable black, welcomed me through the fluted Doric pilasters into the spacious hall. He wasn't the owner, he explained. The owner, a businessman who worked in Malaysia, rented the house to a group of young tenants, all of whom 'tended to be involved in the arts' in one way or another. He spoke of his own passion for the area, its 'decayed shabbiness', its 'vital mix', of how the house itself was 'totally unique'. As a photographer he explained how he particularly loved the quality of light in the house, a translucency almost. I asked him if he knew what happened to the Bengali tenants. He didn't. 'There's no real trace here of the Bengalis, the Bengali presence has been carefully eradicated, carefully erased. I'm not even sure what they could have kept . . .'

I then went round to the relocation site, the converted stables in Heneage Street. I noticed that it had been renamed 'Huguenot Place', which sounded ominous, and noted with growing anxiety the occupations of the present tenants which were listed on the gateway: architect, designer, furniture designer, office services (whatever they were) and Mr Henry George. The familiar heaving of uncut leather between van and workshop and the grasshopper whirr of the sewing machines, familiar sights and sounds on Brick Lane, were noticeably absent.

Entering the designer's 'studio' office, I introduced myself and said I was wondering if any of the original tenants were still using the premises. He said I'd missed the boat, that the last one, a leather cutter, Henry, had moved out just a few weeks previously. He couldn't say for certain why that was, but he could give me his forwarding address. To be honest, he said, he suspected that Henry probably couldn't afford to continue to pay the rent, as well as all the service charges. The landlord had recently put these up.

'And who is the landlord?' I asked

'Mr Morton-Smith. He's just moved into his office on Fournier Street.'

It was only later that the penny dropped. I had come across Morton-Smith before. The owner of Dino's café in Gun Street, just opposite the market, had described him in somewhat colourful terms, after Morton-Smith had refused to renew his tenancy agreement. Negotiating contracts, collecting rents and, no doubt, also relocating tenants, he worked as an agent, in both these cases for the Spitalfields Trust itself. I felt I was on the way to getting my angle for my report. I went back to Ian Lumley.

'You are asking too many questions,' he said, 'there are some things I just can't talk about.'

It was reading through the minutes of the Trust's meetings as they discussed the future of their rag trade tenants and their new accommodation in Heneage Street that I gained a clearer picture of the way the negotiations had developed.

What I discovered was this: that all but one of the tenants at Fournier Street, 'a Jewish dealer in clothes', agreed to move to the new workspaces in Heneage Street but that, fortunately for the Trust, Mr Cohen died before the Trust had to resort to 'peaceable re-entry'. I read how, given the fact that financial viability was always an issue for the trustees, once the rag trade tenants had been relocated in the spring of 1983, they turned their minds to the question of cash flow: 'It was agreed as a fallback that we could always sell the workshops.' Less than a month later the Trust is researching how much the workshops might sell for, and exactly a year later they are put on the market: 'As we were so often in need of large capital sums, it did seem rather a shame to have so much capital tied up in the workshops, though we would have to protect the interests of our Bengali tenants for some years.' The Trust's solicitor suggests seven years.

In September 1984, following a couple of other bids, Rex Morton-Smith, who had acted as the Trust's agent throughout the negotiations, makes an offer of £135,000 against the asking price of £150,000. Following an amount of strategic huffing and puffing, the deal is eventually struck in November 1984, with the Trust settling for a sale, effectively washing its hands of their ragtrade tenants: 'Mr Morton-Smith has agreed to buy the workshops for £140,000 on the understanding that the special price concessions we had given to the 27 Fournier Street tenants should not be carried on further than three years.'

And so it was that the Trust, in spite of all its stated concern that 'locally affordable workspace be created' and 'controlled rents maintained' especially in order to 'sustain the rag trade', found itself putting such tenants for whom it had particular responsibility into the hands of a local estate agent, a man called Rex, who was busily building up his own property kingdom along the City fringe, a promising portfolio of attractive studio and workshop accommodation. Leather workers need not apply.

That's the nature of the deal

What made the Trust's decision to sell its workshop accommodation to its estate agent so peculiar was the fact that there already existed in Spitalfields an organisation dedicated to managing affordable workspaces for the rag trade, namely the Spitalfields Small Business Association. In fact, the SSBA had even been explicitly identified three years previously as the most obvious long-term landlord of the Heneage Street properties in a report prepared for the GLC by an independent consultancy practice, in consultation with the Spitalfields Trust itself. So what happened?

'Oh, the usual cock-up, I should think,' said Kay Jordan, who had coordinated the SSBA's work in Spitalfields since 1984 and had clearly learnt to view the vagaries of running a voluntary organisation on a shoestring with a certain philosophical detachment.

The SSBA was formed in 1980, following the initiative of a few Bangladeshi tenants wanting to improve their living and working conditions in the area, particularly as they saw Spitalfields come increasingly under threat as a result of the City's expansion. Living as many were in condemned buildings, badly lit, without heating, with outmoded and inadequate plumbing, rotting stairways and the full monty of health hazards associated with damp and vermin, they wanted to improve, first and foremost, their immediate environment. With the help of money, both public and private, the SSBA attempted to set up a rolling programme of purchase, in association with the Housing Co-operative, buying mainly mixed-use properties, leasing on the residential sections for improvement and reallocation, and reordering the light industrial sections for use by its tenants. With limited space available in Spitalfields they would try to raise the money for anything appropriate that came on to the market. It was when they were putting together their bid for the Heneage Street properties that the GLC commissioned the report that identified them as the most obvious landlord. In the end, however, it was the Spitalfields Trust, tweaking its City strings, which secured them.

'They're not bad people, they just promote their own interests,' said Kay Jordan on the Spitalfields Trust, 'and whereas their interests are the buildings, our interests are the people. We simply take a different approach, see things differently.'

In fact, the SSBA made its mark in the debate about the redevelopment of the market by seeing things differently; being contrary, especially where property developers were concerned, was Kay Jordan's stock in trade. Passionately loyal to her tenants, she would, by contrast, hector and exasperate 'the boys' from SDG, who, in turn, would regularly complain, in a slightly hang-dog kind of way, that they didn't know where they stood with her, where she was coming from, that she seemed continually to be changing her official line. Unsurprisingly, this is not how she saw it, speaking with emphatic underscorings, in bold type, making sure I didn't miss the point.

'Beckwith and his mob will get away with the very minimum they can get away with. He didn't become a multi-millionaire by handing out all his money to the poor. We've got to do everything we can to make this development work for the local people. I'm quite happy to go and cream his parsnips if it means we'll get some benefit down this end of Brick Lane, but I want to see proof he's moving.'

A clever opportunist, Kay Jordan was also a dab hand at causing well-intentioned philanthropists and City big wigs to take a detour through her workshops and, wherever possible, to empty their pockets into the SSBA's balance of payment accounts. In fact, she had her own Prince Charles story, which was characteristically brazen.

As president of Business in the Community, Prince Charles was due to visit her in her office as part of a scheduled

Spitalfields walkabout. Surely, she suggested, he'd be much more interested if he took a look round the workshops and met some of the actual tenants such as Ezera the pleat maker or Ishrad 'Denim' Ali? The organisers of the visit reluctantly agreed and set in motion the extensive Special Branch vetting procedures and security clearance necessary for such a tour. It was only when the route had finally been planned, the tenants rehearsed and the entourage briefed, that Kay Jordan went out with a colleague and dumped ten wheelbarrow loads of rubble across the designated path, effectively rerouting the royal party through a further workshop at the top of the building.

'Charlie boy was delighted, you could see him get all mischievous as his security men went into flat spins. 'I think I might just take a look in here,' he said, skipping up the stairs and into Fazal's workshop. Once he had gone the press had a field day and, with their help, we managed to get Fazal's problems into all the news bulletins. Almost immediately we were promised the interest-free loan we needed to do up his workshop.'

By profession an architect, in working for the Spitalfields Small Business Association Kay Jordan has also become, by necessity, an unofficial social worker turned rights campaigner, spending long hours with her tenants, either listening to the details of heated family disagreements, filling in forms or simply chewing the samosa late into the evening.

'She's a typically tortured liberal,' said Peter Bradley, speaking as someone frighteningly at ease with himself in his role as the Spitalfields Development Group's PR consultant, 'and she just can't make up her mind about us. Peter Beckwith has put in a lot of time with her but finds the SSBA's position very confusing. I mean, let's be frank, Peter is a very rich man and he knows he's going to make a sizeable profit from Spitalfields. But he's got to the stage now where he doesn't need to count every last penny, he can afford to put some of it back, with his reputation to think of and, let's face it, he's also got his eye on a peerage. He's actually a very straight guy, ready to listen and to help, where he can, but he just can't understand why she says one thing one moment and then another thing the next.

Basically, either she's working with the campaign or she's working with us, that's how he sees it.'

The Campaign to Save Spitalfields from the Developers was indeed one that Beckwith, Bradley and the other boys from SDG were understandably a little cagey about. With its origins in a variety of 'community development initiatives' which had taken root in Spitalfields throughout the 1970s and 1980s, the campaign functioned as an umbrella organisation, claiming signatories, as its newsletter stated, from 'a variety of local pressure and community action groups, small businesses, market residents and and other local residents concerned with the implications for the whole Spitalfields area of a £500 million development scheme'. As a campaign, it condemned the re-development plans outright, scorning any negotiation over planning gain, its no definitely meaning no. But it was only when the parliamentary Bill to revoke the market's royal charter went to the committee stage in the House of Commons in June 1988, after its second reading, that the campaign was able to put on its tin hat and lodge a petition, put its case.

Arguing against the detrimental effect of the redevelopment on the local community, particularly on the clothing industry, whilst highlighting its terrible housing problems as well as its transparent need for more open space, the campaign put up a plucky show. Finding expertise in all sorts of areas it didn't know it had, from the significance of traffic flow computations to the meaning of statistics relating to a possible increase in pollution levels, it also called upon witnesses from as wide a range of advocates as it could muster, canvassing support from MPs, planning consultants and, well yes, from poor old Prince Charles himself. In the course of the hearing, they were also able to ask all those awkward little questions which seem so simple yet invariably require such complicated answers, such as, 'Why do we need more offices?', 'Why here?' and 'What does the community get out of it?'

'We kept them there for ten days,' said Jil Cove, the campaign's not-to-be-outflannelled co-ordinator, 'and it will have cost the City a lot of money. Retaining their lawyer alone must have cost them a small fortune.' The campaign paid its own way, covering what minimal costs it did incur through donations, occasionally also organising a whip-round, 'like in the old days, collecting for the miners'.

In the end, though it congratulated the campaign on the presentation of its case, the House of Commons committee found the terms of the Bill to be such that the legislation before it was, in fact, narrowly concerned with the needs of Spitalfields Market and the will of its traders rather than the likely impact of the redevelopment on the wider community. Such issues as arose here had necessarily to remain outside its field of vision and the scope of its recommendations. In deference to the campaign's case, however, the committee suggested, amongst other things, that the developers should double their planning gain contribution to the community and treble the amount of money that they were to make available for training schemes. It seemed that 'the local community' had won the moral, if not the legal, victory.

In fact, throughout the proceedings 'the local community' had been aerosolled by the campaign in all its multi-ethnic, multifaceted, multi-magimixed glory across the sepia monotony of the City and its property developers' proposals. There certainly could be no doubting what, in the eyes of the campaign, was at stake here: 'The new look for Spitalfields can be either the dry, drab, grey face of the City or the image of a vibrant community enhanced by the injection of much-needed community-directed cash.' Yet, in spite of all this passionate commitment to the 'local community', there seemed to be a question mark over the campaign's representative status, to which the City's lawyer, in his summing up of the case, drew the committee's attention: 'You have heard a lot about the Bengali community. You have not heard, however, from any organisations which represent this community as such . . . You have heard a great deal about the effects on the Bengali community but not one single Bengali trader has been called or put in any statement which suggests he is worried about what will happen.'

He had a point. For most of the ten days, the only visibly active members of the campaign appeared to be the tireless

Cove and a couple of rather earnest research students writing their doctoral theses on the politics of opposition and related development issues. There were certainly other members who attended the committee hearings and the regular 'back bar' planning meetings of the campaign, but there was no significant Bengali contingent amongst these either. Moreover, having never carried out any widespread consultative exercise, claiming instead to know 'instinctively' what the local people wanted, the campaign's credibility was further undermined by the appearance around this time of another representative group within the community, the 'Community Development Group'.

Co-ordinated by two Bengali activists, Nissar Ahmed and Rumman Ahmed, the CDG was effectively sponsored by the government's Task Force in Spitalfields and was seen by Erika Zimmer, its local manager, as part of the Task Force's long-term development plan for the area: 'We wanted to get something up and running which would then be able to take over when we left.' While she herself was running the Task Force in Spitalfields, part of her job, as far as she was concerned, was that of 'honest broker', bringing the different interest groups together, getting them round the polished teak table. There was, moreover, in her approach to such matters something of the missionary zeal of the one who had sent her. As she gave an account of the emergence of the government's Task Force programme throughout the late 1980s, she identified the turning point, the launching initiative, as that occasion in June 1987 when one greater than she had stood on the steps in Downing Street and pledged her commitment to 'those inner cities'.

In her task as bridge-builder and referee, she was a model of even-handedness, combining the tight-lipped discretion of a civil servant with the platitudinous encouragement of a family counsellor. 'There has to be give and take on both sides. The tricky part is that the community are sceptical of the developers, believing them simply to be going through the motions of a consultation, and the developers are worried that they are dealing with a bunch of amateurs. Although there may be an element of truth in both these positions, we've got to overcome that and to keep talking. Basically the developers have got to start being a bit more relaxed and the community have got to become a bit more professional.'

Under Zimmer's guidance, the two Ahmeds proceeded, in their consummately professional way, to worry about mandates and remits, agendas and the circulation of minutes. They asked themselves whether they were facilitators or enablers? Co-ordinators or campaigners? They drew up complicated flow charts which demonstrated the process by which the planning group of the Community Development Group would be transformed, by a series of consultations and working parties, into the steering committee of the Community Development Trust. And for those who were in any doubt as to the purpose of the CDT, they produced numerous information sheets outlining their aims and objectives, detailing how they were to become the 'mechanism through which . . . the negotiations/agreements with the developers were to be implemented, actuated and fully articulated'. In other words, they had their eyes on the dosh, they were in the business of 'accessing funds'.

'Since you're airing it out,' said Rumman Ahmed, responding to my suggestion that, for the PG/SC of the CDG/CDT, any 'negotiation' with the developers was neces-sarily going to be unequal, 'I will air it out too. The first thing I need to say is that for the property developers to retain any credibility in the area they must be seen to be talking to the Bengali community. And as we talk to them we're happy to meet them on their own terms, to use the free market philosophy, to talk figures and uses, to look at spreadsheets and bottom-lines. But we also say that if we're going to talk about a partnership, it has to be about a meaningful partnership. This is the process we've agreed upon in the CDG and I'm here to enable this process. Yes, I'm a professional and yes, I'm good at this role. But in order to get on with the job, I'm prepared to leave my baggage outside. Are you prepared to leave your baggage outside?'

The problem was that those groups which were most opposed to any form of development in the area not only had brought all their baggage with them, but were quite definitely settling in for the duration. Whereas the Community Development Group had apparently swept into the battle zone with its fledgling officers rolling up their sleeves as they unrolled their grand strategies, talking confidently about their protocols and procedures, the Spitalfields Small Business Association and the Campaign to Save Spitalfields from the Developers had dug themselves into the area and were preparing for the long haul, a war of attrition fought from the trenches. Moreover, sponsored by Business in the Community and the Task Force as part of its 'exit strategy', and welcomed by the property developers themselves, who saw in such a group an opportunity to pursue their negotiations to closure, the Community Development Group was looked on by the more seasoned campaigners with downright suspicion.

So, the 'local community', certainly those of its number who considered themselves to be its leaders and activists, who put their name to one of the apparently interchangeable acronyms or pressure groups which operated in the area, was about as politically at odds with itself, as politically intriguing, as it could have been. Yet, as they argued about tactics and priorities, worried about the timetable and focus of regeneration, they all shared the same conviction that the future shape of Spitalfields depended significantly on their present intervention. As with the property developers themselves, their golden age, if they allowed themselves to have one, was just round the corner, over the hill. It would arrive with the dawn.

One dusk, I joined Kay Jordan and her colleagues on the roof of the SSBA's offices on Brick Lane. She pointed out all the derelict sites, those set for 'redevelopment', circling Spitalfields, a new City Wall: 'OK, I realise, there are lots of ways of viewing this, a lot of different perceptions of what is going on here. But the fact is that wherever there is change or transition, there will be casualties. You do one thing, but its always at the expense of something else. That's the nature of the deal and you just hope the deal works for you. You try to minimise the bad and maximise the good. In this situation, here in Spitalfields, we're trying to look after the local Bengali community and, right now, it looks like this community is going to be a casualty of the deal. What can you say? What should you do?'

The cranes, arched and monstrous, swayed magnificently in the gentle evening breeze. 'It's weird,' she said, 'It's just weird.'

Click!

It was surprisingly easy to track down Henry George, the erstwhile tenant of Rex Morton-Smith and before that of the Spitalfields Trust, although it was harder to persuade him I wasn't some kind of ball-breaking henchman, come to settle old scores.

'So what do you want to know?' he said, his voice bassoon-like over the telephone.

'Well, I'd heard you'd moved out of your workshop accommodation in Heneage Street quite recently. I was wondering why that was. I'm doing a bit of research. For the market developers. For the Spitalfields Development Group, the consortium that's going to develop the market site. They've asked me to find out how people in the area feel about the development, how they think it will affect the existing community . . .' I continued to blabber banalities into the receiver, apparently to myself.

'I don't think I can help you.'

'That's a shame, I thought you might have had some information about the Spitalfields Trust and Mr Morton-Smith.'

'What sort of information?'

'General things, the terms and conditions of your lease agreement, rent reviews. I need examples.'

A pause, then 'Maybe you'd better come out here.'

Mr George's new workshop was in Leyton. I took the bus, checking his route instructions against my A–Z, arriving hopelessly late. A big man with a strong handshake and a weary smile, he was younger than I imagined him to be. His denim jacket looked like it had seen racier days; his jeans were modestly flared. A battered old grip with some papers, a thermos and a packet of digestive biscuits lay at his feet. He offered me a chair, and we both sat down. He then unfolded a piece of paper from his jacket pocket, a catalogue of dates and amounts, flattening it out on his knee, glancing to it for reference throughout our conversation.

He took me through the early history, what he remembered of it, the Trust's purchase of 27 Fournier Street, the move to Heneage Street, his satisfaction at having at last a well-equipped workspace. 'You couldn't really complain, it was a very good deal.' He told me how everything seemed fine until, at some point a few years after moving, he became aware that Morton-Smith, the Trust's former agent, had taken over the tenancies. Morton-Smith had become his new landlord, which, co-incidentally, 'was when things started to get bad'. First the old leases were terminated, then the rent was trebled, then the service charge, which had always been kept reasonably modest, became, in his eyes, unreasonably punitive.

'There suddenly seemed to be a lot of things to be done, whether it was keeping the yard clean or whatever, there simply seemed to be a lot of faults, a lot of work being carried out. In fact, thinking about it now, the place was quite simply being fixed up at our expense.'

Though none left immediately, the old Fournier Street tenants fought the rent increase, fearing that Morton-Smith was trying to turn Heneage Street 'into a posh place, where he can get more rent'. By the end of the second lease, however, George was the only original Spitalfields Trust tenant left. And then he, too, received his notice to quit. He remembered that he had been given 'two grounds, the rent wasn't being paid properly and something to do with the state of the building'. George went to see Morton-Smith in his old offices, just opposite Liverpool Street Station. In the end, Morton-Smith relented, offering George a new lease, but with additional terms and further clauses.

'He said he could give me a lease, but that it wouldn't be a three-year lease. And he said he was going to put a clause into that lease, that after eighteen months he could give me notice to quit, whenever he wanted. I said that did not give me much security. He said that that did not mean that he would throw me out, just that he would have the right to do so if he wanted.

Well, I felt that that's the best I'm going to get from him and so I said OK, I'll take it, but deep down inside I knew I couldn't afford it.'

George became ill, was taken to hospital and was told he had developed a duodenal ulcer. He decided he had had enough. When he came out, he handed in his notice, telling Morton-Smith that he couldn't afford the rent. Morton-Smith extended his sympathy, pointing out that the bank was after him too, that it was certainly a tough old world. And as he was leaving, Morton-Smith asked George about his photography, a particular interest of his, and how he was getting on. 'He always asked me about my photography, I think he would have liked that to take off so I wouldn't have to do sewing.'

In fact, George had trained originally as an engineer, although he had pretty much always worked in the leather trade, latterly making up motorcycle jackets, since arriving in Great Britain from the West Indies in 1962. Always seasonal, business recently had quite definitely slowed down and, yes, he recognised that it was probably a dying trade, certainly in Britain, with such competitive markets opening up in the South-East Asia. But, as far as Henry George was concerned, it wasn't the fluctuating world market that had done for him in Spitalfields.

'When I moved in, when the Trust moved me in, I simply never thought I would have to pay so much rent. Looking at it now, I feel the Trust really treated us badly, leaving us for Morton-Smith. They treated us in a secondary way. When the Trust got rid of us from that particular protected house in Fournier Street, as far as they were concerned their job was done and so we were secondary. They just left us to the dogs.'

By this time Morton-Smith had settled into his new office in Fournier Street. In fact, over the previous months I had watched as the building had been vacated by a firm of haberdashery wholesalers, and then done over in readiness for Morton-Smith's arrival. I had seen it knocked through, rebuilt, repointed, plastered, painted, glazed, shuttered and generally touched up. I had seen them hoisting up the electric candelabra and piling in the filing cabinets. One day I had seen what looked suspiciously like an office-warming party. It was some time, however, before I pressed my lips to the intercom system bolted to the Georgian door case and said, 'I was wondering if I could possibly have a word with Mr Morton-Smith?'

'Do come in.'

A tall and extremely lean man, Morton-Smith welcomed me in the reception room downstairs and took me up to his office on the first floor, overlooking the street, overshadowed by Christ Church. I explained how I was doing 'local research' for the market developers, how I had been commissioned to find out what the needs of the 'community' were, how local businesses were faring on the ground, how they saw the likely impact of the redevelopment. That sort of thing. I waved my briefcase around a bit, readjusted my tie, put my tape recorder on his desk, which spread out in front of him, a vast expanse of important-looking emptiness. In fact, his whole office was remarkably clutter-free. Sitting behind his desk, Morton-Smith too looked like a man impatient with mess, given to purges. Remarking on his impressive vantage-point view of Fournier Street I told him how much I loved these old houses, so historical, so hidden away. He was off.

'When I first came here, twenty years ago, I immediately thought, early Georgian houses! I'd come from the West End, from that perspective, and I thought, how can this be? Most people in those days said they were a load of rubbish, that was the feeling in those days. Though everyone now is into preservation and conservation, they weren't in those days. The most amazing thing was when we found so many of the original features intact. Do you know what I mean? If you get fireplaces which are still in situ after two hundred years, it's really quite extraordinary.'

Although Morton-Smith spoke as a property speculator, he was clearly not one without concern for the area, without a feel for the place, a sense of the cultural frisson available here to the passing adventurer. After all, he had seen some changes on Fournier Street over the years, with his earliest memories going back to a time when it was predominantly Jewish, before the Bengali community had really arrived in Spitalfields. Certainly it was different in those days, but he was at pains to instruct me that I wasn't to misunderstand him. I wasn't to misinterpret his professional consideration of the area, his account of Spitalfields from the perspective of a working estate agent, as anything which might remotely smack of racism. He knew there were dangers here and he wanted to avoid them.

'When I'm talking, by the way, I'm not being racial. It's very difficult to say anything without being accused of being racial. I have Jews as friends. If you're working in the area you can't afford to be racial, but it's very difficult and one's sort of terrified of saying things and then being quoted. It's just that my experience of the Bengali community is that probably they are harder than the Jews, as businessmen, if they're successful. I think it's probably an immigrant psychology, probably like the Jews, they've had to fight, to be as hard as nails. But they get away with doing things to their own kind which, were you or I to do them, people would immediately say, racial!'

Or possibly, nonsense! In fact, it was all very well his presenting himself as a prejudice-free property agent, and of course there was no reason to doubt it, but what I really wanted to know was how the deal was working for him, how business was faring. What interested me most was how, as a man with considerable experience of handling tricky tenancy situations, he saw the impact of the City on the fabric of the area. For example, did he have any direct experience of, say, particular tenants who were vulnerable to rent increases as a result of free market activity in the area? And had the Spitalfields Development Group, by its mere presence and stated intention, caused any hiatus in the property market? In short, were rag trade tenants being squeezed out?

'I don't think so. There's a lot of talk about them being squeezed out, I mean I don't know whether they're being squeezed out, I mean there's a lot of song and dance stuff, but I don't know whether they're actually being squeezed out. I think, as far as your development of the market is concerned, they're not being squeezed out there.

'I think in an area like this, with its close proximity to the City, I think you're bound to get a certain demand from firms wanting to service the City. The rents are so cheap here compared to what they are a quarter of a mile away.

'No, they're not being squeezed out by higher rents. We used to rent a lot to suede and leather people, fifteen years ago, you almost didn't bother to ask them what they did, it was bound to be suede and leather. You had suede and leather people in Fournier Street, all over the place, but they can't really afford it now, I suppose one would say. They can't really afford a market rental now.

'But if it's suggested that the market developers are squeezing out the suede and leather people it's a load of bloody bullshit, quite frankly. An awful lot of ideas are being peddled round, which one knows don't actually make any sense on the ground at all. You see, what I think . . .'

Click! My tape had stopped. Morton-Smith peered across his desk. Shock, then panic, crossed his face. I reached out to turn the tape over. He shot up.

'Have you been taping the conversation?'

'Of course, didn't you see me put my recorder on your desk?'

'No I didn't. I mean, I thought it was a pocket calculator.'

'I'm sorry, there seems to have been some kind of confusion.'

'I'd like the tape please.'

'You want the tape? Well, I'm not sure . . .'

'Give me the tape and we can begin again. I'll start the interview again.'

'No, I think I want to keep the tape.'

'Give me the tape and we'll start again and at the end of the day we'll shake on it as friends.'

'No.'

'Give it to me.'

Impasse had descended on our conversation at an alarming rate. Not inclined to enter into negotiation, I exited his office *tout de suite*, muttering something about how I needed a glass of water. I got downstairs. In fact, I got to the front door, but then found myself caught by the interlocking lobby effect of the entrance area, Morton-Smith's foot against the door, trapped with him in a space no more than four foot square, attended by his astonished secretary. Morton-Smith told me if I didn't give him the tape right then he would ring the police. He gave his secretary instructions to ring the police. He told her to stop ringing the police. We stood together, adrenalin gushing, steaming, our arms locked against the door handle, both staring at it, as though we were intensely interested in comparing the width and chalkiness of our pinstripes. I noticed how his long and rather fine fingers had whitened and were trembling slightly. He turned to me.

'What's your name?'

'William Taylor.'

'No, I mean what's your real name?'

'That is my real name.'

'Who are you working for?'

'As I said, I'm doing research for the Spitalfields Development Group.'

'But who are you? Who are you really?'

The door buzzed and swung open. Morton-Smith stepped back. A colleague, who was returning from his lunch, also stood back politely, making way for me to pass, unhindered, on to Fournier Street.

Not personal like that

I was still fizzing when I met my friend Jean at the Aladin restaurant a few hours later. Having spent much of the afternoon pacing my room in the Princelet Street house where I was staying, repeating to myself Mr Morton-Smith's plaintive doorway interrogation – 'Who are you? What's your real name? Who do you really work for?' – I turned up at the Brick Lane restaurant in a state of high spirits. Righteous indignation, especially when unsullied by scruple or self-doubt, is, after all, really quite agreeable.

'My, what a sleuth!' she said, as I told her how, following my meeting with the market developers, I had set about looking into the Spitalfields Trust's activities in the area, how I had pursued the story of the clearance of its prize house in Fournier Street, the decanting of its tenants into nearby Heneage Street and then the sale of this workshop accommodation to its very own agent, Morton-Smith, who had subsequently increased the rents so much that all these original tenants had been forced to move out. I told her how I had tracked down the last one to leave, a leather cutter called Henry George, and, with his story of embattled survival in my head, I had gone to meet Morton-Smith himself. I told her how, having mistakenly assumed a complicity, Morton-Smith had told me what he imagined, no doubt, I had wanted to hear, namely that the notion of there being any identifiable causal link in Spitalfields between the prospect of its market development and the disappearance of its rag trade was, in his professional judgement, 'a load of bloody bullshit'. And then I told her how, when it transpired there had been a confusion about the taping, he had attempted to take the tape and then, when failing to do so, he had thrown me out (I was lying: in fact I had fled). And then I said, thick with emotion, how, in my commitment to Henry George, and others like him, I was determined that this story should be told, that it should see the light of day.

'What story?' she said.

'The story of a man forced out of his community by another man, a man richer and more powerful than himself,' I said.

'But, William, surely you don't think the market is personal like that. Your estate agent, whatever his name is, can't be held personally to account for claiming his market rental and your rag trade tenant isn't the only person to be affected by the collapse of the leather trade in the UK. The fact is we're all caught up in a series of interrelated markets and, although it may be convenient to scapegoat a particular property developer here or a particular estate agent there, it just isn't appropriate given the incredible complexity of the international marketplace.'

Jean, a doctoral student who was writing her thesis on something to do with pollution and social policy, had arranged to spend a few days doing some 'field work' in Tower Hamlets. I found her refusal to be drawn into the black and white of it all frankly a bit annoying and actually quite uncharacteristic of the campaigning activist I had known her to be when we were both students. I hoped she wasn't in the process of becoming the worst sort of prevaricating academic.

'What about civility, taking seriously a sense of neighbourhood, one's responsibility to the communities in which we live
and work, that sort of thing?' I said.

'Well, maybe, although in contemporary circles 'community'
is no longer considered to be exclusively a place-specific
category. Urban geographers talk increasingly about 'community' in terms of 'discourse matrices'. They see community
as an experience which is, above all, generated and sustained
through the medium of conversation. Moreover such conversations are as likely to be pursued over the net, in cyberspace, as
over the wall at the bottom of the garden.' The waiter had
brought our menus, a jug of water and glasses; Jean continued,
pouring out the water and quibbling over her terminology as
though she were at a faculty research seminar, 'I think we need
to be a bit careful, in any case, over our use of the term
'community'. So often it seems to me less a way of defining and
mediating our corporate identity and more a way of codifying
certain practices for the exercise of social control and
domination within particular localised contexts.' She placed the
menu on the table, 'Shall we order?'

As bowls of delicious Indian food were placed in front of us,
spinach and potato and aubergine in delicately curried sauces,
the conversation relaxed into anecdote and convivial gossip. We
caught up on the news and whereabouts of mutual friends, what
they were doing, who they were dating, who they had split up
from. Had I spotted Thomas in the *Standard*? Did she know that
Sebastian had gone to work for the Oxford University Press?
Was I planning on going to Rachel's wedding in Istanbul? She
told me about a recent cycling holiday in Tuscany, how she and
her discourse companion had hopped from hill town to hill
town, and how, for the very first time, she felt that she had
'really managed to engage with the Tuscan landscape'.

I was conscious that the restaurant was filling up. As we fell
silent, finishing our meal, we both became aware of the conversations going on around us, of the various groups crowding
round the other tables, the slightly ludicrous posturing and
performing that often accompany a few drinks and a night out
with friends. It was Jean who returned to our earlier discussion

of the nature of community. Spitalfields, she said rather summarily, was like this restaurant: a series of unrelated communities inhabiting their own discourse matrix and yet somehow coexisting within a single space. I said that that made me feel uncomfortable, that, as a model, it was fundamentally exclusive and excluding. She said that any notion of community was necessarily going to be exclusive, that it was always going to be dependent on the existence of 'the other'. I said that it appeared not only to be dependent on the existence of 'the other', but also, in this instance, on the fact of structural exploitation.

'What about the waiters, the cooks, the cleaners?'

'Precisely so,' she said, 'precisely so, communities are inextricably locked into their market position, defining themselves both according to the existing structures of inequality, as well as over and against them.'

'But surely we need to interrupt these structures, to champion, however inadequately, the needs of the marginalised and the most vulnerable?'

'Why? Who are these people? It's all of us, surely. We're all both inside the circle as well as outside it. The line goes through the middle of us all.'

Maybe Jean was right. Maybe, indeed, in my single-tracked indignation I was too eager to draw falsely conceived distinctions between 'persecutor' and 'victim', between centre and margin. Perhaps I was too eager to perform the ethical equivalent of the zoning of the planning department, their bollarding-in and bollarding-out of urban order and mess. It was certainly more agreeable to do so, keeping the others down below and maintaining for myself, the 'rescuer', an unassailable position up on the moral high ground. In reality, however, weren't we all mixed up together in a complex web of interdependency and mutual exploitation?

The waiter appeared with our bill. He placed it on the table between us along with some filthy-tasting sweets. I felt in my pocket for my wallet. We both put some cash on the table and stood to leave.

The wailing sound of the Indian music stopped and was

replaced by a rather incongruous-sounding news bulletin, which it took me a few moments to place. '. . . His Royal Highness, Prince Charles, visited sweatshops and restaurants down Brick Lane in the East End of London this afternoon. Speaking with restaurant owner Mr Toimus, he said how much he welcomed the generosity and friendliness of the Indian community in this part of London. He was particularly interested to hear of plans amongst the Bangladeshi business community to establish a Bangla Town on Brick Lane, a new tourist attraction in the East End of London.'

The waiter who showed us to the door grinned broadly, 'We play the tape of the BBC radio news when we have requests.' And then, as we passed on to the street, he added, 'We look forward to seeing you again. You are very welcome to the restaurant that Prince Charles likes to visit!'

Negotiation and compromise

'Bangla Town? Bangla Town? It makes it sound like some hideous piece of wrist jewellery,' said Dan Cruickshank, founder member of the Spitalfields Trust and resident of the area. I had gone to see him with my account of how the Trust had handled its former Fournier Street tenants, how it had effectively washed its hands of them, passing the buck while making a few at the same time. I had wanted to hear his side of the story before I went back to the developers; it seemed only fair. Sitting in the walled garden at the back of his Elder Street house, with the early evening sun passing through the vine leaves which shaded our seats, cooled by a light breeze, quenched by a glass of chilled wine, we talked about the way Brick Lane had changed since he moved to Spitalfields. He was pleased to hear of the Bangladeshi community's latest plans to attract business into the area, if slightly bemused by this idea of a 'Bangla Town'.

'I mean, why don't they call it something pretty like Little Bengal?'

Our conversation turned to 27 Fournier Street. When I asked

him what had happened to the Trust's former tenants, Cruickshank was clearly struggling to remember. 'The Trust has always said it never winkled people out, that it never pressurised anyone to move. After buying number 27, we rehoused the tenants into the former stables on Heneage Street. A year or two later we sold this property to Mr Morton-Smith and I have really lost touch with what happened then, I'm afraid it's a story I don't know the end of. I suppose their rights were protected by any agreement we made.'

Well, not exactly. I filled him in on the subsequent course of events, Morton-Smith's rent increase, the expedited clearance of the rag trade tenants, Henry George's exasperated illness. Cruickshank seemed genuinely surprised. 'Of course we never wanted to be landlords, we wanted money to fulfil our aims of buying other Georgian buildings, but it does sound, in the light of what's happened, somewhat short-sighted of us . . . it all sounds a bit of a case of . . . blinkered vision . . . I mean, almost the worst part about this was that it was never discussed. It was obviously a decision which was taken at some kind of level, but it never became an issue for the Trustees at the time when we should have realised the consequences.'

From my reading of the Trust's minutes, it had indeed become an issue for the Trustees, though clearly not for Cruickshank himself. Possibly he had been absent from those meetings when the sale had been discussed. Or possibly he had been distracted momentarily by the catalogue of original features revealed in Fournier Street once the departure of the tenants had taken place. Nevertheless, the sale had gone through. 'It does suggest incredible stupidity. The Trust is always crowing that we did the right thing, that we didn't kick people out, that we put the Fournier Street tenants into Heneage Street, but if the very next chapter is that we simply sold it on to a local businessman then of course it's bad. There's no question about it, the Trust shouldn't have done that.'

To be honest, I wasn't prepared for quite such candour. Clearly, however, I had touched on what was also a contentious issue within the Trust itself. Like a man who had been living through his own private turmoil and had suddenly been released from his vow of silence, Cruickshank began to talk with bean-spilling intensity. 'The real question, it seems to me, is whether the Trust is itself becoming a property developer. I'm not sure, because of the taping, that I can go into all the details, but suffice it to say for the last six months we've been having the most hideous kind of discussions, debates and arguments within the Trust. It's all been focused on our properties in Brushfield Street, the ones adjoining Spitalfields Market.' Collecting himself, Cruickshank paused, hunched over the table. I began to feel I wasn't so much conducting an interview as hearing a confession. 'Basically,' he continued, 'in order to fund our other conservation projects in the borough, we decided we needed to realise some of the value of these buildings, given their quality and the fact of their prime location adjacent to SDG's proposed office development.'

Cruickshank stood up abruptly and disappeared into the house. Was this my signal to go? In a little while he returned with a file from which he extracted a closely typed statement. 'In the end,' he said, 'I wrote a desperate memo to the other Trustees, saying how we would become ridiculous people unless certain conditions were met.' He went on to read a paragraph from this doleful-sounding document:

'Many residents of the area would be shocked, and feel betrayed, if the Trust were revealed as willing partners in a socially and architecturally destructive speculative development, and needless to say its influence with Tower Hamlets council would be at an end. How could it ever again criticise proposals to demolish buildings, and to turn a shop or workshop into offices, if the Trust had done the same itself? The Trust could argue that its descent into commercial development was for an objectively good reason – to raise money to fulfil its declared aims of saving and repairing historic buildings in the borough – but this would be seen as an hypocritical defence by those who feel ends do not necessarily justify means.'

The Spitalfields Trust was facing a dilemma which went to the heart of its credibility as a representative local pressure group and Cruickshank clearly felt himself to be in a bit of a pickle. Whereas the Trust presented itself as a group committed to the highest ideals in town planning, publicly setting itself against the bald commercialism of the Spitalfields Development Group, championing the needs of the rag traders on Brick Lane, standing aloof from the vagaries of the property market, Cruickshank himself told a different story. His story was one of negotiation and compromise, a pursuit of the ultimate deal.

As I walked home later that evening, past the Market into the heart of Georgian Spitalfields – Folgate Street, Commercial Street, Fournier Street, Wilkes Street, Princelet Street – I felt fairly confident I had uncovered enough apparent hypocrisy to enable SDG, through my 'report' and its publicity machine, to launch its own counter-attack against the Trust, exposing its double standard, and reinvent itself, following Angie Peppiatt's strategy, as the self-styled 'community developer'.

When I got home there was a message on my answer machine. It was from Angie herself. 'Something's come up. A Mr Morton-Smith has been on the blower to Brian. There's obviously been a bit of a mix-up and Brian has asked me to sort it out. Can you give me a buzz when you get in? Thanks a lot kiddo!'

I rang in the morning. Angie explained the situation, how Morton-Smith had rung the office to check out my credentials and had needed a bit of talking down. As a local agent, they didn't want to aggravate unnecessarily with the development coming on stream and the sensitive nature of negotiations over the renewed planning application being pursued. She was sure I knew the sort of thing she meant. Particularly now as it looked like the Secretary of State was going to call in the scheme, possibly even for public inquiry. All in all, it was a case of treading softly-softly. 'He also said there was something about a tape and could I drop it by. Of course, we said, we were sure there wouldn't be a problem about that. Probably would be a good idea, don't you think? It doesn't look very good, we don't want to appear unprofessional.'

Inarticulate rage rose in my throat. Was this professionalism?

Smoothing over all inconsistencies, opting for convenience, complicity, tidiness, straight lines? Suddenly Cruickshank's disruptive candour appeared positively heroic.

'Oh yes,' said Angie, cutting across my silence, 'Brian did the cheques on Friday. Yours is ready. Probably best if I give it to you when you bring the tape in, don't you think?'

TURNING ASIDE

Flood

I was shaken by the whole series of events more than I allowed
myself to admit. For the next few days, Mr Morton-Smith's
plaintive doorway interrogation – 'Who are you? What's your
real name? Who do you really work for?' – rang in my ears, like
a stone rattling around in an empty pail. They were all good
questions and ones which I had managed to avoid asking myself
since I had moved to London.

Instead I had been busy asking them of Spitalfields, deconstructing its assorted 'incompatible realities', drawing attention
to the disparity between its various golden age versions and the
complex inner city reality. *Who are you?* I had asked the
Cockney market trader, with his noisily entrepreneurial
individualism and his curiously nostalgic understanding of community. *What's your real name?* I had asked the New Georgian
resident, nursing his snobberies, cradling his insecurities. *Who do
you really work for?* I had asked Mr Professional Spitalfields,
enthusing with the promise of urban regeneration yet oddly
indifferent to the plight of its contemporary residents.

Yet was I prepared to turn the question on its heels? What
was *my* real name?

I decided to go away for the weekend. I felt a strong urge to
get to the sea, to the edge of things, a place where land meets
water. I rang a friend who lived in Suffolk, right on the coast.
He wouldn't actually be there, he said, but I'd be welcome to
hole up for a while. Wonderful! On Friday afternoon, checking

the times of trains and connections, I packed a bag of miscellaneous distractions: playing cards, a couple of novels, a whisky bottle, walking boots, swimming trunks, rolling tobacco, a packet of porridge oats. Randomly scouring my Fournier Street flat, I came across the book my grandmother had written about my grandfather. I put it in the bag.

From Liverpool Street Station I travelled to Ipswich, where I changed on to the local Lowestoft line, getting off at Woodbridge, and then by bus and foot to the cottage. The summer sun was just past the horizon when I arrived, leaving the huge Suffolk sky to bleed its way into night. The breeze was warm and soft and smelt of sea and honeysuckle. I had a bite to eat and then wandered down the shingle bank to throw stones into the water.

The morning arrived early and exultant. The sun, which filled the house, seemed to drag my covers off and demand that the day begin. I knew immediately that the game was up, that there was no chance of just turning over and falling asleep again. I went downstairs and pottered around in the kitchen in a slightly groggy way. I peered into the fridge. I switched the radio on and off. Excavating a pot from the back of the cupboard, boiling water, sniffing milk, prodding tea bags, I began to mull things over in that drowsy pre-caffeine fashion.

So, I asked myself, what *is* your real name? I replied out loud, as it were to the clerk of the court – William Goodacre Campbell-Taylor – and then, once I had spoken, quickly retreated back into internal musing, wondering how the hyphen had found its aspirant way into my surname, like a slightly fancy hinge linking together two pieces of rather plain board. Morton-Smith/Campbell-Taylor: hmm, sounds curiously similar, I thought. Maybe this was what galled me so much. Did I see in him something of my own real self, real name? The water on the cooker had started bubbling and steaming. Yet wasn't this actual name/real name distinction pretty absurd? I poured hot water into the pot and left it to steep. This is an actual teapot, I said to myself, but what, one might ask, is really teapotty about it? What is the nature of its teapotness? What is its essential teapot-*keit*? Snorting to myself, I lifted my grandmother's account of my grandfather's life out of the bag, placing it on the tray next to the teapot, and returned to bed.

Maybe most of the time we only see what we want to see, but there are also times when, for whatever reason, we allow a little truth in. Religious people call it revelation and pray for the grace to receive it. Often, when it strikes, when the penny drops, it is painful. Occasionally it is sweet. Essentially, though, it is a narrative experience; it happens to us in story and in the telling we become retold.

'John Goodacre,' begins my grandmother, 'was born on December the fifth in 1874, in Exeter. There was a flood at the time and the doctor had to use a boat to reach the house. The Goodacres were a family of devoted Church people, and his father was fourth in a line of priests. They were much influenced by the Oxford Movement, which came into being in the first part of the nineteenth century . . .' My grandmother's voice was gentle, loving, containing. Although she had died many years previously I could still recall her Dublin accent, soft and lilting, easing me out of some or other tantrum. I settled into the bed, slurped some tea, and read on.

The facts were already familiar to me. Following his father's illness and mother's early death, he was raised by his grandfather, himself a widower, and his uncle, a bachelor, in a remote North Staffordshire vicarage. Between them, grandfather and uncle had managed to hold on to the incumbency of the poor parish for over fifty years, the son having gone to work for his father as curate and then having stayed on as vicar, once his father retired. For my grandfather it was a strange and loveless childhood – 'but bracing air and plenty of good food,' she writes. At twelve he was sent to Oxford to a school run by the Cowley Fathers, a order of Anglican monks, and from there to Coventry grammar school and subsequently to Cambridge. He was ordained in 1897 and went to work in the Black Country as a young priest.

It was his time in Hanley in the Potteries that caught my imagination. I already knew well the fictional descriptions of the 'Five Towns' in the novels of Arnold Bennett, who, having been born in 1867, was in effect a contemporary of my grandfather's. Set among the blast-furnaces and smoke-stacks of the Potteries, beneath the constant canopy of yellow-tinted smoke, *Anna of the Five Towns* tells the story of its eponymous heroine, daughter of the miserly Ephraim Tellwright, a successful pot-bank owner and all-round tyrant. Inevitably Anna falls for the young Willie Price, whose family, as tenants to Tellwright, are being squeezed out of their accommodation by an increase in rents – where had I heard this before? – business being business, no hard feelings of course. Despite eventually marrying the rather creepy Mr Mynors, himself another successful pot-bank owner – who sees with impressive foresight that the future is in toilet-ware – and then standing by as her father brings about the financial humiliation of Willie's family, Anna is deeply shocked when she hears that Willie's father, Titus Price, has committed suicide. She feels sharply her failure to intervene on his behalf, that she is personally implicated.

This, then, is the context into which my grandfather had gone to minister. 'In 1906,' writes my grandmother, 'John was put in charge of the Mission District of All Saints in Hanley [referred to as 'Hanbridge', in Bennett's book, which itself had been published in 1902].' She continues, 'His work here was a tough proposition, with most of his people working in the pot-banks. Wages were low, hours were long, and the work heavy. One cannot wonder that people found drink their only enjoyment and a means of getting out of their hard lives for some hours ... There was one period of terrible distress when the mines and pot-banks were shut down due to strike action and the suffering caused was acute. John and the other clergy organised soup kitchens and did endless visiting to find the very needy. He described going to one house and the mother refusing to take anything but in the end she broke down and John found she had absolutely nothing in the house.'

I read on late into the morning. I followed her account of his work in Hanley, his raising the money to build a church (to which end he gave his entire personal fortune), his temperance missions, his camping holidays for the young of the parish, his commitment to the cause of the workers in the pot-banks and mines of district. And then I read how he joined up as an army

Chaplain when the First World War broke out, serving alongside many of his men from the parish in the 59th division of the
North Staffs.

His first expedition was not, however, to France. In April
1916 he found himself in Dublin, his division having been sent
to quell the Easter Uprising: 'John told me of the day they were
paraded in the grounds of St Patrick's Cathedral, where there
were gunmen in the houses round. He thought it such a
senseless affair that he told the men to take cover, and did so
himself. Although he was subsequently reprimanded for in-
subordination, he won the respect of his men.' Another story
tells of how, under sniper fire in St Stephen's Green, he
identified the window where the shooting was coming from
and went up to approach the rebel gunman himself, in his dog-
collar and unarmed, with the simple instruction, 'Give me that
gun!' Such was the authority of the Church in those days that,
rather than shooting him dead on the spot, the gunman
obediently handed it over.

With his division pitched in Phoenix Park, he sought
permission of a local Church of Ireland clergyman to baptise
several soldiers in the latter's font. My grandmother allows
herself a little sentiment, 'My father invited him to Sunday
evening supper, and so we met,' she writes, 'little thinking how
that evening would affect us for the rest of our lives.'

When he returned from France, at the end of the war, they
were married. My grandmother moved to Hanley. But the
world had changed; so too had the parish. He found it hard to
re-settle and in 1920 they left the Potteries for the Black
Country. At his Farewell Party, given in the church he had
built, the churchwardens told of how 'one of the most
outstanding results of their Vicar's work in the parish was that
the moral tone of the population had been greatly improved.
Not so many years previously their district had been avoided,
but now it was teeming with solid sober, intelligent and orderly
citizens: indeed it had become almost suburban'.

Suburban! Oh Lord, surely not! The very notion sent me
hurtling back to my own well polished prejudices. I pulled some
clothes on and went outside. As I walked towards the sea I saw

the mast of a sailing ship tilting over at an unlikely angle, stationary, just beyond the bank of stones. I guessed immediately what had happened and as I reached the top of the bank, with a clear view down into the stream of the estuary, I saw that I was right: the boat had run aground on the ebb tide, its owner unused maybe to charting the narrow channel, and would now have to wait for the tide to turn and the river to flood. Fortunately, it was a fine day: a man and woman, presumably the crew, were lying on the far bank, a blanket spread beneath them, enjoying a picnic. What else could they do?

The sun had already warmed the shingle and turned the sea a silvery blue. It was, indeed, a beautiful day. I returned to the cottage and packed my own picnic, feeling an uncertain mixture of pride as well as somehow its opposite, something much sadder, more like failure. With my walking boots on, I found a route beyond the straggle of houses along the top of the shingle bank, a narrow ridge between the water meadow and the sea. Cows grazed nonchalantly in the distance on one side, a few ships arranged themselves along the horizon on the other.

On my narrow path I walked on urgently, my boots giving my step a purposeful deliberate intention, treading here, treading there. The prints of other walkers passed before me, an assortment of soles planted previously in the wet mud, preserved now in the dry dirt. Stepping here, stepping there, pressing on into the midday heat and delicious breeze, my mind relaxed into rhythmic plodding, forward-moving grunts and noises, names and phrases, a steady mantra of simply marching on: *Campbell Taylor, Morton Smith, Morton Taylor, Campbell Smith, A Man Called Rex, A Man Called John, Give me that Tape, Give me that Gun* . . .

Eventually I stopped and lay down on my back. I'm not sure how long I lay there. I may well have fallen asleep and then woken again. I remember thinking at one point how remarkably close the sky looked. And then, from somewhere beneath me, from deep inside the ground, I began to weep, tears of remorse certainly, yet also somehow of joy. I felt I had been unhinged. I wasn't at all sure what was going on.

Sometime, in the late afternoon, I turned around and found my way home. As I reached the top of the shingle bank I looked down into the channel of the river. The tide had turned, the waters had risen. The boat, it appeared, had been swept out to sea.

Turnaround

What is the difference between taking a professional interest and responding to a vocational imperative? How do we ever know we are doing the right thing, in the right place?

Such questions, probably best discussed when one is slightly pissed, began to preoccupy me at this time. After that impromptu weekend in Suffolk, some sort of turnaround in my thinking about ordination seemed to be taking place. I was beginning to see a calling to the priesthood not so much a state of being which, through careful and patient preparation, we may hope eventually to attain, even less a career option we may (heaven knows why) wish to pursue, but rather a promise or a possibility which, unbidden, pursues and inhabits *us*? Like falling in love.

My time in Spitalfields had helped me see this. From that first evening, when I had flung open the door of the old ark of the covenant in the redundant Princelet Street Synagogue, Spitalfields had laid claim on my imagination. I remember feeling that somehow I shared personal responsibility for the area's loss of direction, its variously contested identity. Though I knew such feelings were irrational – displaced, projected, narcissistic – they were nonetheless powerfully motivating. I clearly had something to work out. Spitalfields presented itself to me as the place to do it. I had got involved.

In getting involved in the area I had been able to engage with myself in a different way. I had tried out new voices, put on a wardrobe of unfamiliar roles, articulated all sorts of ugly prejudices – as well as some finer ones. It was a time when I could begin to see what was in there, open up a conversation with myself, rearrange the furniture. Partly through the loss of his ring and my mother's subsequent gift of his book, I had begun to recognise quite how haunted I was by my grandfather's life as a clergyman in the Potteries in the early part of the Twentieth Century. Maybe this was my own version of the golden age. Certainly my head was full of the heroic model of the 'slum priest', one to which I was notably failing remotely to approximate. It even occurred to me that, in my slightly obsessive pursuit of 'parish experience', maybe I was sub-consciously performing some sort of curious act of penance?

But is this not, in any case, what cities are for? More fun than psychotherapy, less exacting (and providing better copy) than the strictures of the confessional, they allow us to participate in the imaginative possibility of regeneration. This possibility, moreover, is often a shared one. Certainly, in the course of my 'parish experience', I found myself caught up in a succession of visions of urban community.

Yet ultimately were these visions, these versions of golden age Spitalfields, nothing but chimeras? Easy to deconstruct, how resistant would such suggestions of local solidarity – Cockney, New Georgian, Professional – actually prove themselves to be when confronted by the impact of the global market? Like the dying embers of the pallet fire continuously kept burning in the car-park of the fruit and vegetable market, they seemed to be stirring into defiant flame at the very moment the old market itself was to make way for the construction of an office develop-ment servicing the international finance community – a development which would extinguish the bonfire once and for all. These imaginary versions of the area seemed, in the end, to signify a reality they were unable actually to sustain.

There was, however, one version of the area I had yet really to engage with: Migrant Spitalfields. In some ways it was the least obviously capable of resisting market forces, certainly the Bengali community was economically the most vulnerable. In other ways it had been the most persistent throughout the area's history. You could even say it was archetypal of an area which, throughout its history, had always been hospitable to marginal groups on the move. Indeed, was not migration – coming and going, merely passing through – the essential nature of modern urban life?

Go and come

Brick Lane was forever being dug up. They would come along, smash the tarmac to pieces, pick-axe the brick, drill down a few feet, spilling the rubble and impacted rubbish all over the pavement. Then they would put up a temporary barrier, surrounding it with a few hazard cones and a sign apologising for the obstruction. They would spend a while poking around, laying a few cables or linking someone up to the mains, before returning a few days later with all the mixers and begin to slop sand and water and cement into a paste which looked a bit like digestive biscuit and shovel it back into the hole. When they had coated the surface over with tar, they would pack up their vans and drive off to another part of the Lane, which they would begin to smash to pieces again.

The traffic on the Lane ran one way from south to north, from Whitechapel High Street to the Bethnal Green Road. It edged past the road works, past the curry houses and clothing wholesalers, the leather shops and saree centres, the travel agents and Ambala Sweets, the primary school, the mosque and all the other sights and sounds which make up the heart of Britain's largest Bangladeshi community.

Pavement life, the shoppers and hangers-out, seemed to take precedence over road life. There was a tacit assumption that it was the car's responsibility to stop, not the pedestrian's to get out of the way. With the road always constipated with vehicles, the shouting and honking of irate drivers became part of the very rhythm of the street, part of its very sociability.

Take Toor. Toor sold belts, hundreds of them, all of different lengths, widths, colours, buckles, 'all leather, very good high class leather', all hung from nails, lining the downstairs corridor of his house. He put a table in the doorway fronting the street and draped examples of his work across it. Sometimes he sat in the window of the shop next door, his shawl completely concealing his shoulders and head, peering out from among yards of cloth like a remaindered mannequin. At other times he would sit in the cool of his corridor, chanting from the Qur'an, or just day-dreaming, watching, waiting.

For Toor, the congestion meant he could observe the street go by, he could study the drivers' faces as they passed and contribute to the angry exchange between cars. One felt that the protracted blockages gave him a sense of belonging to Brick Lane, of participating in its life.

'The people on the Brick Lane, always people going by. Going here, going there. The cars is jammed, many times it is jammed here. The traffic. Loading and unloading. The road narrow. People going in and out. I go and come, I go to Ealing, one year, but I come back. Me living here about 27 years. This is best, this is most best. Everything can I buy here. The shopping. Everything. Late open also. Very late open. Know people. This area I like best.'

I first met Toor one afternoon shortly before I moved out of Spitalfields in the autumn of 1990. I had seen him in his corridor many times over the previous couple of years, from the time when I had first moved into the area and had been a near neighbour of his on Brick Lane, while I was working in the fruit and vegetable market, through my time working as a footman for Julian Humphreys, when I moved into Fournier Street, to my most recent job as a jumped-up community development consultant. I had watched him shuffle up to the mosque on a Friday for prayers. I had seen him bent double over a bowl of curry at all sorts of unlikely times of the day. And occasionally, when I myself had shuffled over to the Pride of Spitalfields for a pint before last orders, I had seen him chatting to the neighbouring grocer, sitting on a stool beside the counter, with his shawl and his cap and the middle-distance stare of a man who had lost the plot somewhere between the flood plains of Bangladesh and the traffic congestion on the Lane. I couldn't honestly say, however, I had ever seen anyone inspecting his wares, let alone witnessed the completion of a sale. I suppose I felt a little sorry for him.

But anyway, on one particular afternoon I stepped into his corridor off Brick Lane to escape a sudden downpour. I had no need of a belt. But as the cloudburst looked like persisting for a while, I found myself comparing buckles, trying on a couple, sniffing the leather and smelling only the damp and the cold.

Toor came and stood directly behind me in a slightly unnerving way.

'You like a very good leather, very strong. Strong!'

'Yes, I want a good strong belt. I want a belt that will last me a few years.'

'Strong! Last!'

Toor brought to my attention one 'very good' belt after another, manipulating each with his bony, curry-yellow fingers, stained no doubt by years of turmeric-enhanced food, insisting each time on the excellent quality of the leather, 'very good, very strong'. I glanced at the street. The rain was already gathering in the cracks of the pavement and the dips of the unevenly tarmacked road.

'You made all of these belts yourself?'

'Made belts. Yes. Very good belts. Very strong.'

'How much is this one?'

'That one? Twelve pound. You pay me ten pound?'

I lifted down from one of the nails a belt with a large asymmetrical buckle. It reminded me of a minaret motif. 'And this one?'

'That one solid brass, very solid brass,' said Toor with surprising conviction, 'Thirteen!' The rhythmic whooshing sound of cars and feet splashing passed the door gave the transaction a slightly back-street secretive flavour. In the narrow corridor our conversation felt oddly confessional as our breath steamed intimately round each other's wary advances. I took the brass-buckled one, with Toor, of course, insisting on cash.

I thought I recognised in this belt salesman a pattern of immigrant labour which had existed in Spitalfields throughout its period of Jewish settlement in the nineteenth century right up to the present day. Was this not the piece-worker short-circuiting his dependence on the alienating chain of middlemen by converting the small remaindered lengths of cloth or leather left over from a commissioned order to pure profit, a direct sale?

Well, no, in fact it wasn't. When I spoke to Kay Jordan, who worked with scores of rag-traders, she said she thought he was probably barely earning enough money to feed the cat, let alone himself. And if he spent the whole day loitering in the half-light of his corridor, when did he find the time to stitch up his leather jackets? Besides, she added, the off-cuts left over by most of the leather work done locally wouldn't normally be sufficiently sturdy to turn into belts. She said he was probably on the dole, making a bit of money on the side. In fact, she wondered, was he not actually from Pakistan, rather than Bangladesh, related to one of the minority of Asian freeholders who had arrived along Brick Lane in the 1960s and bought property at that time from the vacating Jewish community?

Jordan's street wisdom exposed my rather shaky grasp of the realities of life along the Lane. I had spent nearly two years marching up and down it, buying my paper from Muhammad in the corner shop and my mangos from the Taj stores, yet I couldn't say I had really found a way into this community, into this particular version of the area.

All along Brick Lane and its tributary turnings doors opened on to corridors which led up to top flats and back rooms, the apparently impenetrable domain of migrant Spitalfields. Often several bells clustered around a single front door announcing multiple occupancy, a tangle of circumstance. Sometimes you could trace the wiring of a particular line as it climbed the outside of the house to disappear through a window, left permanently ajar. Moreover, relationships between the residents in the area seemed as involved as the wiring up the wall. Was everyone related to everyone else? Kinship networks spread across the Lane, reproducing family patterns established in rural Bangladesh and duplicated in the East End of London. Proprietorship of businesses seemed constantly to shift between relatives. And as shops changed owners and names, the old fronts were often just painted or boarded over, with past lives being obscured beneath the most recently painted façade. Indeed, this had been the pattern for years. On Brick Lane one immigrant history hid behind another – Huguenot, Irish, Jewish, Maltese, Bengali – each making its own contribution to the overall cultural patina of the area.

And yet this community had remained for me a collection of superficial tracings and impressions. Certainly there was a language barrier, but this was only part of a greater cultural barrier. I didn't speak Sylheti, the dialect spoken by most of the community around Brick Lane, named after the area of Bangladesh from which they came, but more significantly I wasn't a first generation Bengali with my family roots in a profoundly rural culture trying to negotiate for myself a new identity (religious, social, economic) in the post-industrial western city.

I went back to Toor a few days later. This time I was a little less circumspect. There were things I wanted to find out. And, somewhat to my surprise, he was ready to tell me. I discovered that Toor was indeed from Pakistan. He had first come across to England as a young man in 1973. He had been just twenty-nine years old. He stayed for two years and then went back, returning to London in 1979. In fact this coming and going seemed to be the pattern he had established over the years, leading to all intents and purposes a dual life, settling in neither country. He was married in Pakistan and it was there that his two sons were born, Abdul and Islam.

Behind the biographical facts there lay a web of aspirations and frustrations. His separation from his family he clearly felt quite keenly. Now they were in their early teens he was hoping to bring them over. He spoke about getting visas, his need to show that he was able to house them and look after them. His account became knotted with self-justifications and hectoring indignation. The house belonged to his brother-in-law, they would be able to live there. They were bright boys too, would get good jobs, could already speak good English. Hopefully they would be here next year. *Inshallah.*

Over the following weeks as I finished writing my report for the developers I called in to see him a number of times. He showed me his paper work and I met his nephew. I too became deliciously indignant at his plight and anxious to do something to help, to write a letter or make a phone call. Then, at the beginning of September, having been recommended for training by one of the Church's recruitment committees, I left Spitalfields. I moved to Cambridge where I began a course of study at theological college. I promptly forgot all about Toor.

As the economy turned

Three years passed before I returned to Spitalfields and, over the course of this period, those years I had spent working and living in the area became 'the 1980s', that decade for hustlers and chancers and money-making adventurers.

On 22 November 1990, the feast day of St Cecilia (the second-century virgin martyr who was suffocated by her retinue while visiting the baths), Margaret Thatcher stood down in the Conservative Party leadership contest and made way for John Major to form a new administration. The Iron Lady wept and somehow the world's whole frame felt out of joint. As recession deepened it became increasingly hard to ignore the human cost of the logic of the market place. In September 1990, the same month that Perrier had withdrawn its bubbly spring water from the international market following a scare that its supply had been contaminated, the British government imposed a statutory ban on the use of specified offal in the manufacture of all animal food after confirmation that a pig had contracted Bovine Spongiform Encephalopathy (BSE).

The movement on the stock market, always a good barometer for public confidence, if not an accurate indication of financial health, charted the shift that was taking place. In January 1990 share prices on the London Stock Exchange had reached their highest value ever; in September of that year Polly Peck was suspended after there were rumours of an investigation into its financial malpractice and by Christmas early jitters showed signs of turning into full-on FTSE panic. The exuberance of the 1980s was exposed as riddled with corruption and double-dealing: a whole new vocabulary entered the columns of political punditry, the language of sleaze.

Certain events punctuate this story in the early years of the 1990s. Robert Maxwell was found floating in the sea somewhere off the Canary Islands. Royal palaces and marriages went up in smoke. The Chancellor of the Exchequer, Mr Lamont, stood on the steps in Downing Street, nonchalantly flicking his fringe from his eyes like some slightly gauche public school boy who had been brought before the headmaster to explain his behaviour, trying to appear cool about the pickle in which he found himself. On 'Black Wednesday' the new global market took on one of the very governments which had invented it, as the City speculators forced the pound out of the Exchange Rate Mechanism.

These were the years of the emergent nation states. Following the collapse of the Berlin Wall in the last months of the 1980s the map of Eastern Europe was being redrawn at every level. At the precise moment the capitalist West seemed to be spiralling out of control, the communist East showed itself to be bankrupt and rotten. There was quite a lot of talk about the end of history, how we had somehow collectively lost the plot, how our meta-narratives were not quite so meta as we thought they were. Certainly, there was a lack of confidence in the future. The Millennium began to loom. In the general election in April 1992 the country decided to stick with the devil it knew. Yet despite John Major's call to bring the country Back to Basics, popular cynicism resisted the appeal of easy slogans and it was clear that there was emerging a profound and widespread disenchantment with the very practice of national politics.

And in Spitalfields there were major changes too. Julian Humphreys' cat died. Closing his Ordinary in Fournier Street, he moved to Ireland and took over the running of a family castle. Yvonne, the landlady at the Ten Bells, who disappeared very suddenly, was rumoured to have run off with one of her 'regulars', a steel erector from Middlesbrough. Meanwhile, the speculators and planners were left gasping as the economy turned, while the City, having expanded so rapidly in the 1980s, contemplated its vast acreage of empty office space. In 1991 the Spitalfields Development Group still owed the Corporation of London, freeholders of the market site, some £50 million and faced a total development cost of £500 million, and by August of the following year the property consortium was reported to be discussing with banks the rollover of a £165 million debt. Plans for the redevelopment of the market site were put on hold. The prospect of the big bonus seemed a thing of the past: Tim Budgen shelved his thoughts of early retirement and began exploring instead the feasibility of starting up a caravan park in

East Anglia. Meanwhile, of course, the fruit and vegetable market, having traded just outside the City wall more or less continuously since the Fire of London, was closed and subsequently relocated (at the end of 1991) to Leyton in the East London borough of Waltham Forest. Spitalfields Market itself became an empty space.

A calling is not a possession

Theological college was also something of an empty space, a time of study and reflection and prayer which those of us who were training for the priesthood filled with our working egos and noisy agendas. Vocation, a funny mixture of vanity, humility and sheer bloody-mindedness, tends to be hard to live with, for the person who 'has' it as well as for anyone who comes into close contact with him or her. They say the best way to treat psychopaths is to lock them all up together so that they can challenge one another into some kind of reality – maybe that's also true for ordinands.

Certainly it was true for me. In 1990 I went to Westcott House, a training college in Cambridge for Anglican clergy, and spent several years – longer, in fact, than I had originally anticipated – preparing for holy orders or, as the college put it, in 'formation'. On one level this was simply a matter of learning to talk the language of the Church, becoming acquainted with the nuts and bolts of parish ministry, being institutionalised. We did courses in canon law and voice projection, we learned about vestments and clergy pension schemes. We were shown how to fold a chasuble, how to light the incense in the thurible, how to hold a baby at a baptism, what to do with our hands when consecrating the elements of bread and wine, and when to genuflect (which knee, how low). We seemed to spend a lot of time getting excited about what John Betjeman refers to, with some fondness, as 'the inessentials of the faith'.

On another level it was a time of radical reorientation. Vocation, it seemed to me when I first arrived, was something terribly austere and absolute, either you had it or you hadn't, like good eyesight or a hairy chest. I came to see it as something more elusive, much stranger, much more rooted in the evolving relationships within a community than a single me-and-my-God thunderbolt from the heavens. I came to see that a calling is not a possession, it is a gift – a grace – and it comes through other people, sometimes surprising people, often painfully. There was an icon in the chapel, in fact the single piece of decoration in an otherwise wonderfully spare space. It presented an image of Christ with a quotation from St John's gospel, 'You have not chosen me, but I have chosen you.' Over the years I was at Westcott House I lit countless candles in front of it.

Naturally, in an institution committed to love and self-sacrificial service, there were heated disagreements and constant fallings-out. The fault-lines were, no doubt, boringly predictable. Some of us took more interest in the arcana of the liturgy, 'the inessentials of the faith', than others, committing to memory, for example, the secret Latin prayers to be mumbled at key moments by the priest when presiding at a celebration of the holy mysteries. Others considered such practices to be so much tosh. There was a constant teasing banter between those who saw themselves as 'high church' and those who saw themselves as 'low church', between the slap-and-tickle catholics and the hard-nut evangelicals. There seemed to be a running feud between those ordinands who talked earnestly about working with people on the fringes of society and those for whom the only fringe that mattered (apparently) was the lacy one at the bottom of their cottas.

In fact, how you defined yourself, how you learnt to carry – or drop – any number of clerical expectations, both the ones you had of yourself as well as those that others had of you, proved to be an important lesson. Certainly, one quickly learnt how to field people's strange and surprising projections. Some, when you told them that you were to be ordained into the Church of England, would smile politely and immediately start relating to you as though you had just confessed to having some terminal illness. If they referred to it at all, they would do so quietly and sensitively, masking their underlying feelings of horror and panic. Others, on the other hand, would take the opportunity to put to you straight-up the questions that had puzzled them for years, such as 'Is the Church of England Catholic or Reformed?', 'Is there a difference between a vicar and a rector?' and 'Are you allowed to, you know, *marry*?' (The answer to all three being 'Yes'.) A few simply wouldn't believe you, would think you were taking the mickey. How could anyone of reasonable intelligence want to do anything so deeply untrendy, so deeply *weird*, as being a vicar?

A few people, however, would want to talk, would open their hearts to you and tell your their secrets. Through such conversations one became aware of the huge privilege of priesthood.

I found being at theological college a disorientating experience, but also one of surprising joy. Hurt from before, always from before, called for attention. Friendship, as ever, saved the day. And it was through friendship that I overcame the terrible embarrassment I had about Jesus, as though he were some crazy vulgar uncle one simply didn't talk about.

And that's basically what we did, We read the bible, wrote essays, led seminars, preached, prayed. We certainly seemed to spend quite a lot of time on our knees. We were biding His time.

Something far more powerful

While I was at Westcott House I did some research into my grandfather, John Goodacre. I imagined him, almost exactly a hundred years previously, a student at Jesus College, just opposite where the college was located. What traditions within the Church had nourished him? What sort of man, actually, was he?

I found a obituary my mother had kept in which he was described as belonging to a well established line of 'Tractarian' priests from the Midlands and I remembered how my grandmother had similarly noted the influence of the 'Oxford Movement' on his family. (I also came across a rather frightening photograph of his great aunt Mary, who was one of the first women to be professed as a nun in the Church of England. She was dressed in her wimple and habit and looked as though she had just swallowed a set of her rosary beads.) When my newly married grandmother arrived in the Potteries from Dublin after the Great War she describes in her account of John's life how, on going into his parish, she had her 'first experience of what we in Ireland call 'High Church Services'. Vestments were used and there were servers and a Sung Eucharist'. She added 'I liked it all very much', which, I guess, was fortunate. Later, when they moved to a parish in West Bromwich, she writes of how he controversially instituted a communion service every Sunday instead of just once a month, as had previously been the case (there were stormings out of the Parochial Church Council meeting by 'better-off business men with Protestant views'). Elsewhere she comments, 'John was an Anglo-Catholic, but a moderate one – a 'Prayer Book Anglo-Catholic' I think he would have called himself.'

A 'Prayer Book Anglo-Catholic' – that sounded rather good, I thought. I wondered if that was what I was. I asked a fellow ordinand, who had done some research into nineteenth-century church history, what it all meant. She said it could mean any number of things. First of all there was the Tractarian movement, which got going in Oxford in July 1833, following a famous sermon by John Keble in which he argued for the spiritual autonomy for the Church, free of Government interference. Looking back to the early Church Fathers and highlighting the place of the sacraments in the revival of Catholic identity in the Church of England, a group of like-minded clerics subsequently produced a series of religious tracts, a sort of party manifesto: They, and their followers, were known as Tractarians. Though connected (she went on) this was not the same as ritual Anglo-Catholicism, which became a political issue in the 1870s when some priests were imprisoned for ceremonial offences (cross-dressing as Roman Catholics) under the Public Worship Regulation Act of 1874. Actually, this bit didn't sound like my grandfather at all. I really couldn't see him getting his tassels in a twist over where you put your tippet and what you did with your maniple.

My ordinand colleague went on to say there was a further tradition within Anglo-Catholicism, that of 'sacramental socialism'. Apparently this was quite big in the East End of London. A group called the Guild of St Matthew, established by the rebel priest Stewart Headlam in Bethnal Green in 1877, met regularly through the last years of the century. Some have even suggested that theirs was the first explicitly socialist gathering in Britain. It was in its stress on the Body of Christ, on communion and sharing, and in its rejection of individualism in religion, that the link between Anglo-Catholicism and Socialism was forged. Headlam would apparently say that 'those who assist at Holy Communion are bound to be holy communists'. I liked the sound of Mr Headlam and wondered how I could find out some more about his 'holy communists'. I asked her. She suggested I try reading some of the books written by Kenneth Leech, a priest working in the Brick Lane area of the East End and pretty much following in this tradition, '. . . and maybe then you might stop pestering me.' Excuse me, sister?

As I read up on my church history, it seemed that, in some places, this subversive tradition within the Anglo-Catholic movement had indeed broken the identification of the Church of England with the Establishment. Not all sacramental socialists, however, were part of this rebel group, which saw the transforming power of God's Kingdom as one which was necessarily disruptive and conflictive, a costly grace, rooted more in solidarity with those who are excluded than in collusion with the proud and the mighty. The social liberals, often the bishops, were far more optimistic about the role of law and the inexorability of progress and many of them had a very high view of the state, one which would have been based more on Aquinas, who saw the state as part of the created order, than on Augustine, who saw it as a result of the Fall. A good example of this sort of social liberal would have been Bishop Westcott himself, a contemporary of Headlam's, whose name had been taken up by my theological college and whose portrait, all whiskers and episcopal gravitas, hung in the dining hall. In an essay on 'The Social Obligation of the National Church', Westcott gives a bold account of his social optimism. Discussing the 'broad laws of social growth' he talks of the 'steady amelioration of life', arguing that because 'the State has a moral end . . . the true ruler will seek to secure the conditions of labour favourable to the development of noble character.'

Of course, it's all too easy, with hindsight, to submit such high-minded twaddle to the acids of scepticism. But how could Bishop Westcott honestly say of the Church (in the 1890s!) that its clergy were 'not a close and isolated caste, but drawn from every class . . .' or of the national polity that 'there is no sharp division of classes among us . . . individuals pass continually from one class to another'? Had my grandfather been similarly dispossessed of his critical faculties? I returned to my grandmother's book.

Unsurprisingly, this was not a question she was really asking. In any case, she had herself only arrived on the scene at the end of his years in the Potteries. Yet in re-reading her account of his life I did come across the following passage, which describes some curious Mickey Mouse before his institution at the Church of St Paul's in Burton-on-Trent in September 1927:

'The patronage of the parish was in the gift of Lord Burton, and as he had died, it was in the gift of his widow. She was a dear old lady, most kind and good. She asked the bishop's advice about a new vicar, and the bishop suggested John, so she invited John to come to see her. They had lunch together, and had a very pleasant talk. I think that John must have had some reputation as being a Socialist after his years in Hanley, for Lady Burton asked him if he were one. John's reply, with a twinkle in his eye, was "I'm not as bad as the bishop!" who was known to have leanings that way. So Lady Burton laughed and asked no more about it.'

It all sounded a bit cosy to me. I rang my mother to see if she had any sense of her father, as a 'Prayer Book Anglo-Catholic', being either a 'holy communist' or 'sacramental socialist'. She said she didn't know what on earth I was talking about, but that she'd found some other papers of his and that she would send them on. A few days later I received a whole bundle through

the post – parish magazines, bits of sermon, messages of con-
dolence following his death – as well as a bound volume of the
letters he had sent back to Hanley from the trenches in the Great
War.

In reading all this stuff, suddenly my grandfather came vividly
and rather disturbingly to life. At first all I could hear was the
late Victorian Church at its most didactic and serious-minded.
The season of Lent he describes as 'the Christian soldier's special
drilling time' and in exhorting his flock to come to the Good
Friday liturgy, he urges them 'most earnestly to put aside all
pleasure on the day of our Saviour's Crucifixion'. Accompanying this disdain for unholy pleasure is an evident wariness
concerning the 'lower passions', which he repeatedly de-
nounces, particularly when acting in the service of 'loose
morality'. In his charge to his parishioners before the 1910
election, he warns them, 'if the majority of England's subjects
are guided in their vote by low and selfish motives, then they
hasten the downfall of the Country; if they are directed by high
and unselfish aims, then they contribute to the nation's welfare.'
These higher qualities, moreover, are learnt in the home, upon
which 'is built up the tone of the parish, the purity of public life,
the welfare of the nation . . . Sap the home of its discipline and
Christian religion, and you strike at the root of England's
strength.'

Help! Were these the words of a keenly ambitious vicar,
burning with a zealous belief in the vocation of the Church of
England to uphold the moral fabric of the nation, or an uptight
and rather troubled young (unmarried) man? Certainly no 'holy
communist', I read this Back to Basics programme with some
alarm and, if I'm honest, disappointment. I wanted my grandfather to be more radical, less card-carrying establishment, more
disruptive. This wasn't the 'slum priest' I had generated in my
fantasy. His world of confident Christian exhortation sounded so
foreign, so remote from those I had inhabited in Spitalfields.
What sense did it make to talk about the purity of public life
amidst such a profusion of hybridity in this locus classicus of
incompatible realities? I then turned to the volume of letters he
had sent back to his parishioners from the front in the Great War.

These unfolded a different story. At first quite upbeat with his description of 'our boys doing wonderful work at close quarters with the rifle, bomb and bayonet' and how 'the Bosche is in many ways a dirty fellow' preferring 'darkness and squalor to light and air', quite soon, however, one gets a sense of his increasing bewilderment at the course of events. His letters are taken over with descriptions of the mud and the rats, the misery of 'trench-fever' and other diseases (and enforced return to 'Blighty') along with increasingly elliptical references to the fighting itself – 'the cost hardly bears thinking about, and there will be many sorrowing and anxious homes in the Midlands.'

At times his impatience with military procedure becomes apparent. In July 1917 he writes of how 'I hate and detest 'parade services' (this is not an official document so I can express an honest opinion of them). I have just been trying to get permission to abandon all 'parade services' for my little lot while in France, and to have purely voluntary attendance in 'loose order' instead.' Elsewhere he describes how he leads a mutiny of fellow chaplains when they are sent behind the lines for a 'course of instruction'. At least, as he reflects, it enables him to 'feel more sympathy with some old stagers, who find themselves being drilled by some beardless strapling of a Sergeant.' There is no more talk here of the 'lower passions' or even of 'higher aims', but rather a touching diffidence in the face of the impossibility of his task of comforting the wounded and dying:

> 'It is very difficult to do the work that lies nearest our heart
> – there are so many obstacles, the patient is either distracted
> with pain, or struggling for breath, or tossed in delirium, or
> again it is so public, and everyone is very shy (even the
> Padre) with respect to religion, and it really is difficult to
> say wisely the things that really matter to a shy suffering
> patient, in the presence of a whole ward of fellows, some
> of whom are sitting on the next bed playing whist or
> cracking jokes round the stove at the foot of the bed . . .'

I suppose we are so used to reading accounts of the horrors of the First World War with its social and psychological fragmentation that it has become a commonplace to see this period as a watershed, as the time when the birds stopped singing. But reading these final letters of my grandfather, sent from the front to his parishioners back in the Potteries, listening to his voice break with the grief of it all, I actually have the opposite sense. My earlier concern about his churchmanship becomes the irrelevance that, of course, it is. Instead, through his stumbling compassion, his earnest attempts to say the right thing, I see something far more powerful. I see a man exposing his belief in the love of God to the misery of the trenches and the lives of the broken-hearted, his own included.

'Victory at last!' he writes in the final letter, posted on Advent Sunday 1918 from the 73rd General Hospital in France, adding:

'. . . but words fail me when I try to think what it means. I can only think in terms of prayer and say "Thank God." At present, I cannot think of the Victory without recollecting the cost, and my mind rushes back to all the good friends I knew and are no more, and I am weighed down with the consciousness of the great responsibility which lies upon those who remain, to see that the fruits of victory are worthy of the lives laid down: I feel that I want to get right away "into the wilderness", and humbly think out the lessons and experiences of the past four years.'

Upon those who remain. Sitting in my room in Westcott House, looking out over the cow parsley and daffodils and Spring bulbs in that part of the college garden we called 'the wilderness', some seventy years on from when these words were written, I felt a sudden surge of respect for their author.

In the event of it, the reality of God breaking into my little life, unravelling my carefully-laid plans, surprising me with all sorts of unforeseen possibilities, arrived, in 1991, from a rather different direction. My girlfriend discovered she was pregnant.

Hiatus ensued. Some very dim views were taken. Whilst we were unsure whether to marry, the college told me I would have to leave (for 'pastoral reasons') and that in due course the

Bishop of Oxford would examine my case and decide whether I should be allowed to return.

Our daughter was born in late August.

A year later, the bishop did, in fact, allow me to return to my training, but made it clear that I was on probation. I was told that he would be reading my end of year reports with particular interest and that he might well want to see me. I was reminded, moreover, that my attendance at theological college did not necessary indicate that I would be allowed to proceed to ordination. Discernment would need to be exercised. There was talk of 'buckling down'.

I have to say that there was a point over the following two years when I really seemed to lose the plot. The college had always encouraged us to integrate our lives into our training, but probably, like most of my friends, I spent many hours peering from behind books about the Oxford Movement or sexual ethics or the Church Fathers at my former life in Spitalfields, feeling only the sharp discontinuity of it all. At the same time I realised how my vocation, such as I had begun to experience it, was caught up with this small area of London. For me, that was where the treasure was buried. I had seen something there which, after several years in Cambridge libraries, I desperately needed to see again. I had unfinished business.

MIGRANT SPITALFIELDS

A sort of placement

With some wisdom, the principal at Westcott House encouraged me to return to Spitalfields, in my final year, on a sort of 'placement' in the East End. He said he wanted me to 'reflect theologically' on the place of the Gospel in its inner-city multicultural environment. Probably he also wanted me out of his hair. Anyway, I was certainly keen to set something up. Apart from anything else, it seemed like a good excuse for a series of jolly trips to the big smoke.

I rang Tassaduq Ahmed, with whom I had remained inter-mittently in contact, and arranged to go and see him at the offices of one of the welfare organisations he was attached to, on Chicksand Street, off the back of Brick Lane. 'And another thing,' said Tassaduq as I explained a little more about my plans over the telephone, 'if you want to be the activist for the Bengali community, you must also learn about the curry cooking.'

I went up to Spitalfields to talk further with Tassaduq about how the project might work out. Walking up from Liverpool Street station, as I had done many times before but not since the market had closed, I was struck by a sudden pang of nostalgia for the good old days of bugger-the-lot-of-you market congestion. Before, with all the traders honking and crashing about and generally disporting themselves noisily throughout the morning, the City had been kept at arm's length. But now, already in the summer of 1993, with the market space occupied by a temporary assembly of cafés, shops, stalls, studios, offices, sports facilities and opera house, it seemed to be adapting itself to the very rhythms of this neighbouring business community. It was June: the Spitalfields Festival banners were flapping in the portico of the church and some of the new restaurants along Brushfield Street had spread their canopies across the pavement to attract the more adventurous al fresco lunchers. Tassaduq was waiting for me in his office in Chicksand Street.

'Now that you are a man of divinity, you will want to bring the ideological programme to work in the context of the local people. From our perspective we need to work with the intelligentsia to promote the class interests of the Bengali community against the profit-hunger of the capitalist developers,' announced Tassaduq before I had even had a chance to sit down. A reconstructed Marxist, he had fortified the innocence of his Bengali romanticism with the insistant logic of dialectical theory.

'And the second thing,' he continued, moving swiftly to details, 'as an activist in the CARP, you will need overnight accommodation in Spitalfields and the necessary creature comforting. You can stay with me in return for the community work, for writing articles for the CARP and for other consultations and feeding-backs.'

'The CARP? Tassaduq, I'm not sure I know what CARP stands for.' Whereas some people will find themselves punning almost involuntarily, Tassaduq was constantly dreaming up new acronyms. I wasn't sure, however, whether this one was of his own coining and was still pretty much at the logo and letterhead stage, or whether it was more generally established.

'The Campaign against Racial Prejudice. You will become part of our media and marketing strategy, to organise and to activate the masses and to protect the local communities from the tentacles of the property developers who are out to swallow the Spitalfields land area in order to satisfy their insatiable profit lust . . .'

As mixed as his metaphors became, Tassaduq was absolutely single-minded in his commitment to his community work in Spitalfields. He had been tramping up and down Brick Lane since the early 1960s, setting up projects, cajoling and encouraging his people, working tirelessly to promote pride in the idea of the Greater Bengal. Although his roots, like those of most of his compatriots, were in rural Bangladesh, his own background was moneyed and privileged and he had arrived in London, after taking his degree at Calcutta University, into a rich network of connections and the prospect of a fine career at the bar. Instead, he became an activist, choosing the route of political engagement. His life of service was recognised in 1989 when he received his MBE.

By his own admission he had lost his way somewhat since his great friend and activist partner Fakruddin Islam had died suddenly in 1985. Tassaduq had always been the ideologue, the fixer, but he was temperamentally unsuited to the hustling and rabble-rousing required in community development work. Despite his rhetoric, he was no man of the people. Charming and testy by turns, he was too remote, too much of a dreamer, to carry his beloved masses with him on his own. He clearly needed someone like Fakruddin to see his strategies through.

Tassaduq and I agreed to be in touch and I gladly accepted the possibility of a bed for the night when I was in the area. I also said I would like to take him up on the offer of cookery classes.

'The curry cooking will be part of your training for divinity,' Tassaduq said as I left him.

It was the late afternoon as I headed back towards Liverpool Street station. As I passed Christ Church primary school on Brick Lane I saw Jimmy Battiwalla, the head teacher, in the downstairs lobby area talking to a some parents who had come to collect the few remaining children from school. Mr Battiwalla, who had converted to Christianity when he came to England as a young man, had the most gently uncompromising approach to matters of faith that one could imagine. In his quietly spoken and unassuming way, he would tell the parents of the children who came to visit the school that he was going to tell them all about Jesus. Paradoxically, however, he seemed to earn their respect. Even the imam in the local mosque was keen to send his children to 'the Christian school', preferring a religious educational ethos for his children, even though it were the wrong one, to the prospect of secularism.

I made my way up Princelet Street towards Wilkes Street. As I approached it, I became conscious of an argument going on at the junction on the right. I slowed down. A man dressed fairly smartly in a suit was shouting at three or four Bengali children, possibly from Christ Church school, just finished for the day. I hovered on the other side of the road, within earshot, curious to know what was going on. I briefly wondered whether I should go back and find Mr Battiwalla. Instead I crossed the road towards them.

'How would you like it if I went into your front room and dumped a load of sand on the carpet?' the man asked the children. The children looked at each other and then back at the man.

'Is that what they've done?' I intervened.

'That's exactly bloody well what they have done,' he said to me and, turning to the children, who were rooted to the spot, he added, 'You should keep out of the site.'

I could see now that he was referring to the boarded up piece of land that made up the corner plot. A makeshift door had been made out of corrugated iron which, it appeared, he had been in the process of trying to open. It struck me, however, that the comparison between this building site and a family front room was a bit rich, even if the children had been trespassing.

'And why don't you shove off too?' he said, turning to me.

'Excuse me?' I was slightly taken aback by his rudeness.

'Why don't you go on and mind your own business, mate?' he repeated, this time a little less bullishly.

Should I say that I was a trainee vicar working for the media division of the Campaign against Racial Prejudice and that, quite frankly, I found his attitude unacceptable? Or should I quietly excuse myself – 'Golly, is that the time?' – and leave them to it? As my fight-or-flight responses were jostling for position, I became aware of a second man behind me. He was wearing dungarees and a pony tail and didn't look as if he were a colleague of Mr Crosspatch here.

'Hi guys! I see we have a little bit of aggro happening here?' he said to the children in that familiar way which Australians have of turning a statement into a hovering question. They didn't bother responding to him, but just rushed through the front door from which it seemed this friend of theirs had appeared.

The man in the suit, now outnumbered by grown-ups, switched from abusive to officious mode. 'As the agent representing the owners of this piece of property, may I remind you that occupation by a third party is considered trespass under the law?'

Our new friend wasn't interested in debating ownership details. Ignoring the property agent, he turned to introduce himself to me. 'I'm Harry,' he said, 'you want a cup of tea?'

I followed him into his house. Almost as an afterthought, Harry turned to our friend, who was busy snapping his briefcase closed, and asked him in his breezy antipodean lilt, 'Can I bring you out a herbal, matey?' I wasn't completely sure he was taking the mickey.

Harry and the children quickly made themselves at home in the downstairs of the house which was open plan and rather haphazardly furnished. The three smallest boys scrunched up together on the sofa, wrestling for a space, all squabbling elbows and knees, whilst the tallest boy, who was presumably the eldest, went over to the kitchen area with Harry. As he pulled the teapot out of the sink from beneath a pile of unwashed dishes and began to pour water through it, he turned to this lad, no older than twelve or thirteen, and said, 'So Delwar, what's the story with the geezer in the suit?'

Delwar began to explain. 'We were in the jungle and there was this shouting and there was someone outside, like, shouting and wanting to come in. For a moment I thought it was you, Harry, pretending you were the police or something. Then Ali had a look out and saw that man and said it was Special Branch.'

The three boys on the sofa exploded into giggles, nudging each other and making siren noises. There were some quick-fire exchanges in Sylheti and then they burst into further giggles. I rather fancied they were talking about me, but also recognised my paranoia for what it was. Harry, who was brewing up, was following the story of what had happened.

'And then, like, we went out and he told us that we should go away. He was quite rude, Harry, when he told us to go away.

[More giggles from the sofa.] He said the jungle didn't belong to us and that it wasn't our playground. And then he said the thing about the front room and that's when you arrived.'

I was taking the opportunity to look around Harry's own 'front room'. With bare unpolished boards on the floor and an accumulation of recycled furniture, it was unlike many of the other Georgian houses along Princelet Street – it certainly hadn't been done up. The kitchen lacked an Aga and the panelling was yet to be exposed, nor were there any candle sconces in evidence, although the open fireplace was clearly a working feature of the room. A couple of bikes lay stacked against the wall by the front door. With the paintwork looking like the advanced stages of a skin disease and the windows badly in need of a bucket of soapy water, it felt more like a student digs than a house in the highly prized conservation area of Spitalfields. In fact, as it turned out, it was a squat.

Harry, who described himself as a storyteller, had moved in six months previously, although the house itself had been squatted by various comers and goers over a period of a few years. The owner, a man who lived in Kent, was said to be happy about the arrangement – the house was kept in reasonable repair, pending the day, with the recession passed, when it would no doubt find its way on to the open market.

The neighbouring piece of derelict land where the Bengali children had set up camp was, as it unsurprisingly transpired, in disputed ownership. A local land agent wanting to build a 'sympathetic' end-of-terrace infill was keen to pursue its claim, based, so far as I could understand it, on the fact that it had purchased the adjoining site on Wilkes Street and it would have been convenient to extend its operation sideways. However, a local resident and friend of the household who also lived in Wilkes Street, a sculptor called Charlie, who had used the derelict site for storage throughout the dark days of the 1970s and 80s and was now happy also to play host to the 'jungle club', also claimed proprietorial ownership as a sitting tenant. Since the deeds had been lost it looked like the dispute might end up in court. Moreover, as a conflict between bald-faced speculative greed and a network of local interests and ownership claims it was, in many ways, typical of the wider disputes over land use in the area. I was keen to get involved.

I came up to Spitalfields a few times over the summer months, staying with Tassaduq and hanging out with Harry and the informal association of local children who continued to play in the derelict site and made up the 'jungle club', shifting sand around and living out their 'jungle' fantasies, before coming next door to Harry's house to make mischief and create further havoc. I got to know them a little, Delwar and his friends, the in-jokes, the regular teases, the fault-lines between friends. I reckoned I had found my 'placement'. And then, as the summer drew to a close and we all began looking towards the autumn, Harry suggested we begin to work on a theatre project together.

'Do you mean wearing funny clothes and saying crazy talking words?' said Ferous.

'Yes,' said Harry, 'and a street party and a play about rival gangs and maybe even a petition to sign.'

'Wow Harry! Cool Harry! Can we be in it too?' said Ali and Ferouk.

'You can all be in it. In fact, you've all got to be in it!'

I thought I could see the way Harry's mind was working and asked if he wanted some help.

'Sure thing,' said Harry, 'Are you any good with raising money?'

'Possibly,' I said, 'how much did you have in mind?'

'Like thirty thousand pounds?'

Dogma is to be left on the doorstep

'Community theatre' was not a new thing in Princelet Street. It was, after all, at number six (formerly number three Princes Street) – in the house directly opposite Harry's squat – that exactly a hundred years previously the Hebrew Dramatic Club had met to perform its repertoire of Yiddish theatrical pieces. It, too, had met with a certain amount of opposition, not to say contempt, not least from the established Anglo-Jewish community in London which saw this as a form of cultural exclusivism and hence threatening the work of assimilation it had achieved.

Latent disapproval became overt censure in the aftermath of a tragedy at this Yiddish theatre in Spitalfields. On 18 January 1887, at a performance of the Hurvitz operetta *Gypsy Princess* which attracted a packed audience, a cry of 'Fire!' from the gallery led to a mad rush to the exit. In the stampede a total of seventeen people were crushed to death, mostly women and children. The *Jewish Chronicle*, mouthpiece for the Anglo-Jewish establishment, was quick to warn its 'foreign brethren' of the dangers which would necessarily follow their self-imposed alienation from English society:

> We plainly tell . . . that one of the most direct causes of the recent disaster has been the persistent isolation in which they have kept themselves from their fellow Jewish workmen in all the social amenities of life. The recent event ought to be a lesson to avoid such performances of strolling minstrels acting in the jargon, and helping to keep up the alienation of the foreign contingent. In making these remarks, we are urged by a consideration of the best interests of these brethren of ours . . . to hasten the process of 'Anglicising'.

In fact this process wasn't one the immigrant Jews of Spitalfields were actually very keen on hastening. They were quite happy with their 'jargon', thank you very much – indeed they used it precisely to foil the possibility of contamination by the host community. They had arrived in the East End of London, fleeing their homeland, torn from their livelihoods and often their families, with the prospect of long-term poverty and destitution. In the circumstances, they were quite ready to remind themselves that this was a temporary state, that they were in *galut* (exile), sojourners in a strange land. And they certainly didn't find it too difficult to resist the enervating lure of Anglicisation. Moreover, by recreating the relational networks of their *heym*, they were able to sustain a link with this absent world whilst simultaneously expressing ambivalence towards their new place of residency.

Once again we see how Spitalfields played host to the imagined world of a community, aliens from a far country, looking to keep alive the dream of homecoming, the hope of return.

It was through the *chevra* – or religious association – that these memories of home were most keenly kept alive. Combining the functions of a benefit office, further education college and social club, the *chevras* were spread out across Spitalfields, often named after the town or district in Russia or Poland from which the majority of its members had emigrated. By 1889 Beatrice Webb had identified quite how widespread and significant they were, with 'thirty or forty of these *chevras* scattered throughout the Jewish quarters' meeting the needs, according to her calculations, 'of some 12,000 to 15,000 foreign Jews'. Each *chevra* had at least one *shtiebl* (small, house-based synagogue) and it was around these *shtiebls* that the *landsleit* (families coming from the same village or town in Russo-Poland) would meet, forming their own street communities, sharing workshops and food-stores, thoughts on the rabbi's sermon as well as tips for the latest gambling scam, snuff-boxes, local gossip, a common past. Then on Friday evenings the narrow alleys and cloistered passages would empty as families gathered at home to observe the arrival of the sabbath, placing candles in the window and joining around the table to sing the songs of Zion in a strange land. Assimilation into some sort of anodyne English, or indeed equally inoffensive Anglo-Jewish, culture was not a priority for these 'ghetto' Jews. Quite the opposite, in fact.

Israel Zangwill writes of this cultural defiance with insight rooted in familiarity. He was himself born in Spitalfields and lived for many years in Fashion Street and knew the particular tensions at work, the dynamics of longing that lay beneath the daily pressures of survival. He knew the way echoes of other worlds and distant possibilities haunted the hearts and minds of his fellow Jews and he knew how to write it up with folksy colour:

'This London Ghetto of ours is a region where, amid uncleanness and squalor, the rose of romance blows yet a little longer in the raw air of English reality; a world which hides

beneath its stony and unlovely surface an inner world of
dreams, fantastic and poetic as the mirage of the Orient
where they were woven, of superstitions grotesque as the
cathedral gargoyles of the Dark Ages in which they had birth.'

His most famous book, *Children of the Ghetto*, explores the
relationship between these 'dreams' and this 'raw air'. Written
almost as a lament for a lost world, it is crammed with reference
to the arcana and exotica of Orthodoxy: like the best kind of
junk shop, it is full of curious and amusing set-pieces –
characters, encounters, liturgical practices – vividly portrayed,
yet oddly without context. The book has no plot to speak of,
other than the trajectory of assimilation, as one generation
succeeds another and the *schnorrers* of the ghetto, with their
cheerful flamboyance and unselfconscious eccentricities, are
replaced by a Jewish community of 'moneyed mediocrity, a
régime of dull respectability'.

Indeed, according to Zangwill, 'respectable' seems to be
everything that the 'ghetto' wasn't. Both concepts recur with
almost mantric frequency in his book and, in their counter-
distinction, establish its dynamic. It is clear where Zangwill's
heart lies. 'Respectability,' he writes, 'crept on to freeze the
blood of the Orient with its frigid finger, and to blur the vivid
tints of the East into the uniform grey of English middle-class
life.' Yet, paradoxically, his very lament for these 'vivid tints of
the East' has the effect of paralysing this lost world of
Yiddishkeit in self-consciousness, by rendering it a mere
amusing curiosity. There is certainly something cloyingly cosy,
if not also rather camp, to the modern sensibility about his
descriptions of immigrant street life in Petticoat Lane, remarking, as he does, on the 'fair fat women, with tender hearts,
who waddled benignantly through life, ever ready to shed the
sympathetic tear', 'the bald, ruddy old men, who ambled about
in faded carpet slippers and passed the snuff-box of peace' and
'the little girls in white pinafores with pink sashes who
brightened the Ghetto on high days and holidays'.

Maybe it is not, therefore, so surprising that he was
championed by the very Anglo-Jewish community he

apparently despised for its 'dull respectability'. Asher Myers, editor of the *Jewish Chronicle* in the 1880s, hailed him as a literary hero and gave him regular column inches to express his art and insights, whilst at the same time, in his own editorials and articles, he treated the Yiddish traits of the immigrants – their religious practices, culture, social organisation and political views – as a regrettable hang-over from the 'old country' to be eliminated as speedily as possible.

'They come mostly from Poland; they, as it were, bring Poland with them, and they retain Poland while they stop here. This is most undesirable; it is more than a misfortune, it is a calamity,' writes Myers with startling bluntness in an editorial in 1881, following the mass arrival of refugees from Eastern Europe. 'It is tolerably clear,' he continues, 'what we wish to do with our foreign poor. We may not be able to make them rich; but we may hope to render them English in feeling and conduct.' Whereas Zangwill feared that the 'raw air' of English middle-class life threatened to blight his tender dreamers from the Orient with an unseasonable frost, Myers was keen to support any initiative, such as the Jewish Working Men's Club, which would root out such fantastical nonsense and enable the immigrants to 'cast off the Oriental shackles which they have imported into this country'.

In the end both Myers and Zangwill were working within the same web of contradictory impulses. As mediators of Jewish identity they needed both to be loyal to their constituency, yet also agreeable to their 'host' community, which was also significantly their readership. Theirs was a classic liberal dilemma: how to articulate difference without threatening the stability of consensus. While focusing on the specific needs and concerns of the Jewish community, as a publication the *Jewish Chronicle* took every opportunity to emphasise how Anglo-Jewry had become intrinsic to the social fabric (of the upper-classes), either by celebrating the appointment of the first Jewish Lord Lieutenant, reporting the graduation of a Jewish huntsman to the position of Master of the Hounds or by running a major feature to coincide with the ennoblement of Sir Nathaniel Rothschild as the first Jewish peer in 1885.

Yet for all their aspirational interests, Myers and his colleagues had a little problem: how were they able to present Judaism as consistently eirenic and accommodating when as a religion it was rooted in the observance of the Law and committed in practice to the protocols of judgement and sacrificial atonement? And in 1880s, with the mass arrival of Jewish refugees, with their keen dependence on the story of their faith, this became a big problem.

It was to Zangwill that Myers turned for some sort of spin on the potentially embarrassing religious enthusiasm exhibited by these immigrant Jews. He was eager to find an ally in the newly fêted author, expressing the hope in an editorial that 'perhaps Mr Zangwill's forthcoming novel, *Children of the Ghetto*, will prove the long-awaited antidote to the literary poison that has been poured in the public ear by several clever and unsympathetic writers.' Already through their joint association with the Maccabeans, a loose gathering of Jewish professionals, Myers knew Zangwill to be an erudite, though not uncritical, voice for the contemporary Jew. Moreover, in a speech the latter delivered to the Maccabeans, Zangwill suggests that 'the only passwords to the clubroom should be character and culture. Dogma is to be left on the doorstep' – a sentiment clearly shared by the editor of the *Jewish Chronicle*.

It is hardly surprising, therefore, that Myers picks up with some enthusiasm on Zangwill's account of the life of faith among the refugee Jews of Spitalfields, an account which, in the end, is very conservative, more picturesque than prophetic. As the Proem to the *Children of the Ghetto* makes clear, Zangwill locates Jewish spirituality not so much in the Talmudic faith of the rabbinate but rather in a historic 'ghetto' which has long since disappeared. His characters, in these terms, are but 'vestiges of the old gaiety and brotherhood . . . the full al fresco flavour [having] evaporated'. This 'ghetto spirituality' of Zangwill's is rooted, moreover, in a sort of holistic time-capsule in which the secular and the sacred were indistinguishable in the constant round of unselfconscious Yiddish cheerfulness. 'The great Reform split did not occur till well on towards the middle of the century, and the Jews of those days were unable to conceive that a man could be a Jew without eating *kosher* meat, and they would have looked upon the modern distinctions between racial and religious Jews as the sophistries of the convert or the missionary.' Even God is benign: 'Worshippers did not pray with bated breath as if afraid the Deity would overhear them. They were at ease in Zion.'

The 'raw air' of the East End, rather than causing the refugees from the Orient to shake off their inner world of dreams and wake up to the reality of life in exile, seemed instead to render a re-enactment of this world all the more necessary, indeed supplied a distinctive 'al fresco flavour' to its retrieval. Moreover, as this 'ghetto spirituality' passed into the folk memory of Jewish Spitalfields, it became the very emblem of respectability, a mark of authentically belonging to the area's past.

Take Nellie, for example. When I first met her she had been living in the same house on Fournier Street for the previous fifty years. Her husband, Hymie, had been a tailor, and a good one, she would say, not like the ones you got nowadays, if you could call them tailors, that is, more like butchers. Nellie would stand by her front door, resting on the railing, her blue house-work apron wrapped loosely around her diminutive body, flicking away stray bits of rubbish from her doorstep with her stick, like so many uninvited memories, until eventually nostalgia turned to resignation and she would say, 'I'll tell you, between us two, I'm glad to sit at home, because I've got bad circulation and I don't go out very often.'

Yet standing on the street she was always happy to share a bit of railing and old times. So when Mrs Schwartz passes her door, on her way back from Elfes, the Jewish stonemason at the top of Brick Lane, they fall into conversation. It turns out that Mrs Schwartz knows a tailor in Fournier Street, Josiah Greenberg, who used to share a work-room with Hymie. The conversation trips into sudden laughter, as waves of trembly, apologetic giggles ripple down the street. Delight all round as the connections which link these two old ladies are established. Like in the endlessly sub-divided and knocked through houses themselves, it doesn't take long to discover the necessary passageway through the warren of rooms and relationships which made up

Fournier Street at another time, to pass through doors now blocked up, between houses now made discrete.

In those days, Nellie would tell you, the street was a sociable place, people were busy making a living, but they would also keep their eyes open, they knew what was going on. 'If you didn't see your neighbour for two days you heard a ring on the bell – 'Are you all right, love?' – but we don't have any neighbours on Fournier Street any more. We used to have tea on the street, parties, clubs. The street used to be full of beautiful people, Jewish people. Well, there's nothing like that now.'

They told each other stories

Of course, certainly on one level, there was nothing like that then either. Its retrospective projection is sentimental and self-deluding. This version of folksy Yiddish familiarity is as easy to deconstruct as the story of cockney camaraderie, with which it has much in common, not least the fact that they both defy the hard facts of late-nineteenth-century poverty in Spitalfields. As Howard Jacobson writes in *Roots Schmoots*, the account he gives of his own search for his Jewish identity, 'Modern Jews idealise a past they wouldn't touch with a barge-pole.'

Life for the newly arrived immigrant was undoubtedly difficult. Arriving with only a letter of introduction or an address, some not even these, the *greeners* would spill out of the steerage deck when the ship docked in the Pool of London, their bodies enfeebled by the cramped and filthy accommodation and an unremitting diet of salt herring. Immediately, then, on touching dry land they would be met by a parasitic mob of opportunistic dealers, offering bogus tickets, promising 'free lodging' to the single women, relieving them of their luggage.

In his autobiography *Still Dancing*, Lew Grade remembers arriving in London with his mother and his three brothers and being met at the docks by his father, who had come to London ahead of the rest of the family to find work and somewhere to live. Recalling his arrival in Spitalfields, Grade writes:

'Our first lodgings were in Brick Lane, in the East End. We were just one of the many Jewish families living in that area, and my initial impressions of the place were not good. I'd never seen so many people in one place and that took some getting used to. Brick Lane was bleak and rather dark, and so were the two rooms we lived in. For the first time in our lives we were really poor, and, on top of this, I could barely make myself understood because all I could speak was Russian.'

Grade's family had come to London from the Ukraine, escaping persecution, leaving behind 'a large house with its own orchard', his own picture of Eden. Living on Brick Lane, his father had drifted into the rag trade. Unlike his son, however, who was quickly learning the way of the street, how to stitch together a good deal as well as an overcoat, he could never really make any money. Lew, on the other hand, had the entre-preneurial spirit of a survivor. Milestones in his life, as he charts his career from immigrant tailor-cum-tapdancer to international show-business impresario, are located not so much around moments of great insight or self-awareness, but at those times of successfully clinching a deal. 'Money, believe it or not, has never been that important to me. During my lifetime I've given away much more of the stuff than I've kept. As far as I'm concerned it's the deal that counts. For me the fun of business is making the deal, not counting up the profits.'

Deals, for Grade, were synonymous with survival, the cut-throat struggle for subsistence. Yiddish conviviality, such as it existed, was rooted not so much in the cooperative cosiness of the *shtiebl* but in the anxious competitive hustle of the market place. Swinging, as the rag trade did, between the busy and the slack seasons, he was always poised between hectic employment and idleness. In a market which saw small workshops pro-liferating on all sides, the rag-trader's continued existence depended ultimately on the cost of labour and his ability to undercut his neighbour.

With the entry of the sewing machine into common usage – the Singer was put on display at the Great Exhibition of 1851 –

this vulnerable labour force also became susceptible to the effects of mechanisation, particularly the greater use of sub-divisional employment – in short the 'sweating' system. A typical street off Brick Lane might have, for example, a whole army of workers, of fixers, basters, fillers, machinists, button-hole hands and pressers, all working simultaneously, each turning out coats by the score. On top of this there could well have been a trimmings shop, a milliner, an embroiderer, an umbrella-maker, a sack and bag dealer, a furrier, a trouser-maker, any number of private tailors and, more likely as not, a couple of sewing machine mechanics. Most jobs were passed on through word of mouth, but for the unemployed *greener* there would have been the humiliating prospect of a trip down to the pig market (*chazar mark*), a sort of employment exchange off Brick Lane where the jobless would hang out and where the masters would come to select their 'hands'.

A reasonably objective picture of life in the rag trade may be got from a *Report of the Lancet Special Sanitary Commission on the Polish Colony of Jew Tailors* which was issued on 3 May 1884. The report declared that 'the principal grievance to be brought against the Jew tailors of the East End is that they work in unwholesome, overcrowded houses where girls and women are kept toiling long after the hours prescribed by the Factory and Workshop Act.' It goes on to describe how the fine Huguenot silk merchants' houses had been sub-divided into lodging rooms which doubled up as workshops and reduced to a condition where decay and foul sanitation were the norm. 'In Hanbury Street we found eighteen workers crowded in a small room measuring eight yards by four and a half yards and not quite eight feet high . . .'

The fact was that the opportunity of becoming a landlord offered the enterprising tailor one route out of his current predicament. Entrepreneurial ambition could certainly lead to improved status and income, albeit for a ruthless (and lucky) minority of immigrant workers, and the possibility drove many forward. As Booth noted in his survey of London, 'the economic strength and weakness of individualism form the economic strength and weakness of the East London Jewish community. Each for himself, unrestrained by the instinct of combination, pushes himself upward in the industrial scale.' Rothstein, an old guard socialist activist who lived in London and was at one point a Soviet candidate for the ambassadorship in England, makes the same point. 'The Jewish worker in England is still the petit-bourgeois fortune-seeker!' Even if the Jewish worker wasn't motivated primarily by a longing to become 'respectable', then he certainly was, it seems, by the possibility of material security, even prosperity.

Yet, and yet. The situation was more complicated than this, intentions more tangled, motivation, as always, a multiple rather than a single thing. The dream of return, the hope of a homecoming, weaved its way through the individual lives of the toiling rag-traders. It gave shape to the contingent circumstances of their lives. It informed their late night *shtiebl* discussions, as described by Israel Zangwill, and circumscribed the various Jewish communities which sought to establish themselves in Spitalfields. The story of this accommodation is, moreover, a dynamic and necessarily conflictive one. As there was an unsteady yet key relationship between the Cockney and his East End context, so too was there one between this fantasy Yiddish community and the pressing demands for survival amongst individual Jews in the ghetto. Drawing on the inheritance of Judaism, these groups defined themselves variously in relation to each other, to the narrative of their particular exile and to their understanding of the imperatives and promises of their faith.

Although religion undoubtedly played a key role in the formation of these settlement communities, its position was certainly contested. Indeed, the clash between the secular and the spiritual was known from time to time to break into a disturbance of the peace. A report from *The Times* on the 20 September 1904 describes such an occasion:

'Religious differences which have for a week past been disturbing the Jews of Spitalfields culminated yesterday afternoon in a riot in the neighbourhood of Brick Lane and Princelet Street, necessitating the drafting of large bodies of police from every station in the H Division. The orthodox Jews were observing the religious fasts in connection with the Day of Atonement. Between three and four o'clock large numbers were walking along the street when a body of Socialist Jews drove a van containing food through the crowded streets. The orthodox Jews resented this and drove the Socialists into their club, from the windows of which glass bottles were thrown.'

There were other groups, like the anarchist cell that held its first meeting in May 1876 at 40 Gun Street, a tiny house in the heart of Spitalfields, which also rejected that faith outright. Aron Lieberman, its prime mover, had arrived in London at the beginning of August 1875, seeking refuge from the Tsarist police. Appalled by the conditions of the workers he met, he asks rhetorically, 'In the narrow, crooked streets of White-chapel, in the smelly and dirty holes and corners of the workshops working twelve to fourteen hours a day for a paltry starvation wage . . . have the Jewish workers of Poland, Russia, Germany, Austria found their better life?' Along with other members of the highly politicised radical intelligentsia which had found itself in East London, such as Leib Wainer, he formed the 'Agudah Ha-sozialistim Chaverim', the cell which committed itself to propagating socialism amongst the Jews. In their manifesto the ten men who met to talk in the smoky attic room of the Gun Street house over the summer months of 1876 – itself a sort of secular *minyan*, the number required to make a congregation quorate – asserted that 'all peoples should have equal rights and rid themselves of religion.' Of these ten, five were tailors and of the rest one was a hat-maker, another a cabinet-maker.

In the end they all fell out horribly with one another. Despite the fact that he saw himself as 'a binder of peoples', Lieberman was accused of being 'selfish and arrogant' with 'a tendency to posture' and was booted out of the tailors' union, which he had helped to form. He went off in a huff back to Russia only to find himself rounded up by the Prussian authorities in Berlin, spending two years in gaol, before returning destitute to

Spitalfields and living at 21 Elder Street. Working in turn as a photographer, a lithographer, a teacher and a shoe shine, he eventually shot himself in Syracuse in America in 1880. Their ideas, however, persisted and come 1914, the anarchists were still one of the most dynamic elements in East End political life. While Anglo-Jewry rejected Yiddish and sought its demise, condemning its use at school prize-givings and even calling on the Board of Guardians to refuse to help anyone who could not speak adequate English, the anarchists elevated it as a prime vehicle for communication, identifying it as the *mameloshn* – the common language or mother tongue – of the working masses.

Israel Zangwill fills in the turbulent story of union organisation in the East End with a vividly drawn chapter, towards the end of the first part of *Children of the Ghetto*, which is set at a socialist rally. The atheist Wolf and the poet Pinchas, equally militant in his irreligion though politically shrewder, vie with one another to capture the imagination of the mainly orthodox, yet profoundly disaffected, audience. Wolf, who speaks the more fluent Yiddish, calls the assembled company to unity in the name of the socialist struggle: 'Have we not enemies enough that we must quarrel and split up into little factions among ourselves?' More astutely, Pinchas appeals to their religious sensibility: 'Brethren in exile the hour has come for laying the sweaters low . . . Our great teacher Moses was the first Socialist. The legislation of the Old Testament, the land laws, the jubilee regulations, the tender care for the poor, the subordination of the rights of property to the interests of the working man, all this is pure Socialism!' Quoting Hillel the Great and other rabbinic authorities, he concludes in a flourish of calculated homiletics, 'We must become better Jews, we must bring on Socialism, for the period of Socialism on earth and of peace and plenty and brotherly love is what all our prophets and great teachers meant by Messiah times.'

Zangwill, himself a champion of yiddishkeit and the cultural vigour of its 'ghetto spirituality', had a similarly ambivalent relationship to the doctrinal specifics of his faith. Naturally, given the fictive nature of his work, Zangwill's own position is not always apparent, certainly not in his novels, as his characters rehearse different positions and, in doing so, explore the tensions within Jewish identity. It is true, however, that certain voices are expressed with greater seeming conviction than others and his work is usually structured around a central dilemma which is 'resolved' only in the final section. Moreover, his satellite essays and speeches indicate the overall direction of his thinking.

The final scene of *Children of the Ghetto* takes place where most of the stories of the Jewish life in the East End begin – at the docks. This time the hero and heroine are leaving for a new life in the New World. For Zangwill, North America came to represent the proper destination for his 'freight of hopes and dreams', his aspiration for a final homecoming, the converse almost to his nostalgic longings for the pre-lapsarian ghetto days in Spitalfields. In focusing our attention on such a destination Zangwill seeks to transcend Jewish particularity. Indeed, in his play *The Melting Pot*, he goes on to articulate a view of America as the universalist ideal implicit at the end of *Children of the Ghetto*. In these terms, America becomes 'God's Crucible, the great Melting Pot, where all the races of Europe are melting and reforming.'

If Zangwill colluded with a construction of Judaism as an outmoded religion, an 'endless coil of laws', this cannot be said to be the case for most of those who worked in the rag trade in Spitalfields in the late nineteenth century. Their faith was simple, affective, parochial. It was concerned with the details of the festivals and the fulfilment of devotional obligations. It was social. They prayed for one another while alive, visited another when sick and buried one another when dead. Organising the *shabes goyim* to stoke the fire on the sabbath, they would also buy the kindling for poor families. To mitigate their nostalgia for the past they had lost and their longing for the future Messianic age to come, and to stave off meaninglessness in the face of their contingent miserable conditions, they told each other stories, stories of exile and return, looking at it this way and looking at it that. And it was in the synagogue, as they enacted the central story of their faith, that the specific stories of their lives were transformed, were given point.

Synagogue life offered a series of recurrent landmarks, ritual and historical, key moments in an evolving covenant relationship with God. They ate unleavened bread at Passover, blessed the moon, and counted the days of the Omer until Pentecost (Shavuot) when the synagogue was dressed with flowers. They passed to the terrors and triumphs of the New Year and the sobriety of repentance on the Great White Fast (Yom Kippur), when they burned long candles and whirled fowls round their heads. They moved on to Tabernacles (Sukkot), when they ran up rough booths in backyards and processed through the streets waving myrtle and palm and willow branches. Then to the Rejoicing of the Law (Simchat Torah), scrambling sweets for the children and parading the scrolls. From the Dedication (Chanukah), with its celebration of the Maccabean deliverance and the miracle of the unwaning oil in the Temple, they passed to Purim; and so back to Passover.

Bernard Homa remembers going along Brick Lane to the Machzike Hadath Synagogue (formerly the Huguenot chapel) in the years before the First World War with its splendid array of Talmudic scholars and a congregation impatient for the Chazan to finish his part so that they could burst out in one loud responsorial chorus. 'One just felt the holiness of the place,' he writes with disarming piety. He particularly remembers the annual occasion on the Feast of Purim when 'a large number of the children of the surrounding district were attracted to the reading of the *megilla* [the name of the particular scroll]. Many were armed with *greggers* [a percussive instrument like a football rattle] or nothing more than their boots with which to demonstrate their contempt for Haman.'

Purim is based on the story of Esther, celebrating her successful intervention as the King of Persia's wife to save the Jews from being killed as a result of the evil conniving of Haman. Through his feeding the King false information, Haman had ghosted a letter, setting out his case against the Jews, for the King to sign and to send to the one hundred and twenty seven provinces of his kingdom: 'We understand that this nation [the Jewish people] stands quite alone in its continual hostility to the human race, that it evades the laws by its strange manner of life, and in disloyalty to our government commits the most grave offences, thus undermining the stability of our kingdom.' Unmasking Haman's jealous rage at the loyal Mordecai, Esther persuades the King to allow her people to defend themselves against this edict which had singled out the Jews as a dangerous and subversive people.

Haman is hanged on the gallows that he himself had intended for Mordecai. The King's new instructions sing a different song: 'We find that the Jews whom this double-dyed villain had consigned to extinction are no evil-doers; on the contrary, they order their lives by the most just of laws and are children of the living God.'

Like most writings of the post-exilic period, the book of Esther is concerned with the painful and urgent problem of how to remain a faithful Jew in a foreign land. It is precisely because they are perceived as unassimilable and disobedient that they are initially indicted. In its narrative the book asks the question: is it possible or even desirable to cling to one's distinctive heritage against such odds? The answer is resounding. And for those who had survived their own pogrom, it was a story which was told and celebrated with particular feeling.

No wonder Homa's account of the festival is so impassioned. In their chanting and banging the Jews of Spitalfields were enacting their own deliverance and calling to mind their own vocation as God's chosen people. It is here, surely, that the possibility of a final homecoming is proclaimed and kept alive:

'The loud din which greeted each mention of Haman's name was like a miniature earthquake, and would last for well over a minute. The noise, usually started by a few adults would grow in volume like a mounting wave, till the whole building on Brick Lane literally shook from the clatter of the rattles and the heavy stamping of hundreds of feet.'

All slightly at odds with one another

Most evenings Mr Uddin gathered his prayer shawl and wandered over to the Brick Lane mosque, the former synagogue and one-time church, to congregate with his fellow Bengalis and perform his religious duties. He would pass Charlie's house on Wilkes Street and the Jungle Club and Harry's squat on Princelet Street as well as the recently renovated houses in that fine Georgian terrace, before crossing over on to Brick Lane and turning right for prayers. No doubt, as he walked passed Harry's front door, he wondered about his son Delwar's involvement with all these funny white people. What did they want with his boy? And as we sat together in Harry's front room, breaking up another pallet to feed the fire, planning a fiesta of community activism and consciousness-raising street theatre, I would watch Mr Uddin pass the shutters, making his way up Princelet Street. I suppose I felt anxious about his possible disapproval.

I raised it with Delwar, who simply shrugged. He said his father had his mind on other things. He was preparing to go on Haj, the pilgrimage to Mecca all Muslims are encouraged to make at least once in their lifetime.

Meanwhile Harry himself was full of fantastic schemes. He spoke to some of his neighbours on Wilkes Street and Princelet Street, sounding them out on the idea of a street party – 'You know, trestles and bunting and Bengali food and a jam session maybe, does anyone play the tabla drums? Let's just sort of see what happens.' He had plans to turn the Jungle Club into a travelling troupe, secure some funding, do a deal maybe with the Spitalfields Festival, maybe even start up a fringe. He drew up leaflets, wrote some sketches and wondered whether there might be some money available from the market developers, the church or from a local youth project. He showed the children how to make juggling balls by filling rubber balloons with rice, and then how to keep three or more of them in the air at once. And when the juggling balls became missiles, exploding their contents all over the room, he counselled calm, 'Hey guys, cool it with the chucking can you, or take the balls next door to the jungle.'

He called a meeting of local residents, asking Delwar to chair it. Delwar told him he didn't want to chair the meeting and that Harry was the boss. Harry said he wasn't the boss, he was just a storyteller and, like, who the hell needs a chairperson anyway? So we sat around on the floor eating chicken pieces out of a large communal pot, talking sensitively to our neighbours and wondering what in fact we were all doing there, until Beth, a Princelet Street resident whose daughters had been a little involved in the Jungle Club activities, asked if there were any specific events planned. Harry said he was working on a few ideas, like exploring the link between rap music and the medieval mummers' tradition, nothing too heavy, just a few ideas. Struggling a little with this concept, we all reached for our diaries. It was the end of September. We flicked ahead into November. Then someone suggested a bonfire night party and there was general agreement. Harry looked crestfallen.

Caroline, a friend of Charlie's who had worked as a drama teacher in a secondary school in Stepney, said she would be happy to help with organising the evening. She said that with these sorts of projects, in her experience, 'process' was as important as 'product'. We all nodded sagely. She said she would happily facilitate and enable the process through a negotiated structure of monitoring and self-evaluation, maybe with the help of a video. We all hummed interest. Harry, who was handing round the fruit bowl and a dish for contributions towards the cost of the meal, had fallen unusually quiet.

'So where do we light the actual bonfire?' I asked.

No one volunteered a back garden, although Ferouk did suggest the roof of his family's flat. Beth wondered whether it would be worth approaching the council. Caroline pointed out that the fire brigade and police would have, in any case, to be informed. Then Andrew, a resident from Wilkes Street, suggested that we approach the development group which had recently bought a large piece of land at the south end of Princelet Street, on the other side of Brick Lane, temporarily boarded up, pending its transfer into the hands of the Spitalfields Housing Co-operative for redevelopment. Maybe they would consider hosting the evening themselves as an opportunity to establish their links with the local community. It sounded plausible.

'What's wrong with the jungle itself?' asked Harry rather plaintively as we all stood, making to leave. The evening broke up amidst a flurry of half-formulated plans of action, all slightly at odds with one another, no one quite sure who had agreed to do what. Everyone, however, danced his or her departure with nervy, self-conscious enthusiasm.

Everyone, that is, except Harry, who was livid. He felt sidelined and steamrollered and ignored. I told him he was talking nonsense, that the evening had been a huge success and that it had all been his initiative. He said no one had listened to him. I said I thought they had listened to him and that we had come up with a workable proposal and that we now needed him to put together some sort of storyline for the club to perform. Harry grunted and went upstairs to sort himself out. I set about clearing up the remains of his chicken and wondered darkly about the feasibility of working with such an unlikely mix of people. When he reappeared, he stood in the doorway for a few moments until he had my attention. He said he had no intention of being monitored and evaluated and that if Caroline attempted to do so he would tell her to stick her product right up her process and he would happily put it all on video for her. I said I thought he was being a little unfair – but only a little. We both laughed.

In fact, over the following few weeks plans for bonfire night came together surprisingly well. Andrew seemed to pull off a deal with the developers, whereby they agreed to allow us to use the vacant site for our bonfire so long as we cleared it with the police. A youth project on Brick Lane loaned us some makeshift percussive instruments. Beth stitched up some fantastic costumes, improvising wonderfully with sheets and ribbons and safety pins. Caroline found a room for us to play in – 'a really accommodating rehearsal space' – and facilitated the club not, in the end, with a video camera, but with a ready supply of biscuits and squash. I even managed to swing some money, through the help of Fr Leech, towards the running costs of the project, my so-called college 'placement'.

Harry appeared to work wonders with the children. He had us all charging around playing 'donkeys and turkeys', 'apples and magpies' and 'giants, goblins and merlins' as well as various other warm-up games, apparently of his own invention, which made the blood rush to our heads and got us all slightly hysterical. In his retelling, the Guy Fawkes plot became a story about rival mobs, scapegoating and gangland executions. Cecil, the Prime Minister, was cast as a deviously manipulative mafioso stage-managing the whole dénouement with sinister precision. Fawkes was the well-meaning foil, disorganised and impetuous, set up from the beginning for entrapment. King James, who staggered around the floor with 'good queen Bess' on his back, was foppish and ineffectual, driven by vanity. The conflict between rival religious interests was exploited, in Harry's version, by Cecil the master politician, eager to pursue his own self-aggrandising ambitions. He was the biggest guy on the block, operating outside the law, paying off his enemies, cheating on his friends, playing one group off against the other.

We got into role and acted out different scenes. Delwar was Fawkes, with Ferouk and Fatar as his sidekick accomplices, Percy and Catesby. Ali took on the role of king, which he did with great gormless enthusiasm, particularly giving the piggy-back to Mary, one of the girls from Princelet Street. Joe, Andrew's son, was a little too charming as Cecil, but, at Harry's direction, became nastier as the weeks went by. Eventually Harry produced scripts and then a song which reworked Guy Fawkes as Chicken Licken on his way to see the king. It all seemed to be coming together.

As we walked back home in the light October drizzle, I fell into conversation with Delwar, who I thought had been quite withdrawn that evening, not wanting to join in the games and bickering uncharacteristically with his brother. It turned out that things were quite difficult at school, that he was being picked on.

'Why is that?' I asked.

'I don't know, maybe they just don't like me.'

'What about your friends, do they help?'

'No not really, they're as wimpy as I am.'

I imagined it was partly because he was so obviously bright that he excited such animosity. It was only later that I found out that the boys who were taunting him were white and had also been racially abusive. I knew that his school in Bethnal Green was quite divided between the Asian and the white students, but I didn't know how much he dreaded the walk home. When he hadn't turned up for several evenings and Ali, his brother, said he couldn't come out at the moment, Harry and I went round to his house. Delwar himself answered the door.

'What's up with you, my friend?' Harry asked.

'My father doesn't want me to come to the club any more,' he said, 'he doesn't think it is the will of Allah, and he's worried about the begging part . . .'

'The begging part?'

'You know, the money for the guy and all that stuff. He says it shames us, makes us look poor and that.' Harry and I look at each other and then at Delwar.

'Can we talk with your father?' I asked.

'Well no, not really . . .'

History will show if we muck up

Mutual misunderstanding and suspicion between immigrant and indigene has been a feature of Spitalfields ever since it hosted its first refugee. Foreigners, after all, bring with them different ways of carrying on – an unfamiliar rhythm – and a seeming self-sufficiency. This, in itself, can be threatening. W. H. Wilkins' description of Brick Lane at the turn of the last century in his book *The Alien Invasion* is as true for any number of moments over the last three centuries, not least today: 'It is easy to imagine oneself to be in a foreign city. Strange habits and customs and foreign faces surround one; and a foreign language is heard on every side.'

He goes on to describe how, along the Lane, 'there were a number of little eating houses with Hebrew letters on the windows, signifying thus 'kosher' – meat prepared in the Jewish fashion – is there supplied.' Only Ramadan has now replaced Passover, Bengali and Punjabi echo around the streets instead of Yiddish, and the kosher restaurants are now serving halal meat, offering, instead of specially smoked sausages from Warsaw, such delicacies as brain mossala (when the Brussels bureaucrats aren't watching) as well as the usual tikkas and baltis and bhajis.

Just as strikingly similar is the reception that certain elements in the East End have given these communities. It has often been full of fear and hostility. For Wilkins, the presence of this immigrant Jewish community in Spitalfields was more lamentable than thrilling and he expressed his opinions in forthright terms, describing the Jewish 'invasion' and its 'corrupting influence on the respectable poor of the East End'. Tassaduq Ahmed remembers similar accusations being turned against the Asian community once it began to settle after the Second World War, such as the 'fact' that they bought no skills with them, that they had come to sponge off the state and, in doing so, displace the honest – and Anglo-Saxon – working man from employment.

If patterns of racist polemic have repeated themselves over the years, so too have the established paths of racial apartheid. When in the 1880s the Jewish ghetto became headline news, the contested area lay between Whitechapel and Bethnal Green, with Brick Lane – and Spitalfields – running between the two. Most Jews, like most Bengalis today, lived at the southern (Whitechapel) end of the Lane, behind Truman's Brewery which functioned as a sort of frontier post. Bethnal Green, with its strong cockney identity, was far less hospitable, not unlike the culture I had encountered while working in the fruit and vegetable market.

At the population peak of 1901, when some parts of Spitalfields were almost exclusively Jewish, the total refugee population of Bethnal Green didn't exceed 3.5 per cent. Even so, the Bishop of Stepney of the day feared that the churches would be 'left like islands in the midst of an alien sea' and the MP for Stepney, Major Evans-Gordon, moved an amendment to the Queen's speech, in which, appealing to the bar-room prejudice of 'the English working-class man in many parts of East London' he argued that these 'strangers from abroad' were parasitic and unwelcome, taking their homes, their jobs, their school places and, if not their wives, then certainly their prostitutes. In the same year Evans-Gordon helped to form the British Brothers League, an organisation designed to stir up anti-immigrant feeling and campaign for 'stringent measures to prohibit the wholesale immigration of pauper foreigners'. In the end the government yielded to pressure, passing the first Aliens Act in 1905. The number of Jews entering London decreased sharply, and by the time war broke out in 1914 immigration had virtually reached a standstill.

These then were the historical nerves touched by the arrival of the Asian community in Brick Lane from the 1950s. Taking over the workshops, the very machines even, of its Jewish predecessors and inheriting its same economic patterns of self-exploitation and internal antagonism, it was this community which spontaneously regenerated Brick Lane. By the 1960s the area had become the main social centre for Pakistanis and by 1970 the stage was set for the widespread immigration from the newly founded sovereign state of Bangladesh.

For many of the immigrants, however, racial conflict and political exclusion were already familiar realities. The particular tensions and histories they brought with them from the sub-continent were worked out in the relationships they established around Brick Lane. This was true for the Pakistani and Bangladeshi communities which necessarily revisited their historical antagonism, as the Pakistani freeholders remained significantly uninterested in the plight of their Bangladeshi leaseholders. It was true for those women turning to Islam to secure for themselves an independent identity in the West, or turning away from its restrictions to escape the controlling and oppressive expectations put upon them by their families from the East. It was also true for those such as Tassaduq Ahmed who watched and supported the liberation struggle of Bangladesh from London and continued to hope for an ultimate rehabilitation of pan-Bengali identity, living this hope out along Brick Lane.

In 1954 Tassaduq had sailed to England from Bombay in the steamship *Ranji*, her last voyage. 'In the ship I realised that as an individual I have no identity. Now I'm not an Indian and I'm not a Pakistani, so what am I? I realised that if I want to be a Bengali I will be struggling to find my identity.' So he came to London to pursue that struggle and now, nearly half a century later, is amused to reflect on the paradox of that choice. 'I left Bangladesh to escape my background and then spent the next forty years exploring what that meant and doing most of that exploration in the Brick Lane of the East End.'

When I went round to stay with him that October, as the Jungle Club prepared its bonfire night extravaganza, I too became conscious of the way distant dramas were being enacted on the Lane. I saw how Tassaduq's championing of Bengali culture was pursued in the face of the political realities imposed by British colonial rule on his homeland. He had come to the heart of an Empire to pursue a cultural identity which that very Empire had, both deliberately and by default, dismantled.

Like many of the contemporary residents of Spitalfields he was born in Sylhet, a district of India (back in 1923) which had been part of Bengal until 1874 and only subsequently part of the newly created colonial province of Assam. Unlike many of his compatriots, however, his family had been middle-class and wealthy and he had arrived in London more as a political than an economic refugee. His father, the deputy magistrate in his home town of Badheswar, an appointee of the British government, was one of the first generation of graduates from the universities set up by the British in India. Owning some land in the area, his father had grown rice (and, on the proceeds, relatively rich) and had managed to establish himself securely within the colonial system. Although Tassaduq remembers it as an idyllic place – 'incredibly beautiful and fertile' – it was also, in other ways, quite divided and divisive. 'It was a feudal background. We had maidservants like in Victorian England, chattels to be used and exploited.' This troubled the idealistic young man who, unlike other members of his family, apparently took seriously Islam's egalitarian ethic.

He recalls an incident from his childhood. His mother was cross with a servant and was waiting for his father to return to punish the girl. Realising this would involve a beating, Tassaduq threw his father's 'thrashing stick' into a pond. It was, he says, his first conscious act of resistance to exploitation – it also caused quite a stir in the family. 'My father was surprised I had the audacity to condemn and criticise. For a number of weeks we stayed in the same house but we were not on speaking terms.' When he was twenty he left home to go to Calcutta University. It was 1943, during the war, and he was quick to ally himself with the strong anti-fascist movement within the student body.

Following the war came Partition, and with Partition came violent bloodshed between Muslim and Hindu as the Greater Bengal was split between Indian West Bengal and the newly formed East Pakistan. 'British rule had always worked in creating the tension and controlling the division. So Mountbatten came and Mountbatten decided to divide and to rule.' Conflict followed division as monsoon follows drought. Much of the conflict, moreover, seemed to be religiously sanctioned, if not directly motivated. Having been bought up a Muslim, raised on the folk stories of Islam's peaceful advance into Sylhet, he was shocked when he saw the same Islam being used by the ruling class in West Pakistan to impose Urdu on the Bengali speakers from the East. 'They were using Islam for advancing their own class interest. This was a major disillusionment for me. Islam as a religion comes with a revolutionary call. They were taking it over and exploiting it for their own ends.'

So he turned to Marxism and its own doctrine of dialectical materialism, becoming actively involved in the Bengali language movement, opposing the government in Karachi and finding himself in danger of imprisonment. He eventually had to leave the country. That was when he came to London.

'Actually,' said Tassaduq, as he expertly gutted a fish, slicing and dissecting with a knowing hand, cutting it lengthways and then crossways, 'I don't believe in the material dialectic, but the dialectic of thinking, of ideas. By arguing, by confronting, we are changing ourselves and we are changing others. All history is based on conflict. But is it in the will of the masses or in the will of the power-hungry élite, that is the question? In your play-acting you are showing a negative thing. You are showing the achievement of crooks and crafty people over the honest toil of the working man.'

'It's a play, Tassaduq. For children. So they can dress up and make a bit of a racket.'

'And another thing, you are presenting the play-acting in the language of the oppressor class. You must present the play-acting in the language of the people.'

I could see Tassaduq was provoking me, but only partly. He was also seriously committed to the promotion of Bengali culture and had organised his life accordingly. His marriage to Rosemary, with whom he was together for over twenty years until she died of cancer in 1982, had been a remarkable partnership based around a shared political vision. 'Our first love had been the unification of East and West Bengal,' Tassaduq would say with breathtaking candour. Together they had run a restaurant, initially in Soho and later in Paddington, a meeting place throughout the 1960s and 1970s both for activists in the Bengali liberation struggle as well as any number of associated political journalists. It was here, at the Ganges, that Tassaduq and Rosemary learnt to cook, through trial and error and then meticulous classification, slowly building up a repertoire of tasty dishes. Theirs was one of the first 'Indian' restaurants in the West End, certainly one of the better known ones.

'What you eat in the Brick Lane isn't the proper Bengali cookery style. It is what you call the bastard cookery. It's curry for the western taste, full of cream and heavy spice and the kebab-type meat. The food of Bengal is lighter, rice and fish, coming from the water.' As he spoke, Tassaduq rubbed salt and turmeric into the filleted fish and then began to fry the separate pieces. As they sputtered cheerily, he prepared some very green-looking bananas and potatoes and aubergines in a separate dish, browning them first in a special spicy oil and then adding the water and finally the fish. He put a lid on the pan and set the timer. He was making stew.

'The fish stew, the *jhol*, is a typical Bengali meal, not too spicy, nice and light in the flavour. Of course there is rivalry for the perfect *jhol* between East and West Bengal. On this or that side of the border it is cooked in different ways.'

In his commitment to ideological purity there seemed to be the seeds of inevitable disappointment, given the fundamental fault-line which ran between East and West Bengal. Nor was it simply a matter of cuisine, but also of faith and state. It gave his single-hearted longing for unification a sense of pathos and his account of his country's recent past an air of unreality. The history of Bangladesh, in his view, was the history of thwarted possibility. 'The masses in action have decided this thing which has become a fact in history, yet crooks have come to use the situation. The masses were not enlightened enough to take the reins into their own hands. A group of people, basically corrupt, have taken over. Bangladesh has become a plaything for the superpowers.'

Maybe it was hardly surprising, therefore, that this was how he also saw the history of Brick Lane. The key theme, again, was betrayal. He had been part of the rise of Bengali consciousness in the 1970s and had actively opposed the National Front following the murder of Altab Ali, a young Bengali leather worker, in 1978. As a community leader he had negotiated housing with the GLC and supported the election of the first Bengali councillors to local government. However, with the rise of a new brand of professional politician he had become marginalised and disillusioned. 'What we see on the Brick Lane now is coach-load politics, the crooked dealers and wheelers with no regard for the common man in the street. It is not the democracy, it is what I call the mobocracy.'

As I got to know him that October, staying in his flat two or three times a week on the evenings the Jungle Club rehearsed their performance, I began to see in his unbending optimism an almost religious quality of steadfastness. Judgement, in Tassaduq's view, would come, not from Allah but from posterity. 'In the end God won't decide what assessment will be made of our work. It will be history. History will show if we muck up.' Yet, according to Tassaduq, was not history itself an agent of corruption? 'There is nothing wrong with new life that is come into existence. Not only are we born free, we are born pure. It is society which is watering the seeds of our negative features, instead of encouraging the blooms of our healthier aspects.' It seemed to me, in some ways, that Tassaduq was doomed to frustration by his own ontology. Was he not still vainly hoping that by throwing away the 'thrashing stick', he could expunge the thrashing impulse?

Tassaduq seasoned the stew and prodded the potatoes to see if they were tender. He turned the heat down and scattered the dish with the coriander leaves I had already chopped. The conversation fell silent in anticipation of food. He set a plate before me and invited me to eat.

'After we have fed you, you will then be ready to write an article for the AIMS?' said Tassaduq, grinning cheekily.

'AIMS, Tassaduq? What is AIMS?'

'The Asian Institute for Media Studies. We will have a series of articles on the regeneration of the Brick Lane, not just the economic regeneration but also the cultural and spiritual regeneration. The AIMS will be our umbrella logo. Do you think it will catch up?'

After death is the judgement

Delwar's father couldn't read English, so it was no good writing him a note. To turn up on his doorstep unannounced, given his wariness about what we were up to, seemed a bit pushy. Telephoning presented itself as a potential minefield of mis-understanding and confusion. How then was I best to make contact?

In the way these things sometimes happen, my opportunity to meet Mr Uddin arrived quite by chance. Rather preoccupied by the casting problems that Delwar's absence would make to our performance, I was wandering up Brushfield Street from the station towards Christ Church one evening. Passing the church, I rounded the corner of Fournier Street and Wilkes Street and was about to walk straight past them when Charlie called over to me. He and Delwar's father were discussing ways of moving a wardrobe, which was too wide to pass up the stairwell of Mr Uddin's house, to its second floor. Charlie, eyeing the front elevation, was coming to the conclusion that ropes were needed, and another pair of hands. I readily volunteered my own and we set about the task of hoisting the cupboard up the wall.

Mr Uddin was quick to ply his workers with cups of tea, instructing his daughter Hafsa to put on the kettle. I went up to the room at the top of the house with the balcony and checked to see whether the wardrobe would, in fact, fit through the window. This also turned out to be the room where his wife and daughters habitually sat, sewed, chatted, watched videos. They were lined up on the sofa when I entered. As I measured the opening and exchanged information with Charlie standing below, I was conscious of them smiling coyly, whispering, and watching with great interest from the corner of the room. Observed by this group of women, I felt uncharacteristically manly as I threw one end of the rope down, attached the other to the railing and began to hoist the wardrobe with a tug-of-war heave-ho. It bounced its way up the side of the house and was delivered, in a rather surreal way, into the middle of this upper room. Everyone was delighted. More tea was ordered, biscuits were offered, we were invited to stay. I said I had, sadly, to go (I was already late for a meeting with Harry) but that it would be nice to meet Mr Uddin again. I said I had heard that he was preparing to go on Haj and that maybe he would tell me about this planned trip to Mecca . . .

'Yes, yes, I tell you all about Haj, you come to the Deedar before prayers?'

'That's the café where my Dad goes to meet his friends,' explained Delwar.

'Which day is good for you?' I said, pulling out my diary.

'Any day, any day,' said Mr Uddin emphatically. I said I looked forward to joining him there. As I was going, I asked Delwar if he were coming to the club that evening.

'Maybe,' he said shiftily, although I could see he meant 'no'. I couldn't work out what was going on for him.

Later that evening, when the Jungle Club – minus Delwar – was done, I went along to the Deedar. It was between the fourth and final prayer of the day, and Mr Uddin was indeed in the café and ready to be bought cups of tea and have a bit of a reminisce. Maybe because he was preparing to go on Haj, the once in a lifetime trip to the holiest of holies in Mecca, he was open to talking, keen to get his story straight. Maybe the prospect of pilgrimage always has that effect, requiring the pilgrim to sort out what was to be taken along, what was to be left behind, focusing a need for detachment, the search for a sense of an overall pattern. Certainly Haj itself offers a particular prospect of closure, a withdrawal from the concerns of the world. There are some Haji (the pilgrim who has returned from Mecca) who will never again refer publicly to the details of their former lives.

Like all good stories, Siraj Uddin's started before he was born. It started, in fact, with his uncle Attar Uddin, who was by all accounts, particularly Siraj's, something of an outlandish character. Attar had been just twenty when, in the late 1930s, he became one of the *Londhoni* (*dhoni* is the Bengali word for rich), an adventurer who was to try to supplement the family income by leaving home, hiking to Calcutta, boarding ship, crossing the seas and sending home his fortune from the golden heart of the Empire, London. Attar made it to the East End, but he was penniless. He spent two years in hiding from the shipping company and then, when he had earned enough money polishing shoes on Bishopsgate to buy himself a sewing machine, he tried to set himself up in the clothing business. 'He worked in Petticoat Lane, where I worked, not the same place, but near the same place.' No doubt, like most rag-traders at the time, he stitched up utility garments for the war, making mantles and overcoats for servicemen. And then, at some point in the late 1940s, having been away from home for about ten years and watched his homeland become part of East Pakistan following Partition, he returned to Sylhet.

It was the return of his uncle Attar and the tales he brought back with him of freedom and wealth in London, of the docks and the big city houses, that first stirred the 'wanderlust' of the the young Siraj Uddin. Up until that point all he knew about England was from what he had heard at school or from what the odd villager had said on returning home. 'England, I was thinking, is like a heaven, very beautiful, like Darjeeling in India, I have not visited to Darjeeling, but I know it is very beautiful.' And now, as his own father's brother, his uncle Attar, was being fêted and questioned about his time in this heavenly land, it suddenly all seemed so deliciously close. It set the young boy Siraj day-dreaming. He began to nurture a rather pleasant fantasy for himself, 'the Hero's Return'.

Siraj went on to describe his arrival in London in 1961. How, settling in Spitalfields, he had initially expected to be back in Sylhet in six months' time. And how, in the event of it, he wasn't to see his village in Sylhet again for ten years. 'I moved around the area, one or two times a year, always move and change. I was sending money back to my father and my brothers, I thought it was my duty, they looked after me when I was young, so my duty now to give them the money.' More and more of Siraj's family came over to join him. His brothers, Nawab and Abdul, came. His cousin Abbas, Attar's eldest boy, came. Then Abbas started talking about bringing over his wife and children and Siraj found it hard to adjust to this idea. It smacked of permanence, of settling down, and, so far as he was concerned, that had never been the deal. Then, just as he had decided to return home, to get his bearings, East Pakistan and West Pakistan went to war. His village was badly hit.

'My father was killed, he was beaten first, and then he died. He was not well. My uncle was beaten as well, two of my brothers were taken away, killed, two other brothers were released, some was hiding, some was running away. The tallest man in the village – he was in England too, in '58 – they killed him. About eleven of our relatives, some not very close, but relatives, were killed in all.'

As soon as it was safe to do so, Siraj had returned to Sylhet. He remembers flying into Dhaka and looking down from the plane at the ravaged city, the upturned cars and buses and war-torn buildings, and then, on leaving the plane, failing to recognise even his brother, who had lost so much weight. His return home was not to be the heroic one about which he had fantasised. It was poignant and remorseful. He felt he had betrayed his family.

As we were talking, the owner of the restaurant, a man called Razzak, Abbas Uddin's son, came and sat with us. Servicing his customers with cross-table smiles and greetings, he spoke quietly, yet with the smooth intensity of the local politician he was apparently seeking to become. He wanted to know what I thought of the newly designed menu, of the sunken spotlights around the bar, of the wall tapestries he had recently bought across from Sylhet, six paddyfield scenes of rural Bangladesh. Razzak, in fact, was only just getting going with his project of interior redecoration. He had Plans with a capital P.

'We want to open a really high class restaurant on Brick Lane, we'll do mixed cocktails, like what you get in the West End, the same sort of meal menu, but more enjoyable atmosphere. We'll have the nice trendy waiters, we're not just going to put any old dickie bird in a white shirt, we'll get someone from a bar in Soho. We're going to get a bit of the West End attitude. For example, with all the office people coming in, we want to maintain accounts, so they don't have to come up with the cash every day, they can use the credit card, pay once a month, that sort of thing.'

Siraj, who was clearly uninterested in Razzak's plans for business expansion, stood to leave. In the distance, we could just hear the amplified voice of the *hafiz* chanting, with a plaintive eloquence, his lament for a lost world, his calling of the Lane to prayer. 'We call him Honey Voice,' Siraj said, downing his tea, which had gone cold and blotchy. 'He has such a sweet voice for the singing.'

As he went off to pray, his place at the table was filled by two other men, 'brothers' as well as business associates, Sadek and Abdul. I said I had just been talking to Siraj about Attar Uddin, the original adventurer.

'He was a pretty way-out guy, my grandfather,' Razzak said.

'Yeah, really daring,' added Sadek, 'really cool.'

I asked them what they did. Sadek said he ran a mini-cab business and helped out in the restaurant. Abdul, it seemed, would likewise lend Razzak a hand. He also had plans to open a clothes shop on Brick Lane, geared towards the City market, offering made-to-measure suits for less than one hundred pounds. 'Very cheap. Very, very cheap. Guaranteed hundred percent, nobody cheaper. Any style, I'll get it made around here, for inside a hundred pounds!' It occurred to me that it was maybe here, with these hustling opportunists, that the spirit of the first Sylheti settlers found its true heirs. If it wasn't with

Siraj Uddin, bound by the rigours of his exacting piety, nor with Tassaduq Ahmed, dreaming of a world purged by ideological purity, it was with these Bangla Town entrepreneurs, full of stories of deals completed and deals projected, that the adventuring spirit of Attar and his *Londhoni* friends lived on.

Take the night before. At nine o clock a man from Richmond had turned up at Razzak's restaurant with a group of friends. On arrival, Razzak had suggested that, were they intending to drink, then they should buy what they wanted from the off-licence just around the corner, since the restaurant wasn't actually licensed to sell alcohol, *sorry sir*. The Richmond customer, telling his friends that this was the whole fun of it, then went round to the off-licence, which happened to be run by Nawab, Razzak's cousin, and returned with a supply of lager. At the end of the meal, after a couple more emergency visits to the off-licence, the Richmond customer decided he was not in a fit state to drive home and (as luck would have it) was presented with the number of Sadek's mini-cab service along with the after-curry mints and the bill. He then asked Razzak to order him one, which meant that he had to walk over to Sadek's office opposite in order to pass on the booking to Hasmat, Sadek's friend, who was looking after the rank at the time. Hasmat then called Sadek, who had in fact been helping Nawab in the off-licence that evening, and told him that there was a job on, could he come round.

As the Richmond customer had got into the car, half-recognising Sadek from an earlier trip to the off-licence, he was heard to mumble to his friends how they all looked the same, these Pakis. He was very drunk.

Sadek told this story of deftly coordinated go-gettism with some pride. Clearly enterprising, he was also bristling with ideas for expansion, eager to build up a reliable crew of about twenty or thirty cars. With car ownership attracting such high prestige with the young people, he found there were quite a number of drivers in the cat-walk congestion of Brick Lane keen to make a bit of money out of their status symbol. Whereas at the moment he depended on these drivers keeping in touch themselves, circling the block, hanging out in the cafés, he had plans in the future to install a system of radio contact. He had fantasies of walkie-talkie control.

'We should do OK if we organise ourselves a bit better. Charge less rent from our drivers, attract more drivers, get more jobs. More jobs, more drivers – more drivers, more jobs. More money.'

What struck me as he spoke was the similarity, both in his manner and his concerns, between this young Bangladeshi man and his friends and the cockney traders I had encountered in the market. Slightly flash, unsentimental, with an eye for the main chance, they both pursued a logic which was unashamedly bottom-line. Both groups were also essentially tribal, hiding behind a narrow sense of who was in the gang and who was out of it. This affinity had also, it seemed to me, a darker side. In standing up to the white racists, had not some of the Bengali youths resorted to the same brand of defiant prejudice to which they had been subjected? Had not retaliation led, in some measure, to emulation?

This was most obvious among the disaffected youth of Brick Lane, sitting around in their designer clothes and American baseball caps, chucking their bravado around as confidently as they tossed the football from one to the other. 'The way I see it,' said one of the regulars down at the Chicksand Youth Club, 'before things changed, the whites used to come down here and give us all sorts of abuse. Then we got together and now we don't take no shit no more, know what I mean? We fight for ourselves, we stand up for ourselves.'

'Yeah, that's right,' agreed another, 'We learnt how to stay together, there was safety in numbers. When you're with your gang you feel totally cool, know what I mean? We fight for ourselves, we stand up for ourselves.'

'Yeah man,' chimed in a third, 'That's right man, in the seventies, like there were a lot of riots, skinheads and that sort of thing, down Brick Lane, especially on Sundays, because of the market and that, but that was before we were around. We came on the scene in the eighties and we retaliated, got ourselves together, same as with the blacks. When the blacks first came to this country they were kicked about, but no one kicks them about now, do they?'

This was in 1993. Already there were drug problems apparent within this Bangladeshi subculture and it wouldn't be long before heroin in particular was to take its toll. Although heroin addiction is no respecter of racial origin – 'All the kids round here are doing it, blacks, whites, Asians,' said a local substance-abuse worker – the Bangladeshi population was particularly vulnerable. Because of their large families and overcrowded living conditions, Bangladeshi youth spent a lot of time on the street and were more likely, therefore, to come into contact with both pushers and abusers. Youth workers said that children as young as eleven were already addicted. Some, too young for acne, were covered in the tiny pimples bought on by smoking the drug. In 1998 a third of the young drug-users attending the Community Drugs Team facilities would be Bangladeshi boys, often brought along by their concerned sisters.

In the early 1990s, however, cannabis was still the thing. In fact, maybe Siraj Uddin's concern about Delwar's involvement in the Jungle Club – although, to be honest I didn't detect much in our conversation – was because of the widespread fear amongst his generation that their children were going to be corrupted into white and western ways through over-familiarity. Was this his particular fear? I wondered whether to raise this directly with Mr Uddin when I went along to find him at the Deedar the following evening. In the event, he didn't give me much chance. He wanted to pick up where he left off the previous night and continued to tell me his story of his return to Spitalfields as together we sweated deliriously through a plate of burning hot peppers.

'Where the father stay is the children's home. When he dies, you have no home. Now my father died, I had no home.'

While he was alive, his loyalty to his father meant that Siraj was never able to see his life in Spitalfields as anything more than temporary. But now his father had died he had begun to feel the same about Sylhet, that there was nothing really to keep him there. Certainly, with six brothers, he wasn't needed on the small family farm. He also began missing the freedom of

London, his relative economic independence, even the climate. He had grown so used to the more moderate temperatures, even his skin colour changed.

Siraj stayed in Sylhet for three years. He got married and his first children were born there. But in 1975 he returned to Spitalfields. His cousins had stayed in London and it was they who accommodated him and his family on his return and helped him find work. He soon got a job as a tailor and readily picked up his cutting scissors again. At least he now had some kind of independence, his own trade. He also managed to get his wife some piece-work to do at home. And then, just after Delwar was born in 1981 his family moved into a housing association house just off Princelet Street, their own place.

'Did your wife manage to make friends when she came to Spitalfields?'

'Friends.' Siraj looked puzzled, 'Yes, yes, friends. My wife stay at home. Spitalfields not a good place for the women, a dangerous place for the women.'

He had returned at a point in the history of Brick Lane when there was a growing tide of racial threat and violence. In particular, the murder of Altab Ali, the 24-year-old Bangladeshi clothing worker, at the beginning of May in 1978, had sparked off a series of demonstrations and galvanised the anti-racist movement into action. On 14 May about seven thousand Bengalis held a protest march from Brick Lane to Downing Street behind Altab Ali's coffin. Throughout the summer there were violent clashes, mainly on and around Brick Lane, between the National Front and the Anti-Nazi League. Local resistance to these pernicious groups spilled over into the community's opposition to the GLC's plans to segregate, supposedly for their own protection, all the Bengali families within their own housing estates. To the increasingly politically self-conscious Bengalis, this smacked of 'ghettoisation'. They stopped it happening.

The Bengali community on Brick Lane suddenly became the subject of numerous reports and surveys, each detailing the horrifying enormity of the area's problems as though they had just been discovered. With their setting-up of programmes of regeneration and their putting together of agendas for reform, they seemed to become a self-perpetuating cry of complaint; of reports which recommended further reports which called for further reports. The account they give of multiple deprivation certainly makes for pretty grim reading.

Citing statistics, however, is like quoting chapter and verse: it's a rather bullying form of evangelism. It tells a story, but it tells it baldly, it leaves no room for aspiration. How do you quantify another person's hope? How do you table their despair? How do you explain that, despite all the statistical woe, most of the Bangladeshi householders wanted to remain in the Spitalfields ward, that they felt it to be their home?

I wanted to ask Siraj about this and so, joining him as he left the Deedar to go to prayers, I did so. 'Did Spitalfields become your home, then, when you moved back in 1975?'

'Spitalfields is only the temporary home, like Sylhet. We are moving, poor people are always moving. They will be like the Jewish people. The Bengalis will not stay here, they will not tie themselves to a certain place. This place, this Spitalfields, is always giving rest to another group. Now the rich people is moving in, it will not be a place for the poor people.'

We were standing at the door of the mosque. Men dressed in their baggy *shalwar* trousers and *thoki* prayer caps arrived from all directions, climbing the steps in front of us with steady deliberation.

'Is that a good or a bad thing?' I asked. If Tassaduq Ahmed was hopelessly committed to transforming the material conditions of the Bengalis along Brick Lane, Siraj Uddin seemed remarkably quiescent, almost indifferent to his community's physical plight. For both, however, there was more at stake than simple economic regeneration. Their concerns were ultimate.

'After death is the judgement,' Siraj said, with undoubted conviction. 'There is one good place to live and one bad place. In the good place everyone will help you and make your satisfactions, in the bad place there is only fire and so you will be burning hot all the time.'

I could see I had to bite the bullet, whilst still engaged so intensely in these matters.

'So do you think our performance with the Jungle Club is a bad thing? Do you think it is against the will of Allah?'

Siraj looked at me rather blankly, then shrugged.

'In this matter you need to talk to the imam, he is a very holy man. He will be helping you in your problem with the jungle.'

A dream

In fact Siraj became quite insistent. He felt I should certainly ask the imam about 'my problem with the jungle'. He said that there was much for me to learn about the beauty of the faith. He told me I should just go and introduce myself, to just say I was a friend of his. It was OK, he told me, they came from neighbouring villages in Sylhet, their families shared farm machinery, he had gone to school with his uncle, his niece had married one of the imam's cousins and so on and so on.

Yes, yes, I said, I would go and introduce myself. OK, fine, I agreed, I would go and talk to him.

Now I felt trapped. I felt I had been bounced into seeking permission from the imam for something which was actually none of his business. What had started out as respectful deference to Siraj Uddin's religious sensibility was fast becoming bothersome accountability to the authority of the mosque. Why shouldn't we put on a little play with the children? What on earth could be the objection to an evening of jolly social fun, a fantastic opportunity for the families living in the conservation area to get to know one another? I could see nothing in the performance which defamed Islam or called into question the integrity of the faith.

Nevertheless, the next morning I put on a tie. I practised my Arabic greeting – *Assalaamu Walaikum*. And I thought through how I would present my case, maybe suggesting to the imam that cooperation needed to be based on mutual understanding and respect. Full of apprehension, I then walked round to the mosque. There were a couple of people performing their ablutions in the wash room by the main entrance and I could see a couple more saying private prayers in the large prayer room off the hallway. No one was particularly interested in me. Siraj Uddin had said I should speak to Imam Mahmudur Rahman, the second in command. A man in a long blue overall, carrying a broom, appeared from a large reception room to my right.

'Imam Rahman?' I said.

'Up,' he said, pointing the stick up the staircase, repeating, 'up.'

I found what I thought was the imam's room on the second floor of the mosque, at the top of the rather fine eighteenth-century staircase, presumably part of the original Huguenot chapel. It was overlooking Brick Lane. A collection of sandals had gathered on the floor. A Qur'anic inscription was stuck to the door. I knocked. Silence was broken by the sound of mucus finding its way out of a throat into a jug.

Bleary-eyed, a man opened the door. 'Ah,' he said, half in acknowledgement, half in annoyance.

'Imam Rahman?'

'Ah!' he repeated.

We shook hands. Unfortunately in our introductory shadow-boxing Siraj Uddin's name drew a complete blank with the imam. In fact most things I said drew a blank with him. My little speech about the need for mutual understanding was met with a total lack of comprehension. 'No sleeping,' he said, 'Up at four-thirty for the morning prayer. People disturbing. No good. No holidays. Always busy.' As he spoke, I noticed that he had been sleeping on the floor rather than on the bed, which was itself piled high with books and I wondered whether this arrangement was contributing to his insomnia. 'I'm getting ready,' he said, quite abruptly, and shut the door.

I went downstairs where the man wearing the long blue apron made me a cup of tea. We smiled a lot at each other. And nodded and gesticulated. And uttered a few nonsensical monosyllables. I think I told him the imam was on his way down. I think he told me to take a seat. Quite soon Imam Rahman did appear and gave the man wearing the long blue apron some brisk sounding instructions. He scuttled off. Then the imam sat down, coughed a little, and then began to talk.

'You want to know Islam?' he said.

'Yes, I should like to understand more about your faith . . .'

'Faith, yes. My English is bad.' Imam Rahman cleared a space in front of him on the table, shifting papers and books into a pile, moving a dirty plate to one side. 'You teach me English. I teach you Islam.' I was slightly nonplussed by his directness.

'That sounds like a good deal,' I said. The aproned man had returned with more tea which he placed in front of us. The imam gave me a further mug and took one for himself, heaping into it several spoons of sugar. Then he said he wanted to talk to me about 'bounden duty'.

'For the perfect Muslim, there is five bounden duty. The first bounden duty is that there is one God and Mohammed is His messenger, peace be upon him. The second bounden duty is for the daily Prayer. The third bounden duty is for the Ramadan fasting. The fourth bounden duty is for the rich man to give money to the poor. The fifth bounden duty is for Haj, the trip to Mecca. These are the five bounden duty.'

Imam Rahman was a small man. He had very dark hair and lots of it, all over his face and pulled into a pointy beard at the bottom of his chin. The effect was certainly startling. He would sit on the edge of his seat, stroking his beard, with his head cocked attentively to one side, until he had something he wanted to say, at which point he would pounce on his words and accompany his sentences with a whole series of brusque hand gestures, of flickings and proddings and pokings.

We talked a bit about bounden duty and we thought up some alternative expressions such as 'obligation' and 'responsibility'. I suggested that if he really wanted to impress his friends with his idiomatic English he could try 'pillars of belief' or 'tenets of faith'. He asked me what a 'tenet' was. I said it was something you held on to. Like this, he said, pretending he was steering a car. Yes, I said, a bit like a 'steering wheel'. He repeated it several times, emphatically, 'steering wheel', 'steering wheel', 'steering wheel'. Then he began again with that look of sweet innocence. 'For the perfect Muslim,' he said, 'there is five steering wheel . . .'

It was at this junction that our conversation veered off the road. We had been joined by a man carrying a bottle of Lucozade who stood at the door until he was beckoned closer.

When he came over, he explained something to the imam and then offered up his bottle, which the imam took, unscrewed and peered inside. Imam Rahman then carried it over to the other side of the room and proceeded to blow on top of the water – I took it to be water and not Lucozade – whilst murmuring a few prayers. When he had finished, the imam handed it back and nodded a rather cursory farewell. After the man with the bottle had left, he made some fed-up sort of grunting noises and then said, 'Ah! People always disturbing. It's no good. This man, his child ill, he want me to make some water good with the prayers, for his son to be better. People always asking, always disturbing.'

'Why don't you suggest he goes to see a doctor?'

'Doctor no good. They want the prayers of the imam. They want the blessing of the holy man. They come to the mosque, they not come to the hospital.'

It wasn't clear to me whether he approved of this practice or not. Clearly he resented the intrusion, yet enjoyed the authority and wielded it with undoubted confidence. In any case, maybe the bottle-blessing worked, maybe it did its job. Maybe the man's son would become well. Imam Rahman stood up. The lesson had ended. It was time for prayer.

The following day, the imam was waiting for me. So was some tea and a plate of Bengali sweets. 'Eat! Eat!' he insisted, offering me the plate. Then he sat silently, stirring his sugar into his tea, apparently waiting for me to begin.

'Today we're going to look at the role of the family,' I announced grandly, adding a little more circumspectly, 'according to the law of Islam.'

'According to the law of Islam,' began the imam boldly, picking up on my deference, 'the husband is super-powerful and the wife is respectful to the husband. It is forbidden for the husband or for the wife to go without marriage to any other man or woman. Forbidden! By the law of Islam! But for man there is opportunity to marry several times, if his strength is enough or his work is enough to look after, he can take two or three or four women if he wants.'

'Does this happen at all in Spitalfields?'

The imam hedged. 'It does happen. It is the opportunity, you understand. It does happen, but not regular, it is the opportunity. Women are too much agitated in mind. When two of the women come together: quarrelling! Quarrelling! You understand? Too much noisy!'

I said I understood exactly what he was talking about and shared a moment of blissfully unregenerate anything-for-a-quiet-life chauvinism. He went on, 'According to the law of Islam, it is necessary to be obedient to your father. It is saying by the Holy Prophet Mohammed – praises be upon his name – if a child is disobedient to his father and mother he will not be coming to heaven. In this country too many Bengalis are exciting about their children, because they are disobedient of their parents. Everybody crying. They are coming to me and asking for a blessing for the children to be obedient.'

Imam Rahman was leaning over the table towards me, half excited, half angry. 'Here the girls don't have the shame from the home country. They are open. They go to the market, they talk in the street, they don't cover the face. In Bangladesh it is so pure, so lovely, and we are losing that in this place. In the Islamic way the women stay inside the house, forbidden to come out. They are subject to the husband. But in Spitalfields the Bengali women are going out, they will not stay in the house and work in the house, they are not soft-minded.'

He settled back in his chair. 'In Islam it is also necessary to look after the family. I have a father in Bangladesh. It is necessary for me to be looking after him, and finding out what is the problem and what is the economic problem and what is the physical problem. Then he will give a blessing for me and I will go to heaven. With parents, everything is bounden duty for us, you understand?'

Back to bounden duty. Islam was looking to be very good at the business of social responsibility, of underlining the need for a strong sense of family and of community loyalty. Yet I also wondered about the cost at which this came. In particular, along with most people educated in the western liberal tradition, I found his attitude towards women to be quite problematic, although I was also aware how many young Muslim women, who had 'reverted' to the faith of their parents, were finding in Islam a means of gaining independence and respect, a real source of empowerment. Many wore the *hijab*, the headscarf, with an almost defiant confidence. It was hard to see, however, how much of this was reactive, a response to the prevalent liberal agenda, and how much of it expressed a genuine commitment to the inheritance of faith. These gender roles were certainly much more sharply defined in Spitalfields than they were in Sylhet, where, so I was told, women actually enjoyed far greater freedom, far less discrimination.

'It must be difficult for you to keep in touch with your family in Bangladesh, while you are living on your own in Spitalfields,' I flannelled.

'Difficult,' he repeated in agreement, and again, savouring the word, 'Difficult.' I felt him sigh at the weighty impossibility of it all.

We then started discussing the relative efficiency of the postal service as compared to the inordinate expense of the telephone. (This was before e-mail.) He told me that he never wrote directly to his wife, but would only communicate with her through an open correspondence with his father. After a while, however, it was time to pray. And that was the end of our second lesson.

When I came the following week for our third lesson I found Imam Rahman in the company of three very serious-looking Bengali gentlemen, somewhat older than him, I thought. As I stepped out of my Doctor Martens and rather selfconsciously left them amongst the assorted pairs of slip-on sandals by the door, their conversation turned to silence.

'Please, sit!' commanded one of the assembled company, lightly touching the back of one of the empty chairs. He then continued, speaking apparently on behalf of the other members of the reception company, 'We understand from Mahmudur Rahman that you have some questions concerning the Islamic faith.'

'Yes,' I replied somewhat shiftily, 'It's clearly an important aspect of your life in Spitalfields.'

'What are the questions you are wanting to ask?'

'Well,' I continued, trying to pretend my mind hadn't gone

a complete blank, 'I'm very interested in the differences in attitude between the older and the younger Muslims in Spital-fields . . . and how you feel the changes which are taking place in the area will affect the whole worshipping community here . . .'

'In our Holy Qur'an it is written that the prophet Moham-med – peace be upon him – is very perfect and that his followers are very perfect, but today there is no real example of the perfect Muslim. You can always find fault, but that is not the fault of the religion, do you understand? This is because we are not correct perfect Muslims. I think proper Muslims have a light in their souls and their hearts, and this light is the light of Islam, but nowadays there are none like this, with this light, do you understand?'

He was talking quickly, chanting almost, urgently running his sentences into each other. 'There are many teachers in the UK, but you should remember that they are not perfect Muslims. If you want to speak to a perfect Muslim, you must speak to a perfect mullah. Holy Qur'an is a very hard book to understand and if you are not beloved to Allah, you will not understand the original meaning, you will understand the word meaning, but that is not sufficient, that is not the original meaning, do you understand? If you want to understand the original meaning you must speak to a mullah, not an ordinary mullah, but an extra-ordinary mullah. In fact, if you are really wanting to understand the original meaning I think it would be better for you to meet a great Muslim saint.'

I was beginning to feel rather embarrassed for Imam Rahman, who may not have been the absolute tops, Muslim-wise, but struck me as being a very decent sort of fellow.

'And do you know of any such person?' I asked.

'I do!' he replied, triumphantly.

'So where does this perfect Muslim live?'

'He lives in Peckham, in the High Street.'

'He is the brother of this Mr Ali,' interrupted the imam pertly, introducing me, with a cheeky wink and a sudden movement of the hand, to my interrogator.

I took the brother's name, this 'perfect Muslim saint', and left, slightly bemused by the whole encounter. So that was the end of the third lesson.

The following day Imam Rahman was waiting for me. As I sat down he poured me a cup of tea and offered me some onion bhaji. Then he said,

'I had a dream.' And he began to tell me his dream,

'I see one – what's the name? – a snake. I see a black snake going in front of me and my friend. My friend, he has a stick in his hand. I tell him to beat the snake. He beat one time and the snake is going into the hole of the earth. Then the snake is turning his head and I catch the stick from my friend's hand and beat the snake, I beat the snake seriously. Then he had died. Died. Finished. I wake up. What is the meaning?'

I was astonished. One didn't need to be an expert in Freudian dream analysis to know that snakes and holes and sticks could be referring to other things. Yet to whom or to what? It wasn't clear to me. In fact, what his dream actually meant didn't seem at first as important as the fact that it required interpretation, that its meaning was apparently hidden. I wanted to know how the imam would deal with this. Given Islam's resistance to the procedures of interpretation in relation to the Qur'an – which most Muslims and certainly all 'perfect Muslim saints' see as the unmediated word of God – I was intrigued to know what the imam would do with his own dream.

'What do *you* think it means?' I asked.

'The snake is the small enemy of me, the snake is the enemy of my mind. Maybe some disease, maybe a particular man, maybe a particular ghost. It is the success of my life that I kill the snake.'

'So where do you think the dream came from?'

'Sometimes the dream is the thinking of the mind, sometimes the dream is coming from Almighty Allah, a sign of the goodness, sometimes the dream is coming from Satan.'

'And how can you tell which dream is which?'

'It depends on the condition of the dream. When you see the peaceful and good dream, it has come from Almighty Allah. When you see fearness and anything of bad, you know it has come from Satan.'

'And when does the dream come from your own head, from your imagination?'

'If you are dreaming about something you think about or something you see, then it is coming from the mind.'

'So where did last night's dream come from?'

'I think my dream came from Satan.'

'What about either of the other two?'

'No.'

'Not from your imagination or Almighty Allah?'

'No. Satan sent to me a snake to kill me and I was strong.'

But how did he know? How could he be so sure? It was his absolute clarity that I found so disarming, indeed alien. It also played, of course, into all my liberal anxieties about Islamic 'fundamentalism'. So, in my wisdom, I thought I would try to tease out of him a sense of textual multivalence, the appreciation that all our interpretations are necessarily partial, necessarily defined by the hermeneutic circles we inhabit . . .

'If you killed the snake, you must have been participating in your dream, so maybe part of it came from your own mind, your imagination?'

'Ah!'

'Although if the dream was a warning that a snake was going to kill you, that it was about to happen, then the dream might have come from Almighty Allah, warning you to be ready . . .?'

'Ah!'

'Or is it possible that the dream came from more than one place, or possibly from all three, from Almighty Allah, from Satan and from your own imagination . . .?'

'No!' he said, standing up abruptly, apparently indicating that he wished to curtail the conversation, 'Satan sent to me a snake to kill me and I was strong.'

Suddenly, in the force behind his statement, I realised there was more at stake here than simply the interpretation of his dream. He was suspicious of me. He was warning me. As far as Imam Rahman was concerned one thing was now becoming clear to me: I was the snake.

In liturgy as in life

It has to be said that Salman Rushdie found himself in hot water with his own attempts at dream analysis in his novel *The Satanic Verses*. Reworking the original story of the 'satanic verses' into one of his character's extended dream sequences, he engages in a ninth-century debate within Islam about the status of these 'revelations' with all the hocus pocus of a late twentieth century novelist. In doing so he revisits the political battles (disguised as polemical disputes) between a group of theologians known as the 'Mu'tazilis' and their opponents the 'Hadith folk'. The former tradition, which more readily employed *iftihad* – creative interpretation of the divine texts and innovation in law – was suppressed by the more conservative latter tradition. The 'Hadith folk' recognised no authority outside the divine text and as a result they initiated a tendency which led towards the deification not only of the Prophet, but also of the Qur'an, as the 'uncreated' word of God, a kind of eternal cosmic entity, something of God himself.

This version of Islam provides Rushdie with a usefully conservative philosophical system upon which he is able to perform his deconstructive acrobatics, exercise his distinctive postmodern *jouissance*. Having spotted how there can be no exact correspondence between words and their referent (or, as contemporary French philosophers would say, between the *signifiant* and *signifié*) he sets about exposing the apparent illusion of all those fixed systems of representation which draw their authority from a 'foundational meta-narrative.' It is this that gives his attack on the Qur'an – a text whose semantic structure is such an essential part of its divine significance – its subversive energy. By focussing on the linguistic instabilities that prevent us from picturing the world coherently or *in toto*, we come to see how easy it is to slip between worlds, between subjective versions, between 'incompatible realities'. Pitching the 'truth of the tale' against the 'unarguable absolutes of religion' Rushdie seeks to offer us a 'secular definition of transcendence', to fly his kite without a breeze.

Now, although Islam isn't particularly my thing, I know

enough about it to recognise how Rushdie's depiction – as well as its populist book-burning response – both rely on a distortion of the historic faith. Islamic law is not a set of unambiguous commands deriving from bald scriptural statements, but is rather a vast corpus of writings, an assembly of analogical connections, rhetorical methods and lexical procedures which stretches back over centuries and a vast expanse of territory. It is arcane, highly technical and essentially concerned with the interpretation of precedents and general principles. Over the last hundred years it has also, in some places, been increasingly open to reform or *iftihad*. It is as much a perversion of Islamic law for Rushdie to refer to its 'unarguable absolutes' as it is a nonsense to call for its neat 'application' – as some Islamic ideologues have done – as though it were the latest cookery book by Delia Smith.

In his setting of the 'truth of the tale' against the 'unarguable absolutes of religion', it is clear that Rushdie simply hadn't got his head around the way in which any belief in God is inhabited precisely through the enactment of stories, in liturgy as in life. Faith is an art – as much as pursuing the craft of a novelist is a calling. Your field becomes the site of your tilth, the earth into which you dig your deepest longings and out of which you harvest your dreams. It is a place of bright hope as well as dark despair. It is the very ground of regeneration.

I had seen this most clearly since returning to Spitalfields. I recognised it in the accounts of Yiddish Spitalfields as the Jewish refugees sustained their sense that they were merely in *galut*, sojourners in a foreign land, through their noisily hospitable *chevras* and synagogue lament. In Tassaduq Ahmed's commitment to working out his vision of the Greater Bengal along Brick Lane I had similarly witnessed a life in the service of a larger story, as I had also seen in Siraj Uddin's vivid sense – no doubt accentuated by his preparations for going on Haj – that Spitalfields, though his chosen place of residence, would only ever be a 'temporary home' in the context of the ultimate journey of his faith. Indeed I wondered whether this heightened sense of the narrative nature of faith was a particular feature of a migrant community in exile, as it collectively remembers – and re-enacts – that world now lost to it?

Of course there are as many 'Islams' as there are Muslims, as many 'Christianities' as there are Christians. Not all Muslims would concur, for example, with Imam Rahman's account of the normative relations between men and women – as not all Christians would find it easy to condone the personal circumstances in which I found myself becoming a father. Yet Christianity is rooted in the mysterious entanglements of judgement and forgiveness, experienced as grace, and any religious tradition is sustained by debate and disagreement, is kept alive through its adherents' loyal dissent and critical solidarity. It needs continually to be broken and remade. Each tradition has its own blind spots and strengths (Islam's straightforwardness about some of the biological imperatives of sexual desire is something that Christianity, with its tendency to abstract and etherealise, could benefit from) yet in its ability to change and evolve each also attests to the fact that faith is a living thing.

So too vocation. My conception of being called to the priesthood had also changed and evolved over the previous six years, since first going to see the Bishop of Oxford. Whereas, in the beginning, I had seen it as essentially a private and inward matter – even a career decision I had taken with a nodding reference to God – I now saw it in a much more lateral way, as a way of participating with the Church in solidarity with the broken-hearted and vulnerable. Was I simply becoming institutionalised? I hoped not. Through my time in Spitalfields, sorting through my particular inheritance of faith, especially in relation to my grandfather, and more recently in conversation with Ken Leech, I had found within the Church a tradition of radical political Christian protest and proclamation which felt authentic to the Gospel charge. How could a movement founded around the life and startling teaching of Jesus not be subversive and defiantly eccentric?

Essentially I had come to recognise the unlikely inclusivity of the City of God. Who are we to bar entry? In its urgent call for participation in the common life of the Kingdom, there is little in the Gospel that would support an attempt to privatise its membership. Rather, the persistent thrust of the New Testament is towards the New Creation, the new humanity *en*

Christo, anticipating the arrival of the City of social joys, the site for the healing and renewal of the nations. It is crazily generous. And rather exposed the vaguely sensible mumbo-jumbo and well-meaning platitudes that had a tendency to fall from my lips in a rather embarrassing way.

Paradoxically the very experience that had exposed me to myself, that had really bought all this into focus – the birth of my daughter in my first year at theological college – also seemed now to be the one that might still disqualify me from ordination. I had yet to return to the bishop for his final judgement on the matter. Maybe, as if I were a little boy about to be deprived of his favourite toy, just at the moment at which the prospect of priesthood in the Church looked like it might be withdrawn from me it appeared all the more urgent and important. I began to pester Ken Leech, who was supervising my bonfire night placement. What should I say to the bishop? Should I write him a letter? Stand my ground? Beg his forgiveness? Leech would look at me, nod very attentively, and then change the subject. He seemed to be more interested in telling me how, as a lad in Manchester, they used to make mushy peas and parkin for Guy Fawkes night.

'Don't you have any suggestions?' I eventually asked, maybe a little petulantly.

He told me a story. He told me how, before he was Archbishop, Michael Ramsey had been asked to lead a mission in Oxford. The planning group had finished their meeting and as he rose to leave one of the younger clergy present said, 'Don't you think we should say a prayer for the success of the mission?'

'"Oh yes," says Ramsey . . .' said Leech, imitating a plummy episcopal stutter, '". . . prayer, very important, yes we should certainly say a little prayer."'

Ramsey put his hands together and bowed his head. Everyone waited for him to begin. As he continued to sit there, his head bent over, the room of clerics became increasingly agitated.

'Eventually he stands up, thanks everyone for coming and walks out.'

'I see,' I said, not, in fact, seeing at all.

Everything was burned

In the end I had left without asking the imam his thoughts on dramatic representations. Actually I'd got it all wrong anyway. It turned out that Delwar's withdrawal from the Jungle Club had nothing to do with any religious scruples his father may have entertained, nor any particular concern he may have had about Delwar's exposure to drugs, nor indeed with any particular family shame associated with collecting money for the guy. Nor had it anything to do with the fact that Delwar was being picked on at school, though he was. With Delwar's assistance, I had been busy dreaming up all sorts of reasons for his opting out of the club which weren't in fact the case. In the meantime, I had missed the way that he had become miserably distracted by a complicated and painful family disagreement in which he had found himself increasingly involved.

It was Harry who eventually discovered what had been going on. Delwar had come to him for advice on ways of reconciling his father to his eldest sister, Dipali. Siraj had refused to speak with her since she had run away, at the beginning of the summer, to move in with her boyfriend, a young Bengali she had met at school. She had gone to join him with his family in Bethnal Green. This was bad enough, but two other factors had almost simultaneously compounded the public humiliation for Siraj. First, Dipali had fallen pregnant. But far worse, as far as her father was concerned, she was already promised in marriage to the son of a friend of his in Bangladesh. In fact the wedding had been due to take place that summer in Sylhet, with the whole family flying out. It was only two weeks before they were due to leave – the tickets had been booked, injections taken, wedding arrangements made – that Dipali disappeared.

Siraj had refused to take her phone calls and instructed other members of the family to do the same. Angry with everyone, not least the boy's parents for taking his daughter in, he withdrew into himself, spending a lot of time on his own. Delwar's mother was particularly concerned about the progress of the pregnancy and encouraged Delwar, as the eldest boy, to try and make contact with her. She knew her husband was also worried about Dipali, but, in his pride, had cut himself off from these feelings. She knew, in his shame, he felt only rage but hoped that this would pass. She encouraged him to spend more time at the mosque. If only there was a way of bringing them together, she would say to Delwar, if only he could arrange for them all to meet . . .

Now Delwar was himself in despair. He felt the burden of responsibility for his family's happiness, but found himself trapped by divided loyalties. Unbeknownst to his father, he had visited Dipali in Bethnal Green, taking her specially prepared food from her mother and letters and some money. Dipali was keen to come home, for her family to meet her boyfriend, Ayub, who she knew they would like. She knew she had done a bad thing, just disappearing like that, but had felt herself trapped by all sorts of expectations and knew that she would never have been happy returning to Bangladesh for an arranged marriage. In any case, she loved Ayub and was now expecting a baby and wanted more than anything else to be reconciled with her family and, in particular, with her father.

'So what shall I do then Harry?' Delwar said, as we sat around the kitchen table, folding invitations to the bonfire night party.

'You know what I think, my friend?' said Harry, with a characteristic twinkle in his eye, 'I reckon you ought to invite them all along to the show. Ring-side seats. Give them all a hot potato and they'll all be best mates in next to no time.'

Delwar and I both smiled at the cheek of it, 'Do you think so?'

'Sure do. Means you've got to star as Guy Fawkes though. No good inviting them along if you don't burn. Isn't that right, Will? You've got to be a human sacrifice, if you want to get your folks talking to one another again.'

Delwar, it seemed, had backed himself into appearing at our bonfire night extravaganza. We finished folding the invitation in high spirits, thinking of all the unlikely people we could invite along. It amused me to think of bringing together all the different groups of people in Spitalfields, the cockneys, the conservationists, the developers, Gilbert and George, the imam.

In fact, I did take an invitation round to the mosque. I hadn't seen Imam Mahmudur Rahman for a couple of weeks and felt bad about the way the conversation had ended so abruptly. When I arrived the man in the long blue apron told me the imam was in the kitchen. I went down the stairs and found him in the middle of eating his breakfast. He didn't appear in the least surprised to see me.

'Eat! Eat!' he said, passing me a clean plate and cutting off a slice of his pancake which had been doused in golden syrup. The kitchen itself felt coldly inhospitable. Against one wall was a large gas cooker, piled high with empty vat-like pans. In the corner was a stone sink. Above our heads dangled an electric bulb. On the wall behind where the imam was sitting hung a photograph of Mecca. The overwhelming sense of bachelor austerity was compounded by an oddly incongruous packet of Sugar Puffs which sat on the table at the his elbow.

'I brought you this,' I said, passing over the invitation. He looked at it and placed it along with some other correspondence, which he shuffled around, checking the contents of various brown enveloped letters. Then he sighed a most profound sigh.

'No sleeping. This room in mosque, too noisy, all the night, noisy, noisy. People ringing. Always disturbing. Ache in the head.'

'You don't sound very well.'

'No well! No well! I need holiday.'

At this point he unfolded one of the other letters he had in front of him, which he flattened decisively on the table. He then gave it to me to read. It had all the markings of official correspondence – reference numbers, telephone extensions, an illegible signature – and was headed with a PO Box for the immigration department of the Home Office. It read something like this:

'Dear Mr Rahman,

'Thank you for your letter of September 15th. Your application for an extended-stay exit-visa is under consideration at the moment. Unfortunately due to the back-log of applications we will not be in a position to inform you of our decision until December of this year. May I ask you, however, to complete the enclosed form and return it to us, in the envelope provided, as soon as possible. This will assist us greatly in processing your application.

'Thank you for your cooperation, yours sincerely, etc.'

Imam Rahman was staring at me hopefully. Did he want me to draft a response for him? I suddenly remembered Toor, the belt salesman on Brick Lane who had similarly been trying to arrange for his wife and children to come over to London, and then imagined all the other families in Spitalfields, like the imam's, like Delwar's, like Toor's, which had somehow become fragmented in transit. The imam said he was hoping to return to Bangladesh for several months that coming winter. As he started explaining to me how he hadn't seen his wife and two children for over a year (he had never, in fact, seen his younger son), I began wondering why on earth he had come to London in the first place. I asked him.

'Imam in Spitalfields is a good job,' he said, 'lots of money. Also, big respect. Most important is peace of mind. It is good for the day after death.'

'What about the loneliness, being separated from your family and your home?'

'Loneliness is bad. Bangladesh is a beautiful country, very beautiful.'

Imam Rahman thoughtfully wiped his plate clean. Then he reached into his billowy shirt shawl and brought out a small envelope. He drew out from the envelope a number of photographs. Dealing them out on to the table like so many cards, occasionally interjecting a name or a description, he showed them to me: father – farm building – wife – boy – a boat for sailing – fields – sister, she died – me and father. The man in the apron brought in a tray with two bowls of yoghurt and a cup of tea for me. We ate our yoghurt, which turned out to be more like semolina, in silence. I contemplated the scene. Here was the imam, sitting beneath his portrait of Mecca, weeping silently for a world apparently lost to him. My heart went out to him.

Then, after a while, he began again, 'So you find me a good lady, a nice English lady?' I couldn't think, at first, what he meant. He went on, 'She must be a Muslim, very pious, easily understanding what I say and what I want. She must be good cook also. But cooking is not main thing. Main thing is support for my mind, not quarrelling. You find me a lady with a soft mind?'

'What shall I tell her you have to offer, apart that is from your excellent career prospects and dashing good looks?' He laughed and tweaked his beard self-mockingly.

'If she want anything I will provide her. Money, anything, lots of money, if she wants.' Imam Rahman was clearly enjoying himself, slipping suddenly into his sing-song voice. 'Money is sweeter than honey! Money is sweeter than honey! Money is sweeter than honey!' It was only then, as he broke out into this unlikely refrain, repeating it again and again, nearly falling off his chair with delight, did I fully realise that he was laughing at himself, at us both, that he was teasing me something rotten.

He didn't come to the bonfire night party. Some weeks later when I went along to the mosque to hear how his visa application was going, the man in the blue apron told me that he had been taken into the London Hospital for tests. I subsequently discovered he had been diagnosed a diabetic and was returning to Bangladesh to convalesce.

On the morning of the 5th of November the developers changed their minds. They felt that it was too much of a security risk, hosting the bonfire, and wondered whether we could possibly find another venue, sorry about that. So there were no surprises there.

Harry did a bit of telephoning and by noon we had relocated ourselves to Spitalfields Farm on Weavers Field. The afternoon was spent making masks and hats and painting prompt signs for the audience: 'Boo Hiss', 'Hurrah', 'The End'. Delwar went off with Ali and Ferouk and came back with an armful of sparklers. Beth brought her face paints round and set to work on the cast and anyone else who got in the way. Charlie organised for a stack of wood to be taken over to the farm and then, in the early evening, turned up at Harry's house with a huge bag of chestnuts. Caroline and I cleaned the Taj stores out of potatoes. Half an hour before we were due to roll, Joe went round to one of the halal butchers on Brick Lane, returning with a sheep's heart for the guy.

'Look,' he said, waving it in our faces, causing the girls to rush off screaming, 'It's still beating!'

After dark we all lined up outside Harry's house. Pushing the guy in a wheelbarrow, Delwar and Harry led the way along Princelet Street, down Brick Lane, up Woodseer Street and then across Weavers Field to the farm. We all followed on behind, banging on drums, waving sparklers, practising our song, tripping each other up, forming a motley collection of rowdies, threading our high-spirited way through the still beating heart of Spitalfields.

The fire was already alight when we got there. Harry identified a space near it for the performance and then lined everyone up behind a chicken shed for a little pep-talk. The farm was filling up rapidly with friends and family and the passing curious. Although it was dark and smoke from the fire palled over the gathering crowd, I'm sure I was able to identify some familiar faces. There was Kay from the Spitalfields Small Business Association, talking with Ken Leech and Hadip and Jessica from the mannequin studio on Princelet Street. There was Tassaduq plotting the revolution with a man who looked like Tim Budgen, the former site assembly agent for the Spitalfields Market Developers and now one of the good guys, working as secretary for the Spitalfields Market Community Development Trust. Jimmy Battiwalla and his wife Jan had come to support his children from Christ Church primary school. Dennis Severs had come along with Rodney Archer, my former landlord on Fournier Street, and Julian Humphreys, my former 'master', who was over from Ireland for a few weeks and had very sweetly baked some rock buns, hard as bullets, for the occasion. As the action started they were joined by another man, who looked very much like Dan Cruickshank, Dennis' near neighbour in Elder Street. And over there, in a relatively quiet corner by the stable, was Siraj

Uddin talking to a young couple, their heads bowed in earnest conversation.

The performance was complete chaos. Harry stood at the side, keeping his troupe just about on cue whilst simultaneously providing a running commentary on the action to the bemused but delighted audience. Cecil was duly booed, King James laughed at, Guy Fawkes cheered. We all sang our Chicken Licken song about the sky falling on our heads. Harry's version had successfully inverted the whole story. As little Fatar was pushed on with the sign declaring 'The End', there was huge enthusiastic applause. I felt absurdly proud. Fatar stood there, grinning with amazement, with his funny sign now fallen to his side, upside down, 'The End'.

Then, turning aside to the fire, everything was burned. We tossed the guy on to the fire, we tossed on the hats, the signs, the scripts, the masks, the still beating heart. We consigned our costumes to the flames. We had done it.

THE WORLD TO COME

A melting-pot of sorts

Embedded in the narrative sprawl of *The Satanic Verses* is the story of the lamp. Throughout his childhood Saladin Chamcha, one of the novel's two key protagonists, longs for the day when it will be his, when he will inherit it from his father, the over-bearing and rather alarming Changez Chamchawala. He covets it, whenever in his father's study, up there next to a ten-volume set of the *Arabian Nights*, 'Aladdin's very own genie-container: a lamp begging to be rubbed'. To the growing boy the lamp promises the customary granting of secret wishes, it seems to extend to him the possibility that 'one day his troubles would end and his innermost desires would be gratified.' Unfortunately he falls out big-time with his father and, full of anger and hurt, turns his back his family, their religion, as well as his own rightful inheritance – the lamp – choosing instead to reinvent himself in London as a 'goodandproper Englishman'. He becomes an impersonator, a simulator of other people's voices. Socially, he buries his origins. Philosophically, he rejects the notion that identity is a stable thing. He goes into voluntary exile.

Gibreel Farishta, Chamcha's co-hero and alternative ego in *The Satanic Verses*, also has a bit of a lamp fixation. Or, more accurately, he comes to see himself as a proto wish-granter, 'the quencher of desires, the slaker of lusts, the fulfiller of dreams.' Farishta plays genie to Chamcha's Aladdin. Like Chamcha (indeed, like Rushdie too), Farishta comes from Bombay, a

307

successful movie star who already specialises in 'God stuff', portraying such diverse deities as Krishna and Gautama and Hanuman the monkey king, in the popular genre known to the film world as 'theologicals'. At the time of the plane crash which projects these two characters on their respective journeys, he is travelling to England to be with his latest love interest, the coldly beautiful Alleluia Cone, whom he has met on the rebound from belief in Allah. Recovering from a serious illness, he loses his faith and falls for the Allie the 'ice queen' in one seamless moment of revelation. Pursuing her to London, he tumbles from the sky, in the opening sequence of the book, himself a spiritual refugee.

Both Chamcha and Farishta are painfully divided, looking for some sort of wholeness, a way home. Yet over the course of the novel, following their unexpected ejection from the plane, they each seem to reach a very different conclusion. Once separated at Hastings, where Chamcha is arrested and Farishta sets off on his own to London, the narrative jumps backwards and forwards between them, setting up implicit, if not explicit, comparisons. For both characters, however, the main action of the novel (as opposed to the dream-sequence detours) is set in the capital, much of it along a fictionalised version of Brick Lane in Spitalfields ('Brickhall Fields'). This area becomes for them an archetypal 'zone of transition', a place for experiment and speculation, for dreaming and being dreamt upon. It is where they are able to come to terms (or not) with their loss and plot a path towards some sort of restitution. It is where they find sanctuary, the space to reconstruct an identity, a melting-pot of sorts.

And so, too, has it been for us.

Rubbing their lamps

In fact, since it first emerged as an industrial suburb in the early eighteenth century Spitalfields has been an area where all sorts and conditions of people have gathered in order to reinvent themselves. First came the Huguenots, then the Irish, the Jews, the Maltese and more recently the Pakistani and Bangladeshi communities. Over the years numerous political and religious refugees have made it their home, finding in this parish, which grew up outside the walls of the City of London, east of Aldgate and Bishopsgate, across the ancient Houndsditch, an essentially *hospitable* space, free of oppressive church and state authority. Etymologically, this is, of course, entirely appropriate: the area derives its name from the manor land (Fields) leased by the Bishop of London, initially in 1498, to the Augustinian Priory or Hospital (Spital) of St Mary.

At the heart of the area has been the fruit and vegetable market, established in the 1680s, relocated in the 1980s, the fixed point for a small orbit of satellite entrepreneurial activities. Not only has it directly supported a number of traders (the latter-day costers) in the local network of street markets, as well as a range of dependent businesses along its periphery (cafés, pubs, garages, the Commercial Street prostitutes), but also, and more importantly, Spitalfields Market has protected the area from the advance of the City. While it continued to trade in E1, with its noise and filth and crazy congestion, land values in Spitalfields remained considerably lower than those to be found two hundred yards to the west, in EC1.

With the prospect of the market redevelopment, however, all this changed. And as land values have risen in recent years, so too have market rentals. Many small businesses and sole traders, such as the leather worker Henry George, not being able to afford the new levels, have had to move out further east to Stratford or East Ham or Manor Park or Leytonstone. The cumulative effect of this piecemeal exodus has been the steady erosion of the rag trade in Spitalfields, an industry which actually depends for its survival on all its constituent workers – machinists, pattern cutters, trimmings' suppliers and so on – working near one another, not to say in close proximity to a mosque, a halal butcher and a travel agent which can book cheap flights to Sylhet. In fact, in their continuing inter-dependence the Bengalis who work the rag trade in Spitalfields have managed, until now, to establish and sustain a wonderfully intricate, albeit extremely vulnerable, economic community.

Unfortunately, it is also a very unselfconscious community. As Kay Jordan, the coordinator of the Spitalfields Small Business Association points out, 'They don't see the change happening around them until it actually hits them in the face and they have to pack their bags and leave.'

From about 1984, the year Tim Budgen sketched out his development plans on the back of an envelope, the prospect of change did, indeed, begin to hit Spitalfields in the face. It became a contested space, giving rise to a number of different versions of itself, often contradictory and sometimes really quite fantastic. Individuals, claiming to speak for communities, boldly asserted the legitimacy of their account – and often in the face of other, equally convinced, individuals. Jostling for position, they have argued it out, be it across Julian Humphreys' damask-strewn dining table or in a committee room of the House of Commons or at a 'planning-for-real' exercise organised by the Spitalfields Development Group in some chilly community hall.

In the different sections of this book I have tried to identify what I have come to see as the four main versions of Spitalfields. Broadly speaking these four versions also coincide with four fairly distinct class identities: The entrepreneurial 'working-class' cockney, the 'upper-class' new georgian, the 'middle-class' managerial professional and what we might rather un-fashionably call the 'artisanal' migrant rag-trade worker existing at the bottom of the heap. How consciously these class identities are owned by their constituent communities is debatable. (Certainly they are changing very rapidly.) That the assumptions they bring with them shape the terms of the negotiation over the future of Spitalfields is, as I hope I have shown, less so.

Now that we are all notionally somewhere in the middle, class identity is much more intriguing than simply an indication of economic status. For those of us who play the game, the language of class tends to be aspirational, based more on gesture and the nuances of allusion than hard fact. It is also, by definition, social, tribal even. It makes friends and enemies – and hence neighbours – of strangers. And because of this it is also one of the few ways we have of asserting some sense of cor-porate belonging, of telling our story in a way which defines us as public people, with a shared history and moving within a particular context. Most languages we use to describe our journey through life are private – psychotherapeutic or confessional – often masquerading as 'spiritual' or 'religious', with the most important trip we make being the one between our mother's nipple and our lover's embrace. But the genie which comes out of the lamp marked 'class' is called 'community', a notion indeed to conjure with.

As we've seen, Spitalfields is full of individuals busily rubbing their lamps and bringing to mind some lost or pending Eden of sweet conviviality, some golden age when we used to have 'genuine neighbours' and not just the people-who-live-next-door, or some promised urban utopia, a total work–and–leisure 'environment' for people who have 'lifestyles' rather than lives. For the market trader it is focused around 'cockney' Spitalfields, a cultural identity which has its roots in the heyday of late nineteenth-century music hall and wheeler-dealer coster-mongering and is still powerfully present today in the imaginations of white 'working class' East Enders. For the gentrifying resident of the conservation area, it is 'Georgian' Spitalfields with its commitment to an aesthetic of symmetry and unfussy elegance as well as a notion of upstairs-downstairs social equilibrium, as illustrated by the accounts given of the Liberty of Norton Folgate by Dan Cruickshank and others. For the migrant communities in Spitalfields, it tends to be located back home, across the seven seas and thirteen rivers, in the villages of Sylhet (or, as formerly, in the *shtiebls* of Poland) and then recreated on the Lane, as most recently evidenced by the launch of 'Bangla Town'.

For the professional community of social entrepreneurs the golden age is just around the corner, certain to arrive with the new millennium. In its marketing material for the latest scheme of its proposed development, the Spitalfields Development Group outlines what it rather ominously calls 'the vision'. It is, of course, pure poetry. 'Welcome to Spitalfields,' it reads, 'London's exciting new financial quarter, master-planned to accommodate the workplace and lifestyles of the world's most discerning occupiers. The development is a landmark in the financial heart of the capital, with buildings to be individually designed to meet the specific needs of companies looking forward to the 21st Century ... Spitalfields will create an environment where one can enjoy the finer aspects of both work and leisure.' Hmmm. Oh really?

The virtue economy

Spitalfields has proved to be a 'locus classicus of incompatible realities' exactly as defined by Rushdie. On our travels we have noted many such juxtapositions. We have seen the way the global economy of the City has overshadowed the manu-facturing base of the rag trade along Brick Lane and the way a virtual financial market has been lined up to replace a produce market at heart of the area. There have been other incompatible realities: a Christian primary school whose student population is almost exclusively Muslim; an upmarket music festival in a fine example of early English Baroque architecture operating above a hostel for homeless alcoholics; a strong racist presence in the street markets which punctuate the very area with the highest proportion of Bangladeshi residents of anywhere in the UK.

Yet we need also to note how behind many of these apparently ironic juxtapositions – such as the one between those who don't use electricity in the conservation area because it isn't authentic to the eighteenth century and those who don't use electricity on the Chicksand Estate because they haven't got the money for the meter – lie substantive inequalities. 'In the end, it's an 'us' and 'them' thing,' says Jil Cove, coordinator of the Campaign to Save Spitalfields from the Developers, 'They want our market and we want to keep it for Spitalfields. We think it belongs to the East End and not in the City. We want to draw a line.'

In fact, 'drawing a line' is what the Campaign has spent much of the last decade doing. And although the redoubtable Cove has at times appeared like Canute on the sinking sands of Bishopsgate, protesting helplessly against the incoming tide of capital 'investment' and the swirling waters of urban 'regeneration', the most extraordinary fact of the matter is that, more than ten years after the developers first received planning permission to raze the old fruit and vegetable market to the ground, it is still standing. And so why is that?

It's due to a number of factors, some easier to pin than others. It's certainly due to the Campaign's harrying opposition to successive development proposals. At crucial moments in the proceedings they have held up the smooth passage of the developer's plan through the various statutory committees and rubber-stamping authorities, causing, in the process, un-expected, expensive and highly inconvenient disruption. For example, following the Campaign's successful delay in the granting of the Act of Parliament by which the royal charter on the old market was lifted, the Spitalfields Development Group found itself eventually free to move only as the economy was tipping into recession. In this instance local and global forces conspired, in a wholly unforeseeable way, temporarily to frustrate the construction of the developers's 'new creation'.

Other groups have also played their part. The Spitalfields Trust, that group of residents particularly concerned about preserving the stock of Georgian houses in the area, managed to furnish the papers with well-placed editorial objections to a particular version of the scheme just as it was passing before the planning department. The result was a peremptory change of architects (coincidental, of course) and a further setback for our benighted developers. Nor should we forget that the Trust itself traces its origins as a conservation pressure group back to 1977 and the illegal squatting of two half-demolished weavers houses in Elder Street ('with integral leaded loom lights') in defiance of a property company, bulldozers at the ready. In general, the various pressure and interest groups in Spitalfields may dislike and distrust each other but they dislike and distrust the Spitalfields Development Group more. Opposition to office development generates, it seems, an acquaintance between strange bedfellows.

Yet the shenanigans of neighbourhood politics in contem-porary Spitalfields is only the surface expression of an opposition with much deeper roots and much wider implications. As we have seen time and time again this corner of the East End has, throughout its history, displayed a slightly anarchic resistance to most forms of imposed government and institutional authority. State religion, as expressed in the aspirations of the Fifty New Churches Act of 1711 which led to the construction of Christ Church, has never really taken root in Spitalfields. Rather it has always been a place of theological non-conformity and minority belief, as evidenced by the multiple lives of the Huguenot church at the other end of Fournier Street, as well as the pro-liferation, throughout the area's history, of small associational gatherings, of chapels and meeting-houses and synagogues and *chevras*.

Religious dissent and political radicalism have, moreover, tended to exist together in Spitalfields (with some notable exceptions, such as those Jewish Socialists who taunted their orthodox kinsmen at the Great Synagogue on Brick Lane with a provoking show of revelry on the Day of Atonement). The Quakers, for example, who had a unique presence in the parish through the Buxton family, the Quaker brewers, were a chief source of support to the silk weavers in times of trade distress. And the weavers themselves, many of whose families were originally religious refugees from France, became notable political agitators in the eighteenth century. Coming from a relatively prosperous artisan class, they were part of an emergent tradition of opposition to government and the market, which also included those who gathered at the local trade clubs, tavern societies and chapels. Under the direction of the campaigning radical John Wilkes and following the religious and consti-tutional struggles of the previous century, the weavers boldly asserted the 'rights' and 'liberties' of all Englishmen.

Did the root of their political confidence lie in the vocational nature of their trade? Certainly the Calvinistic ethic assigned a high value to work, which was considered to be the practical exercise of a calling appointed by God. For subsequent generations the calling may not have been divinely inspired, yet the sense of 'vocation' has persisted: Spitalfields has been a place where people discover their *field*, where they acquire the necessary skills and experience to move from being an apprentice to being a journeyman and the necessary pride in their work (and political nous) to organise into guilds and friendly societies and trade unions. Of the ten Jewish anarchists who met at 40 Gun Street in 1876 for the first time, five were tailors and of the rest one was a hat-maker and the other a cabinet-maker. In the 1990s Gun Street was similarly occupied by a number of graduates from the nearby London College of Furniture such as Jim the Joiner who makes exquisite reproduction furniture for local residents or Robert the Carver who has specialised in cutting most of the replica door case consoles in the conservation area. Similarly, to this day, Brick Lane is bursting with skilled leather workers organised informally around small workshops.

Kay Jordan, the coordinator of the Spitalfields Small Business Association, believes this strong tradition of small scale manufacturing work expresses something essential about the genius of the area. 'It's something the boys from SDG have never really got, they've never really understood it. They talk about 'design task' this and 'professional project' that and then they go back and hide behind their computer screens. But Spitalfields has always been about hands-on inventiveness and improvisation, about people making goods and making good.'

There have been times, however, when skilled labour has struggled for survival amidst the general poverty of the area. Philanthropy (professional do-gooding) became much more visible, and indeed necessary, in the nineteenth century, as Spitalfields tried to absorb the effects of industrialisation. Yet even here it's wrong to be taken in by those commentators, such as Jack London, who have seen the East End as marked exclusively by depression and dreariness. Of course, it's often the urban planners and regenerators, those side-kick associates of the property developers, who are the keenest spotters of squalor. Theirs, after all, is a professional eye. And although they may very well see the poverty, what they always seem to miss, however, is the burlesquing defiance of the poor people themselves.

This, after all, is what being cockney is all about, a carry-on spirit of making do, scraping by, sorting deals, against the odds.

Found in the street markets of the area – Petticoat Lane, Brick Lane, Columbia Row, Whitechapel Waste – it survives in the banter and performing badinage of the traders. Social historian and long-time resident of Elder Street Raphael Samuel comments, 'The most historical feature of Spitalfields, to my mind, was not the buildings at all but the open-air market which on Sundays brought thousands of street sellers to the area.' In this tradition, he identifies a resistance to the bottom-line logic of the developers, one which was echoed by Mr Starns, a one-time fruit and veg trader in Spitalfields Market, when appearing before the City's barrister in the commons committee. Starns is at pains to draw a distinction between 'efficiency' and 'atmosphere': 'Markets are not about bricks and mortar. They are about people and that is atmosphere. Efficiency is a totally different thing.' Political theorist Maurice Glasman, who also lives in the area, sees in this 'virtue economy' (as distinct from the 'virtual economy' of the City) traces of solidarity and hope. 'Go and have some of Clyde's salt beef at the market café and you'll soon find yourself actively subverting the logic of the free market.'

In his book *Unnecessary Suffering* he draws out the implications of this distinction. 'Sustainable economic activity,' he writes, 'presupposes a society characterised by robust non-market institutions entangled within the economy which are best described as vocational.' Spitalfields has always been a nexus of such entanglements, not only in the trades which have persisted throughout its history, but also in the very higgledy-piggledy street plan of the area, which has encouraged a particular kind of interplay between the different orbits of its economic activity. As we've also seen, the myth of cockney (or, indeed, Jewish) Spitalfields offers these respective communities a sort of vision social inter-dependence which needs to be set against their everyday cut and thrust of economic survival.

In one of its newsletters The Spitalfields Trust makes a similar point about life along Brick Lane: 'Despite its nondescript architectural character, it is one of the most successful thoroughfares in town planning terms in the whole of London . . . Drivers may curse its narrowness and lack of parking or unloading facilities, but as a focus of a thriving community Brick Lane really works.' The cursing and congestion are, of course, all part of it, as is the animated display of Bengali entrepreneurialism. This, after all, is street theatre at its most dynamic and inclusive, in which everyone has a front-row seat and everyone has a walk-on role: Joan the cat lady, John the street sweeper, Patsy the prostitute, Delwar, his father, Imam Rahman, his assistant, the owner of the Taj Stores, each of us in fact, even Gilbert and George: 'Hello!', 'Hello!' they chorus on the up-beat, before turning into Fournier Street.

With its tradition of radicalism and dissent, its history of small-scale artisan workshops as well as a wheeler-dealing defiance of authority, along with its tendency to slightly anarchic self-government, it is hardly surprising Spitalfields pits its strong sense of 'us-ness' against the perceived 'them-ness' of the Spitalfields Development Group. Paradoxically, this strong sense of belonging is rooted in the area's very tradition of hospitality, of permeability. For three hundred years Spitalfields has provided a transit-camp for 'survivors', passers-through. Yet redevelopment and community regeneration will inevitably bring closure. They herald the spectre of respectability and uniformity, the hideous prospect of becoming just another semi-smart suburb for the financial services of the City of London, the death of having finally 'arrived'.

Sense of solidarity

In the end, when I went to see him, the Bishop of Oxford showed mercy.

'I'm very glad that this door has opened for you,' he said, wishing me well as we stood to part at the end of the meeting. And then, as I had a sudden Scooby Doo vision of a trapdoor opening beneath me and plunging me to some subterranean depth, he pulled one of his own books down from the shelf (*Prayer and the Pursuit of Happiness*) and handed it to me, asking,

'What is it, William, that excites you most about the Gospel?'

I was ready this time.

'You never know quite where it's going to land you.'

Which is, unfortunately, true.

When I left theological college in 1994 and was sent by the Bishop of Barking to be a curate in Chingford I was frankly appalled. After my time in Spitalfields I fancied myself tramping the mean streets of the East End; I certainly did not see myself touring the 'avenues' and 'drives' and 'rises' in the White Highlands of suburban East London. After all, Chingford was where you escaped to, once you had made a bit of money and moved up in the world. It was Mile End made good, itself a place of arrival and respectability, a stronghold for Middle England – it was Norman Tebbit's former parliamentary constituency, for heaven's sake – and certainly no zone of transition. Or so I thought.

In fact, over the three years I lived and worked there, I underwent something of a conversion experience. If not exactly to love it, I certainly grew to see the point of Chingford. Twenty-six minutes one way and you were in Liverpool Street station and the heart of the City of London; in the same length of time, heading out of town, you could be ambling through the hornbeam and beech trees of Epping Forest. I also spotted how, beneath the stone cladding, behind the ornamental squirrels and sculpted pineapples, people's lives could be every bit as tragic or exalted, and certainly as tangled, as I had found them to be in Spitalfields or Whitechapel or wherever. Although suburbia seemed to nurture a particular kind of subterranean existence, an unsung and unseen heroism, its residents were potentially no less on the move, no less transient, than those who lived anywhere else.

Of course it also had its fair share of eccentrics, of individuals as crazy as the paving which adorned their front terraces. One woman, convinced my cassock was a dress and that I was a transvestite, would invariably stop me in Station Road and encourage me in my defiance of sartorial and sexual convention. I would happily banter with her about hem lines and colour co-ordination and the rest: I suppose I assumed that, at some level, she was simply taking the piss. And then one day I opened my front door to discover a little box of carefully wrapped cotton blouses and floral outfits – castoffs, apparently – with a brief note expressing the hope I would like them. Oxfam certainly did. The next time I saw her in the High Street I made a big point of inviting her to join us all at mass on Sunday. She was polite, but firm: She didn't *do* church, thank you very much. We never spoke again of frills and furbelows.

Maybe such a rich fantasy world indicated a life lived in lonely isolation. Certainly there was a lot of it about in Chingford. How often I would find myself talking to the relatives of someone who had died, after a long life, much of it lived in the parish, to be told, when I inquired after the deceased friends and associations, his wider life in the community, that, in fact, 'he had never really socialised very much,' how, in fact, 'he was essentially very . . .' 'Private?' I would venture. 'Yes,' they would repeat, with some relief, 'private, a very private person.' Of course, I saw there could be dignity in privacy; I also saw there could be desperate loneliness there too.

I spent much of my time in Chingford helping to bury the last generation of white cockneys, those who had been born, before the war, in Whitechapel or Bethnal Green or, indeed, in Spitalfields, and who had subsequently moved out through the Lea Valley as their prospects improved and their families expanded. It was a well trodden path. Indeed, while working in the parish we hosted the entourage for Ronnie (or was it Reggie?) Kray's funeral, that fiesta of mawkish sentimentality which had weaved its way from the family home in Bethnal Green, through East London, up to Chingford Mount Cemetery. Most bizarrely of all, a few weeks after I was ordained, I found myself buying my spuds from Phil Barry, the owner of the stand in the old fruit and vegetable market which had employed me, five or six years previously, to do the early morning delivery round. I think he was as surprised as I was to make the reacquaintance. When Spitalfields Market had moved to Leyton he had apparently switched his operation from wholesale to retail, pitching his stall on Chingford Mount.

Chingford as a whole, however, had an ambivalent relation-ship with its identity as a suburb for East End success stories. Many was the old boy who lived in 'the village', the posher part of the parish, who would prefer to be seen, like Saladin Chamcha, as a 'goodandproper Englishman' as opposed to a bit of an old *ice cream freezer* made good. And, on one level, who could blame him? Yet, over the time I spent in Chingford, my own attitude to matters cockney changed. Whereas formerly I had expended my energy, in the market and the pub, deconstructing what I saw to be a nonsense fabrication, a narrow and excluding version of Spitalfields which denied the reality of the area's multicultural life, I now sought to rehabilitate it in Chingford as a beautiful lie. I recognised how it actually brought people together, how it provided a shared language and established some degree of solidarity in the face of the great impersonalities of life and death and modern suburban living.

This was particularly apparent in the church community, which would rub the cockney lamp with real vigour. Not only at the charity quiz nights, the pie and mash dinners (filthy muck, actually), fish and chip evenings, sing-songs around the old *joanna,* but also in the tender, down-to-earth capacity of a group of people to care for one another and for those around them, I saw something of real value. I saw an essential quality of *hospitality*, one that I had missed earlier. I like to think it was because we were all busily being transformed by the renewing of our minds into the likeness of Christ; it may, of course, have been because I had become a little less snobby.

One evening I was rung by an elderly member of the congregation, one of my sick communicants, who was in a bit of a state. She was going through a bad patch, could I come round? As we sat and talked, comparing neuroses, exchanging herbal remedies, restoring some normality over hot tea and chatter, the telephone rang. She went to answer it. Through in the hall, where the receiver was located, I heard her ask if she could return the call later: 'I can't talk, now, love,' she said, 'My priest is here.' For a brief moment I wondered who she meant – I thought we had been alone. Then, the penny dropping, I blushed self-consciously and then blushed again at my blushing. Oh dear! When she returned into the room I said something foolish about how hot it was, how heavy these serge cassocks were, and how, maybe, could I have another cup of tea, after all?

Within the assortment of roles I was able to inhabit as the curate I encountered a real sense of solidarity. For a few years I made my home here; I belonged. I may not have chosen to go to Chingford, but, in the end, I felt a strong identification with its people. I was learning to care.

Your field

In parishes, amongst the faithful, trying to live a life of Christian discipleship makes some sense for much of the time. For some, it makes too much sense, nearly all the time. For others, looking in from the outside, it makes very little sense at any time. I don't think this is hostility – although occasionally it clearly is – I think it is more usually just benign bafflement. What is 'ordination'? What does 'sacramental' *mean*? How are you supposed to respond to a man dressed head to foot in synthetic fibres and clutching a floppy black bible in his hand, when he says he wants to tell you all about what God is doing for Man in Jesus?

The key thing is that belief is enacted in communities of the faithful. It is relational. There's no such thing as freelance discipleship. Ordination articulates this reality. You are ordained, first as a deacon and then, normally a year later, as a priest to serve in a particular parish – a particular people in a particular place. You are charged to 'teach and encourage', to be 'messengers, watchmen, and stewards', to 'call to repentance' and to 'declare the forgiveness of sins'. You are instructed to 'lead the people in prayer' as well as to 'minister to the sick and prepare the dying for their death'. The parish is your field. The people are your treasure. Their lives the bright miracle of the lit bush.

It is catholicity which pulls the plug on narrow parochialism. It demands that all the world is seen in this grain of sand. It reaches beyond the particular to the universal, across time and in space, and transforms the parish into a global village of the divine economy. Moreover, it makes for the sacramental, for the sense in which we are able to enter into the mystery of eternity through the accidents and anomalies of the material world.

I was ordained in Chelmsford's bijou cathedral at the end of June 1995. It was a hot day, not really one for wearing layers of weighty robes. As I stood in front of the bishop as he performed his declaration of the priestly task to us, I adjusted my stole – a long and narrow strip of linen worn over one's shoulders indicating the priestly calling (mine had been appliquéd with some threadbare patches of Spitalfields silk) – as one might shuffle a jacket before going in for interview. It all felt a little unlikely, veering somewhere between splendour and absurdity. How would the laying on of the bishop's slightly pudgy hands transmit to us the charism of holy orders?

'. . . In the name of our Lord we bid you remember the greatness of the trust now to be committed to your charge, about which you have been taught in your preparation for ministry. You are to be messengers . . . to teach . . . to minister . . . and to search for his children in the wilderness of this world's temptations and to guide them through its confusion . . .'

I was reminded of my grandfather's letters from France during the Great War. I thought of his final one, in which he had spoken of his need to go out into 'the wilderness', to think through the lessons of the war years. In some ways, at the other end of the twentieth century, it felt as though we were still very much in that wilderness, still thinking through those lessons. Is not the life of faith now as much the life of deferred doubt? Intermittently we may enjoy moments of seizure and clarity but is not the rest mostly a tentative turning over of possibilities, like beachcombing for amber after the high tide? The infrastructure of commonly held Christian assumptions has been broken up on the rocks of pluralism and secularity. To suggest, as my grandfather had done, that 'the root of England's strength' was located in the Christian faith seems now a fantastic notion. Meanwhile the insistent tide of the free market has kept sweeping ashore the random trappings of belief, a hotch-potch of different lifestyle options, of self-help manuals and guide-books to the esoterica of some lost wisdom, which lie exposed at the top of the beach like so much spiritual jetsam.

As I went forward to kneel before the ordaining scrum of bishops and supporting clergy, which gathered around me like surgeons at an operating table, I found myself repeating, without knowing quite why, some lines of a poem by Yeats, almost as if it were a mantra, almost as though it were in protest against my crow's nest of little doubts,

> '. . . But Love has pitched his mansion in
> The place of excrement;
> For nothing can be sole or whole
> That has not been rent . . .'

I knelt beneath an encircling wall of clerics. For a brief moment it went dark. I crossed myself. Words were pronounced. I stood a priest.

After the service, when I joined my family, my mother handed me a small package. It was a ring, newly minted, made from the broken sapphire of my grandfather's old ring. The original stone, damaged by the jeweller, had now been reset, off-centre, on a plain gold mount.

'Try not to lose this one', she said.

A few days later, back in Chingford, on my thirtieth birthday, I presided at a celebration of the mass for the first time. Ken Leech came to preach. It was to be a rather grand affair with incense, trumpets, anthems, processions and, naturally, extremely fine vestments. A friend had given me a bottle of a 1986 Sauternes, a very good year, to use for the communion. I had also been lent, for the occasion, a beautiful early nineteenth-century fiddleback chasuble (the type of poncho worn by the presiding priest) – richly embroidered with roses and crowns on cloth of gold – and was conscious of looking really rather splendid. I was a little concerned, therefore, when Fr. Leech arrived in a T-shirt with a picture of a turtle on it, and we hurriedly had to dig him out a suitably tailored liturgical outfit.

His text was the account of Jacob's dream in the book of Genesis. In this story, as he crosses the desert, Jacob has a sleeping vision of a ladder reaching up into heaven, with angels going up and coming down, and of God, who reaffirms his covenant relationship with Jacob and his descendants. When he wakes, Jacob is gung-ho with excitement, shouting out loud, in the middle of absolutely nowhere, 'This is none other but the house of God and this is the gate of heaven.' Leech spoke of how it was the priest's task, wherever he found himself, crossing the desert, travelling home, to point to the Glory of God.

At the end of the service, as we turned to depart, with Charlie the thurifer going full pelt with the incense, inducing a series of asthmatic attacks amongst the good people of the parish, I followed out behind everyone else, sweeping by in my French chasuble, a worthy sign pointing indeed to the Glory of God. Where else? Yet, as the altar procession passed into the nave of the church, through the congregation, I heard my young daughter turn to a friend standing beside her and ask, with crushing precision, 'Why is my daddy wearing a hot water bottle cover?'

There had clearly been an unfortunate break in the signifying chain.

Walking towards the fire

Of course, the signifying chain is constantly breaking apart and frustrating our efforts to plot a straight path out of exile and towards home. No sooner does it look like we've set the ladder on *terra firma*, with the top resting happily in the heavens, than the ground begins to shift under our feet and the clouds gather to obscure our view of the skies. Many would refer this state of affairs, this slippage between dream and reality, to what Lyotard called, in 1979, *La Condition Postmoderne*, drawing our attention to the 'discontinuity' between our 'incompatible realities' (as Rushdie would have it) and the inevitable 'fragmentation of truth' in a world lacking any 'totalised explanations'. Although somewhat less *au courant*, I would rather put my money on the doctrine of original sin.

Saint Augustine of Hippo had a thing or two to say about this. In fact, in his various works, most notably *The City of God*, he offers a refreshingly bleak portrait of human nature. There is little here to support the belief that the future will bring any lasting accommodation between warring hearts and minds. He starts from the premise that the world is a fallen and contested space, a zone of transition no less, comprising 'a society of aliens speaking all languages' through which the 'the Heavenly City is on pilgrimage'. In fact, one imagines that Salman Rushdie and the great doctor of the Latin Church would find a good deal to talk about.

Apart from the fact that they both write long books and ones which address the big potatoes of life and death, they also both know what it is to speak out of the experience of exile, literal as well as existential. Identifying himself as an Indian writer in England, Rushdie places himself in a particular tradition of migration and displacement, indeed, one that draws our attention back to the 'locus classicus' that is Spitalfields: 'We can quite legitimately claim as our ancestors the Huguenots, the Irish, the Jews; the past to which we belong is an English past, the history of immigrant Britain,' he writes in the title essay of his collection *Imaginary Homelands*. In the same way Augustine, who was born and raised in North Africa in the second half of the fourth century, subsequently moving to imperial Italy, spends much of his life away from home. Schooled as a Roman rhetorician, he is also exposed to the philosophy of the Greeks before converting to Christianity in 386. In his theology he draws heavily on these various thought worlds – this is its achievement – producing a rich synthesis of 'joinings and co-joinings and hybridisations and fusings' in his talk about God. Indeed, Augustine is surely proof of Rushdie's thesis that it is possible to *gain* an identity – as well as lose one – in translation.

The particular contribution Augustine makes to Christian theology is his adaptation of New Testament eschatology – the belief that the early followers of Jesus had that they were living in the End Time of history – to the expectations of a continuing story. In his writings Augustine is circumspect about too literal a reading of the mathematics of the book of Revelation, his principal source material for much of his exposition. He writes reassuringly, 'The author may have intended the thousand years to stand for the whole period of the world's history, signifying the entirety of time by a perfect number.' In any case, his advice to anyone keenly anticipating the final apocalypse is not to go and stand on a hill and stare up at the empty skies, wide-eyed and open-armed, awaiting the onset of the 'rapture', but rather to continue as normal in one's daily business, 'sweeping one's cell' as he puts it. One reason for this business-as-usual approach is precisely because we are already living in the End Time, and always have been. Our lives, he suggests, have only ever pointed towards their ultimate fulfilment in the *eschaton*, the divinely ordained climax and conclusion to history. We exist in a place of tension between times, between the old aeon and the age to come. 'The City of God,' writes Augustine 'has been coming down from heaven since its beginning.'

Our dreams are richly woven with this hope of home-coming. One only has to look at Spitalfields with its variously imagined accounts of the golden age, its competing attempts to realise its different versions of the 'reign of peace' to wonder at our capacity for inhabiting this possibility. It is a possibility, moreover, that those people, referred to usually as 'religious', anticipate in the journey of their faith, rubbing their lamp, looking for home. In Christian terms it is a possibility which heralds the topsy-turvy enactment of justice, the putting down of the mighty from their seat and the exalting of the humble and meek. Similarly, the successive migrant communities of Spitalfields, gathering weekly in the Brick Lane Mosque, sometime synagogue, onetime chapel, have, in their own songs of lament and promise, attended faithfully to this prospect.

Siraj Uddin, knowing the Qur'an's repeated reference to the 'day after death', with almost every sura referring to the physical rewards and punishments of heaven and hell, the Garden and the Fire, clearly had a strong sense of his merely passing through Spitalfields en route for some more final destination. 'Spitalfields is only the temporary home,' he had told me, standing on the steps of the mosque. 'We are moving, poor people are always moving.' Similarly we saw, through Bernard Homa's account of the festival of Purim in the Machzike Hadath Synagogue, how the Jewish community enacted its own hope of an ultimate homecoming. Certainly in their boisterous celebration of the story of Esther's timely intervention at the King of Persia's court to save her compatriot Jews, we can begin to understand how the Jews of Spitalfields were enabled, like the psalmist, to 'sing the Lord's song in a strange land'.

Just as the vagrants and vagabonds (or whatever synonymously euphemistic term one might use for the transient homeless of Spitalfields) would gather around the burning pallets in front of the fruit and vegetable market, sharing warmth and stories, so too have generations of passers-through remained defiantly hopeful, finding a niche outside the City of London, a bit of camaraderie, even the chance to make good, to inhabit a dream. And so it is here, in the liberty of Norton Folgate, that Dennis Severs has found the space and imaginative freedom to accommodate his fantasy family from the eighteenth century. It is here, along Brick Lane, that Tassaduq Ahmed continues to work towards the unity of East and West Bengal. And it is here, surveying the world from the roof of their Fournier Street house, that Gilbert and George can 'push out the possibilities of their art', can think the unthinkable, including the possibility of unassisted flight.

An awareness that we live our lives between the 'City of God' and 'City of Man', however defined, between Kairos and Chronos, between dream and reality, magic and logic, elegy and irony, that we are always already walking towards the fire, helps to remind us that, in the end, we are all only ever comers and goers and itinerants in this zone of transition.

EPILOGUE –
SPITALFIELDS 2000

As I was busy being a curate in Chingford, the countdown to the Millennium began in earnest. Apocalyptic groups, with their thumb stuck in the Book of Revelation, read the signs of the time with gathering excitement. Already in 1993 we had seen the Davidian cult at Waco ignite itself in an eschatological frenzy and then in Tokyo in 1995, following a poison attack on the subway, we saw how a deeply sinister doomsday sect had grown up in the middle of a peace-loving Buddhist community. Following a CIA report which said that the wetlands of Southern Iraq had been transformed into a barren desert after a campaign of drainage and burning by President Saddam Hussein, Nostradamus was brought in to help hand out roles for the incipient drama of the End Time. Some roles, however, were taken up voluntarily – in April 1995 Jonathan Aitken wielded his Sword of Truth to slay, once and for all, the Guardian newspaper over its reports about his business activities and shady dealings. A somewhat rash act of heroism, as it turned out.

Meanwhile postmodern 'joinings and co-joinings, hybridisations and fusings' continued to alarm as the Health Secretary (Stephen Dorrell) announced in March 1996 that the most likely cause of a new strain of Creutsfeld-Jakob disease (CJD) was beef from cows with BSE eaten before some types of offal had been banned in 1990. Then a couple of months later baby formula milk became the latest locus classicus of incompatible realities when it was discovered by the Ministry of Agriculture that phthalates, chemicals used to soften plastics, had been identified in some brands. Yet who was to take the blame? In our increasingly complex global economy, it wasn't always clear. For example, when the 'Sea Empress' spilled 65,000 tons of crude oil along the Welsh coast in February 1996 it was discovered that she had been built in Spain and was owned by a Norwegian, registered in Cyprus, managed from Glasgow, chartered by the French, crewed by Russians, flying a Liberian flag and carrying an American cargo. The imperatives of international trade rendered the restrictions imposed by individual states increasingly irrelevant.

Generally speaking, the Opposition blamed the Government, whilst the Government, which had been in power for nearly two decades, scapegoated where they could. We were told that under New Labour 'things could only get better', which didn't seem necessarily a good reason to vote for them, although 31.4 per cent of the electorate did, effecting a landslide and allowing Tony Blair to form a government and John Major to go and watch the cricket. In May 1997 expectations were running high but, unlike New Labour's 'things', they could only go down. 'Spin' replaced 'sleaze' as the pundits favourite tag.

In fact not a lot changed. The Labour Government took over the Conservative Government's spending commitments, beef problems, dome proposals. Quite soon it also had its first resignations from high office as both Peter Mandelson and Geoffrey Robinson left the Cabinet just before Christmas in 1998. In the end both parties were basically working out the same free market philosophy, struggling to adapt to those changes which were driving forward the global economy. The new administration sought, as the song instructed, to accentuate the positive, eliminate the negative, latch on to the affirmative (and not mess with Mr Inbetween). Mr Blair called it the Third Way.

But what were these global forces? One was clearly the emergence of the internet, the virtual revolution. Websites started appearing on advertisers' hoardings, as people at parties began exchanging their email addresses at the end of the evening as they had once exchanged telephone numbers. In September 1998 Microsoft replaced General Electric as the world's biggest company when its market share value reached US $267 billion. Yet information dissemination did not necessarily work only to the advantage of the powerful multinationals – in the same month that Microsoft took its place at the top of the league of biggest boys on the block, the World Wide Fund for Nature published a report which said that a third of the Earth's natural resources had been lost in the previous 25 years. Global communication, it seemed, could also be put to work for the sake of the environment as well as the poor and oppressed. Much of the momentum for Jubilee 2000's campaign for the cancellation of Third World debt was generated through cyber-technology.

Mr Inbetween also found himself in a new position. As the old bonds of solidarity were fast becoming irrelevant, categories of class, religion and profession all looked sadly hasbeen in our madly mobile wannabe society. Yet at the same time commentators and social scientists had begun talking about the importance of what they called 'social capital', 'civic culture' and 'the common good' – that level of interaction which exists between the individual and the state, the unit we used to call the parish. In my time in Spitalfields I had become something of an expert in this. I had traced the various attempts to share a residual vision of corporate belonging. But now when I looked I saw how the cockney working class identity had increasingly become merely an affectation for middle class young men and women ('mocknies') hanging out in the low-slung cafés and trendy bars along Brick Lane. Similarly I saw how the New Georgian fantasy had exploded in a series of petty scandals and speculative house sales. Where this particular upper-class affectation wasn't masking something much dodgier it now just looked silly.

In late 1999, when I went to visit Dennis Severs, who was unwell at the time, he was wondering what should be done with his own remarkable house, his timewarp theatre of the imagination. A week before he died in December 1999, he sold it to the Spitalfields Trust, who subsequently decided to turn it into a museum. What else could they do? The Severs show had ended.

The Spitalfields Development Group similarly foundered in its attempt to recreate Spitalfields. Having given up hope of successfully marketing a speculative development, they moved to the idea of purpose-built office accommodation. They sold the land to the London International Financial Futures Exchange (LIFFE) which, with one eye on the progress of the Euro and another on the demise of the open out-cry dealing floors, hedged its bets (as is its wont) on the prospect of a move. Losing its share of the market to their hi-tech continental rivals, especially in Frankfurt, LIFFE decided in September 1998 to stay put in the City and develop instead a screen-based system. It sold its Spitalfields Market plot back to the Corporation of London. Once more the Campaign to Save Spitalfields from the Developers was assisted in its task of local democracy by an unlikely alliance with technology and the vicissitudes of global finance.

There was mayhem on Brick Lane following the explosion of a racist nail bomb outside the Café Naz in May 1999. Yet the community's robust answer came a few weeks later. Following Bangladesh's surprising victory over Pakistan in the world cup cricket, Brick Lane became a honking carnival of defiant Bengali nationalism. Nearly causing a riot outside the mosque, however, was a small group of Islamic purists, members of the *al-muhajiroun* who were provocatively waving their own banner, a call to pan-Islamic allegiance, in the face of the young revellers. When I described the scene to the imam a few weeks later – not Imam Rahman, who had died on Haj – he said with some dismay, 'Extremists, both groups'.

Of course the imam was right. Once again extremisms seemed to be taking root in these fields outside the City. But with potentially so little sense of local solidarity how else will the next generation face the inevitable instabilities of modern urban life?

With all the students gathered in the chaplain's rooms I will normally begin with a reading from Saint Augustine, possibly the one about the Heavenly City on its pilgrimage through the world, or, if they seem to be a particularly sleepy lot, then something a bit more colourful and apocalyptic. Blank faces will give way to bemusement as they look from me to one another. Hadn't he invited us on a walk through Spitalfields rather than an extended meditation on the state of the nation and the end of history? And then, before dissent has an opportunity to break out, we all troop downstairs to the front of the building where I now work, Calcutta House, just off Petticoat Lane market, to begin our tour of the area.

I moved from Chingford back to Spitalfields in 1997 to take up the post of Sir John Cass's Chaplain to London Guildhall University, a grand title for, well, an equally grand job. This highly international university, spread out across the City of London and the foothills of the East End, also seeks to serve the communities in which it is located, which it does with imagination and vigour. It hosts the highest proportion of Bangladeshi students as any university in the UK and continues to attract more through its flexible and intriguing courses.

We head up Old Castle Street, past the old wash–house, built in 1846 and now scheduled for redevelopment as the National Library for Women, a jewel in the university's tiara. Passing through Wentworth Street and Middlesex Street, where Jewish and cockney traders flaunt their silly prices and special deals, we arrive round the back of Cutler's Yard. It's possible to stand here on the very border between the City and the East End, as EC1 becomes E1. I ask the security man at the entrance to the building what he's guarding and from whom. He doesn't seem to know.

Following the intersection of streets along the City fringe, we cut back into Spitalfields, through Artillery Lane, where Ayub Ali held open house to those *Londhoni* who had jumped ship, through Gun Street, where the first meeting of the Jewish anarchist cell had met in 1876, and on to Brushfield Street. And it is here, with the former offices of the Spitalfields Development Group behind us and the fine view of Christ Church in front of us, all columns and arches, that we stand on the very spot, right next to the former fruit and vegetable market, where for so many years the dossers would gather to burn pallets and keep themselves warm. But no more. The site is now in the process of being developed. A Dutch bank on Bishopsgate dwarfs the site of the former market car park and the hoarding in front of us indicate that excavation work is in hand. The Sptalfields Development Group have, in the meantime, opened up their marketing suite in one of the units in the western edge of the market, hoping to lure in biddable office tenants with their shiny vision of 'London's new financial quarter'.

Meanwhile the local interest groups and old networks of resistance – including the Spitalfields Historic Buildings Trust, the Spitalfields Community Association, the Spitalfields Small Business Association – have regrouped with new energy and purpose, forming an unholy alliance as Spitalfields Market Under Threat, or SMUT for short. Launching a website – smut.org.uk – they appeal for widespread support, recognising that theirs is a battle being fought out across London, indeed across urban landscapes everywhere. Is regeneration primarily an economic project or a social grace? I remember the words of Tassaduq Ahmed, now recovering from a stroke in an East London nursing home. 'Williams,' he would say to me, 'please remember that the regeneration is not about the monies but about the morals.'

This is where I give my little talk about markets. Increasingly since the seventeenth century, I begin, the market has played a greater part in the exchange of goods and services and cultural meaning, taking over from such institutions as the Church, the City, professional guilds. Over the same period, as a consideration of means as opposed to ends became the proper concern of the thinking person, students of the Enlightenment sought to develop an objective science which established a universal morality without any needless reference to the oppressive conventions of religion or myth or tradition. Human nature, it was assumed, would regulate itself, just as markets, through their free operation, would supply adequate controls, internal checks and balances, a certain 'hidden hand', to militate against dysfunction.

Yet, in what sense, I go on to ask, do we check the operation of the market? On what grounds do we, in fact, limit the free play of its 'forces'? Whence come the bonds of solidarity to set against its atomising influence? And then I place this question locally, in the context of the redevelopment of the old fruit and vegetable market site, owned by the Corporation of the City of London but situated in the neighbouring borough of Tower Hamlets. What is the responsibility of the one to the other? On what grounds should we privilege the interests of the international money markets and a group of corporate lawyers – the potential tenants – over those of the comers and goers and itinerants which pass continually through this hospitable zone of transition, London's first industrial suburb? Do we actually need more offices here or more public space that will engage our imagination and nourish our sense of moral citizenship? Whose fields are these?

We pass in front of the market and on into Folgate Street where Dennis Severs would once have transported us back to the eighteenth century. We go into the front room which offers up a rich enchantment of signs and smells, a feast for the imagination. I can still hear Dennis whispering urgent stage directions, 'It's all in what you don't see, what you don't hear, neither right nor left, neither here nor there, neither tick nor tock, but . . . in the space between.' It occurs to me that Dennis, himself a bit of a genie, knew a thing or two about living between the aeons.

From 17 Folgate Street we head across Commercial Street, that 'ghastly Victorian invention' (as described by Dan Cruickshank), peering through the doors of the Ten Bells pub, formerly Jack the Ripper, which now offers exotic dancing rather than exotic cocktails. Up Fournier Street, past Julian Humphreys' Ordinary, now a private residence again, we join Brick Lane by the mosque. I have arranged to meet the imam in the school rooms at the top of the building where the children come after school to learn to recite the Qur'an by heart. He welcomes us warmly and asks if we have any questions. I look at my motley little group hoping someone will open their mouth. Will it be Anna, a secularised Jew, whose family arrived in London from Poland before the war, but who has spent much of her own life in Scotland? Or Dom, a black Canadian computer scientist with a Plymouth Brethren background and his own webpage? Or Hanne, a Danish art student with Buddhist leanings and a very Zen way of staring you out? Or Andrew, who grew up in Stratford in East London but as President of the University's Salsa Society is learning to swivel his hips with a certain Latin brio?

'Would the children know the five pillars of Islam?' I ask.

The imam instructs one of his boys to stand and recite them. When he reaches *Zakat*, the obligation to help the poor, the boy struggles to explain. He looks nervously at the imam. Anna steps in.

'It sounds like what my father would call *tsedekah*.'

Here, I reflect, is the common good in action.

We have one last treat in store. Andrew Byrne, the new assistant secretary to the Spitalfields Trust, has opened up the Princelet Street synagogue for us, which we file into quietly, respectfully. Andrew gives us a little history about this extra-ordinarily evocative memorial to a former Spitalfields community in exile. He explains how it would have been very much the local synagogue, linked to a *chevra* of Yiddish-speaking Polish Jews. I wonder whether communities actually need to be in exile in order to function as such. Maybe, in the end, 'community' is not something you can bolt on, an added extra, like a brass plaque or a company logo but is, rather, only ever the moment's response to the moment's needs, the moment's answer to the moment's question. It is something you find rather than fashion, requiring essentially a recognition of being part of the common fellowship of ignorance and error, a certain humility. I stand in front of the ark, whose doors now rest open against the crumbling walls of the apse, and wonder whether I should share with the students a few final words of sententious wisdom.

By this time, however, I can see that they are thinking more about their stomachs than the curious conundrum that is Spitalfields and so, without further unwanted reflections, we all head round the corner to the Aladin restaurant for some food.

Next Easter Eve I will stand with others in front of the great portico of St Paul's where business-like virgers will set a small brazier on the cathedral steps. The congregation, emerging from the crypt, traditionally the place of the dead, will shuffle warily across the immense forecourt, nervous of getting too close to the posse of curiously robed clergy and choir. Aware that something is about to happen, no one quite sure what, we will gather in the shadow of this great cathedral and mill, quietly exchanging expectant looks, while the brazier is stoked and cajoled into flame and a new fire is lit.

In the hiatus I will bring to mind how, three hundred years previously, similar crowds would have daily pressed together, trading, exchanging gossip and goods in the network of streets and markets around old St Paul's, before the Great Fire put a stop to all that in 1666. It was then, with the rebuilding of the cathedral, that they would have had to find a new pitch for their stalls, this time outside the walls of the City of London, through Aldgate or Bishopsgate, or maybe even over in the fields by the old Augustinian Spital of Saint Mary . . .

Repeating an action performed throughout the world and across history, indeed appropriating one which has its roots in the pagan festivals of the pre-Christian era, the Bishop of London will bless the new fire. And then, using the new fire to light the Paschal candle, the light of Christ, he will trace the outline of the Greek letters 'alpha' and 'omega' on its shaft and inscribe it with the numerals of the current year and pierce it with grains of incense. With this single candle held aloft the choir, the clergy and the whole people of God will then follow through the porch, through the huge west door of the cathedral into the great ark of the darkened nave, where she will raise her voice, beneath London's original dome, to sing the ancient anthems of the City of God as it passes on its pilgrimage through the City of Man.

Lumen verum inluminans omnem hominem in hunc mundum venientem.
(This is the true light which illuminates all in the world to come.)

ACKNOWLEDGEMENTS

Travel books are significantly about the people one bumps into on one's journey and this one has been no exception. Many have appeared by name in the book, others are submerged in the telling of the story. I would like to thank them all. Especially I would like to thank Andrew Byrne, Angie Peppiatt, Brian Cheetham, Charlie Brandt, Dan Cruikshank, 'itchy' Dave, Delwar and family, Eddie Stride, Gilbert and George, Harry the Storyteller, Henry George, Ian Lumley, Isobel Barker, Jessica Thomas, Jimmy Battiwalla, Jim the Nightman, Jil Cove, Joan the cat lady, John Gaze, Julian Humphreys, Kay Jordan, Ken Leech, Paul Duncan, Phyllis and Clyde, Rex Morton-Smith, Richard MacCormac, Rodney Archer, Steve Medway, Phil Barry, Tassaduq Ahmed, Tim Budgen, and 'Ten Bells' Yvonne. Sadly some fellow travellers – Dennis Severs, Mahmudur Rahman, Michael Gillingham and Raphael Samuel – have died whilst I have been writing this book.

The most exhilarating travelling necessarily involves a bit of trespassing and so my apologies must go to those into whose fields I have (un)wittingly erred. My particular thanks, however, to those who have been kind enough to offer route directions when they found me wandering around hopelessly lost. Specifically I would like to gratefully acknowledge the help of Ben Quash, David Mazower, Edward Kessler, Flora Gathorne-Hardy, John Shaw, Jonathan Clark, Jean Strahan, Jeremy Morris, Jenny Wallace, Kate Zebiri, Louis Ayres, Maurice Glasman, Nupu Chowdhury and Shaffique Rahman, all of whom have read bits of the book, making corrections and offering helpful suggestions.

Although writing a book is necessarily a bit of a lonely trek, I have also happily hitched a number of lifts. I would particularly like to thank Yorick Blumenfeld and Adam Nicolson for getting me going, Jenny Dereham and Stephen Hayward for taking me part of the way and Ariane Bankes and Louise Moore for their help when I found myself in the ditch. Along with my agent, Georgina Capel, whose engine turns over with impressive top-end thrust, I would like to thank my publisher at Methuen, Max Eilenberg, as well as my editor, Eleanor Rees, both of whom have cunningly chauffeured me round some bends I hadn't originally bargained for.

There are a clutch of reverends whose good humoured friendship has made for true companionship: Andrew Meldrum, Andrew Wilson, Edward Dowler, James Buxton, Jonathan Beswick, Kerry Ramsay, Lucy Winkett, Mark Oakley and William Gulliford. My particular thanks go to Michael Roberts and the community at Westcott House, along with Nicholas Edwards and the good people of Chingford, for their support and encouragement; likewise to my colleagues – staff and students – at London Guildhall University and in the Diocese of London for their interest and input. The Sir John Cass's Foundation has also been an informed and sympathetic patron, for which I am very grateful.

Thanks also to Rémy Blumenfeld for originally supplying the tickets to ride; Rose Verney for her continuing commitment to the M11; Tim Miller for his way-side hospitality; Markéta Luskacova and Richard Kraft for supplementing my holiday snaps of Spitalfields with some photographs of genius; as well as Sylvia Hutchinson and co for help in repacking my baggage en route. I would also like to thank Richard Harries, the Bishop of Oxford, for stamping my passport when it looked like I was going to be turned away by border control.

I'm not sure that I've actually learnt the prescribed humility, but maybe that's no bad thing. In the book the bishop gave me, *Prayer and the Pursuit of Happiness*, I read the following passage with interest, not to say a little annoyance: why didn't he tell me this in the beginning? 'Humility,' he writes, 'cannot be acquired just by going for it. Indeed, just the opposite. Some of the most sophisticated and deepset forms of pride hide under the guise of humility. Humility can cloak some hideous forms of arrogance. So the first and continuing task is to try to be as aware of our motivation as possible . . . Clergy are not always as aware as they might be of their own hidden springs of action.'

As for these springs of action, maybe they need to remain hidden. Maybe the most one can hope for is a good map. Following his first heart attack and before a second and fatal one, my father was given a tape recorder, rather like the one in *Krapp's Last Tape*, a great clanking device with unwieldy detachable spools. During his convalescence, as he lay in bed drugged up to the eyeballs, he recorded some of his favourite poems and passages of scripture, including psalms 121 and 137. From a young age I knew these off by heart. As psalms of promise and privation – the one is a celebration of the prospect of homecoming, the other a cry of despair from a place of exile – they seem to articulate that complex of hopeful longing which is such a central experience of the life of Christian faith. Certainly I have used them to help me find my way into this particular bright field. My thanks to Beaumont Stevenson, a good friend, for helping me to plot the route.

Final and fondest thanks to my brother Rod, my daughter Harriet, truly gracious, and my mother Jeanie. It is to her, and to the memory of my father, that I have dedicated this travel book in one place, with love.

SELECT BIBLIOGRAPHY & FURTHER READING

Ackroyd, Peter, *Hawksmoor*, London, 1985
Adams, Caroline, *Across Seven Seas and Thirteen Rivers*, London, 1987
Artley, Alexandra, *The New Georgian Handbook*, London, 1985
Archbishop's Commission, *Faith in the City*, London 1985
Aziz Al-Azmeh, *Islams and Modernities*, London, 1993
Berman, Marshall, *All That is Solid Melts into Air*, New York, 1982
Besant, Walter, *East London*, London, 1903
The Bible, Oxford and Cambridge
Briggs, Asa, *Toynbee Hall*, London, 1984
Cruickshank, Dan, *London: The Art of Georgian Building*, London, 1975
Cupitt, Don, *What is a story?*, London, 1991
Englander (ed.), *Documentary History of Jewish Immigration*, Leicester, 1993
Fishman, William, *East End 1888*, London, 1988
—— *East End Jewish Radicals 1875-1914*, London, 1975
Forman, Charlie, *Spitalfields: a battle for land*, London, 1989
Gellner, Ernest, *Postmodernism, Reason and Religion*, London, 1992
Giddens, Anthony, *The Third Way*, London, 1998
Girouard, Mark et al, *The Saving of Spitalfields*, London, 1989
Glasman, Maurice, *Unnecessary Suffering*, London, 1996
Grade, Lew, *Still Dancing*, London 1987
Gray, John, *False Dawn*, London, 1998
Harrison, Paul, *Inside the Inner City*, London, 1983
Harvey, David, *The Condition of Postmodernity*, Oxford, 1989
Hewison, Robert, *The Heritage Industry*, London, 1987
Hobbs, Dick, *Doing the Business*, Oxford, 1988
Howard, Ebenezer, *A Peaceful Path to Reform*, London, 1898
Ignatieff, Michael, *The Needs of Strangers*, London, 1984
Jacobs, Jane M, *Edge o Empire*, London, 1996
Jacobs, Jane, *The Death and Life of Great American Cities*, London, 1962
Jacobson, Howard, *Roots Schmoots*, London, 1993
Jahn, Wolf, *The Art of Gilbert and George*, London, 1989
Jencks, Charles, *What is Post-Modernism?*, London, 1986
Kant, Immanuel, *Political Writings*, Cambridge, 1972
Khan, L, *Bangladeshi Information Handbook*, London, 1990
Le Corbusier, *The Radiant City*, London, 1933
Leech, Kenneth, *Brick Lane 1978*, London, 1994

——, *The Sky is Red*, London, 1997
London, Jack, *The People of the Abyss*, London, 1903
Luttwak, Edward, *Turbo Capitalism*, London, 1998
Lynch, Kevin, *The Image of the City*, Boston, US, 1960
Macintyre, Alasdair, *After Virtue*, London, 1981
Mayhew, Henry, *London Labour and the London Poor*, London, 1861
Mearns, Andrew, *The Bitter Cry of Outcast London*, London 1883
Milbank, John et al, *Radical Orthodoxy*, London, 1999
Morrison, Arthur, *A Child of the Jago*, London, 1896
More, Thomas, *Utopia* (trans. Paul Turner), London, 1961
Murdoch, Iris, *The Fire and the Sun*, London, 1978
Neil, Stephen, *Crises of Belief*, London, 1984
Palmer, Alan, *The East End*, London, 1989
Pearson, John, *The Profession of Violence*, London 1972
Porter, Roy, *London – A Social History*, London, 1994
The Qur'an, trans. Marmaduke Pickthall, New York, 1930
Raban, Jonathan, *Soft City*, London, 1974
Rude, George, *Wilkes and Liberty*, London, 1962
Rushdie, Salman, *Imaginary Homelands*, London, 1991
—— *The Satanic Verses*, London, 1988
Ruthven, Malise, *A Satanic Affair*, London, 1990
—— *Islam in the World*, London, 1994
Runnymede Publications, *Islamophobia*, London, 1991
Samuel, Raphael, *East End Underworld*, London, 1981
—— *Theatres of Memory*, London, 1994
Sennett, Richard, *The Conscience of the Eye*, London, 1990
Sinclair, Iain, *White Chappell, Scarlet Tracings*, London, 1987
Smith, Neil, *Gentrification of the City*, Boston, US, 1986
Smith, Adam, *The Wealth of Nations*, London, 1970
Soskice, Janet, *Metaphor and Religious Language*, Oxford 1985
St Augustine of Hippo, *City of God* (trans. Henry Bettenson), London, 1972
Stedman Jones, Gareth (ed.), *Metropolis*, London, 1989
Sudjic, Deyan, *The 100 Mile City*, London, 1992
Survey of London, vol 27, London, 1957
Tabori, Paul, *The Anatomy of Exile*, London, 1972
Vallely Paul (ed.), *The New Politics*, London, 1998
Wright, Patrick, *Journey Through the Ruins*, London, 1991
Zangwill, Israel, *Children of the Ghetto*, London, 1893
Zebiri, Kate, *Muslims and Christians Face to Face*, Oxford, 1997
Zola, Emile, *L'Assommoir* (trans. Leonard Tancock), London, 1970

Two guide books are indispensable. For a very beautiful account of the origin of peace between the heavenly society and the earthly city I would especially recommend chapter 17 of book 19 of St Augustine's *City of God*. Then for hours of armchair route planning there's the London A–Z. Bon voyage!

William Taylor
Easter 2000